At the
USS A.

At the Helm of USS *America*

*The Aircraft Carrier and
Its 23 Commanders,
1965–1996*

James E. Wise, Jr.,
and Scott Baron

McFarland & Company, Inc., Publishers
Jefferson, North Carolina

*Coauthor James E. Wise, Jr., died in July 2013, when
the manuscript for this book was nearly complete.
His assistant Natalie Hall and coauthor Scott Baron
carried out the remaining work.*

LIBRARY OF CONGRESS CATALOGUING-IN-PUBLICATION DATA

Wise, James E., 1930–[2013]
    At the helm of USS America : the aircraft carrier and its 23
commanders, 1965–1996 / James E. Wise, Jr., and Scott Baron.
        p.   cm.
    Includes bibliographical references and index.

    ISBN 978-0-7864-7656-5 (softcover : acid free paper) ∞

    ISBN 978-1-4766-1568-4 (ebook)

    1. America (Aircraft carrier) 2. Ship captains—United
States—Biography. I. Baron, Scott, 1954– II. Title.
    VA65.A53W57 2014
    359.0092'273—dc23   2014025258

BRITISH LIBRARY CATALOGUING DATA ARE AVAILABLE

On the cover: The USS *America* (CV-66) with planes from
Carrier Air Wing One (National Archives)

Printed in the United States of America

*McFarland & Company, Inc., Publishers
    Box 611, Jefferson, North Carolina 28640
    www.mcfarlandpub.com*

To the men and women who served aboard
the USS *America* (CVA-66/CV-66),
and to the pilots and air crewmen
who flew from USS *America* in war and peace,
with gratitude for their great service to our nation
—*James E. Wise, Jr., and Scott Baron*

In remembrance of James E. Wise, Jr.
(December 11, 1930–July 7, 2013),
my coauthor, friend, mentor, surrogate father,
and one of the finest, most decent
people I have ever known.
Godspeed old friend, and smooth sailing.
—*Scott Baron*

Acknowledgments

First and foremost, the authors wish to acknowledge the very valuable contribution of our long-time editor, Natalie Hall. Her attention to detail and professionalism remain at the highest level. She is truly an indispensable member of our team.

In addition, we would like to acknowledge the encouragement and support we received from Nicholas J. Thrasher and the Naval Aviation Museum Foundation. Additionally, thanks are due to Diane Delletorre, Kevin Reem, and Scott Johnson for advice and inspiration.

We also wish to thank the skippers of the USS *America*, and others, who took the time, often while engaged in other projects, to be interviewed, and answer what must have seemed endless questions.

Finally, we would like to acknowledge the officers and sailors of the USS *America* who for over thirty years sailed the oceans, often in harm's way, to preserve and protect America. Your service has kept us free.

Contents

Preface

This book is about extraordinary men who commanded an extraordinary ship which for more than thirty years traveled the oceans of the world and sailed in harm's way three times during the war with Vietnam, and once each to Libya, the Persian Gulf, and Bosnia.

The twenty-three navy captains who commanded the *America* during her time in service were a unique collection of men. Most were combat veterans who served during World War II, Korea, Vietnam, Mayaguez Rescue Operations, Lebanon, Haiti, Libya, Bosnia, or Desert Storm. Four were Naval Academy graduates; seven were test pilots; one became Inspector General of the Navy; one wore both Navy Wings and Submariner Dolphins; and one was a prisoner of war from July 1967 to March 1973. Many joined through the Naval Aviation Officer Candidate and the Naval Aviation Cadet Programs. All were aviators; one later became a Navy Flight Officer due to loss of visual acuity. Two retired as Admirals (one was Chief of Naval Operations); five as Vice Admirals; and eleven as Rear Admirals.

Their cumulative medals and awards are impressive, including three Navy Crosses; five Silver Stars; twenty Distinguished Flying Crosses; thirty Legion of Merit medals; ten Bronze Stars, five with Combat "V"; two Purple Hearts; 33 Navy Commendation medals, 24 with Combat "V"; 150 Air medals, Individual and Strike Flight; one POW medal plus many more distinguished medals. The Knight Commander of the Order of the British Empire (OBE) was also awarded to one. The major premise of the book is that only extraordinary men were selected for command of the ship.

The book includes profiles of those twenty-three men and is based upon official biographies, published memoirs, interviews with the surviving commanding officers of the *America* and families of the deceased skippers. Some profiles are more extensive than others depending on available materials and interviews. The profiles also include operational occurrences while

Indian Ocean. Front air-to-air view of an F-14A Tomcat from Fighter Squadron 102 just after taking off from the aircraft carrier USS *America* (CV-66). The aircraft is armed with two AIM-54 Phoenix missiles, centerline, two AIM-7 Sparrow and two AIM-9 Sidewinder missiles mounted on the wing fighter pylons (Peter Mersky Collection).

Crew spells out "America" on the flight deck of CV-66, August 1965 (official U.S. Navy photograph).

these men commanded the carrier, thus providing a history of the ship's service.

The ship itself, one of the *Kitty Hawk* class super-carriers built in the early sixties, stands apart for being "where the action was." The decision to deliberately sink the ship in weapons testing rather than establish it as a floating museum resulted in a controversy that continues. Despite being the target of numerous and varied weapons and enduring explosions and live fire tests, the ship proved stubbornly unsinkable, and had to be scuttled to sink her.

Also covered are the effects of the scuttling, the efforts to name a new USS *America* to the fleet, and the resulting commissioning of USS *America* (LHA-6).

Finally, the present work is both a study in leadership and a tribute to the thousands of sailors who served aboard the *America* and is, to the best of the authors' knowledge, the only work of its kind.

Addendum by Scott Baron: James E. Wise, Jr., the first-named author of this book and my long-time friend and mentor, died suddenly on July 7, 2013, as we were finishing the manuscript to submit to the publisher. Less than two weeks earlier we had spent three days together assembling photographs, writing captions and wrapping up various details. After Jim's death, editor Natalie Hall and I finished the manuscript.

Scuttling of a U.S. Naval Super Aircraft Carrier

There were bright blue skies that Friday morning, and the scent of salt water floated in the air as people gathered along the Virginia shore. They came from all corners of the nation to say farewell as an old friend went reluctantly into retirement after a distinguished 31-year career.

On 9 August 1996, more than 1,000 spectators came to a dockside ceremony at Norfolk Naval Shipyard to say their goodbyes to the USS *America* (CV-66), many of them former crew members, as she was decommissioned and struck from the rolls of the active fleet.

Among the spectators were nineteen of *America's* twenty-three "skippers" who had commanded her, extraordinary men in their own right. Many others were former crew members whose short naval careers had ended decades earlier, but who had never forgotten and took pride in their service aboard her in war and peace. There were more than a few tears as her colors were lowered for the last time. Some like Sal Tallarico, a former Seaman Apprentice who served on her first crew, explained, "You're part of the ship. I mean, it's a great honor, I think, to be on the first crew and then be able to be here when she's taken out of service. It's a once-in-a-lifetime thing."[1]

Former Petty Officer Dan O'Halloran, who worked as a crash and salvage petty officer on her decks from 1967 to 1971, recalled her for a different reason: "I went to war twice on her. I became a man on her."[2]

Above all else, *America* was a warrior. On at least six cruises, she sailed into harm's way: three to Vietnam, and one each to Libya, the Persian Gulf, and Bosnia. Her decorations are extensive: three Meritorious Unit Commendations, three Navy "E"s, four Navy Expeditionary medals, three National Defense Service medals, eleven Southwest Asia Deployment medals, a Republic of Vietnam Gallantry Cross Unit Citation, NATO medal,

Republic of Vietnam Campaign medal, Kuwait Liberation medal (Saudi Arabia), Kuwait Liberation medal (Kuwait) and many Battle Efficiency awards, including eight Battle Stars for service in Vietnam.[3]

On her last deployment, her squadrons flew 250 combat missions over the skies of Bosnia and Herzegovina, and during Operation Desert Storm, the *America* was the only carrier to launch strikes against Iraqi targets from both sides of the Arabian Peninsula, from Red Sea and the Persian Gulf.[4]

The USS *America* was a victim of the post–Cold War budget cuts. Originally scheduled to undergo Navy Service Life Extension Program (SLEP) she was instead retired early as a cost saving measure and harbored at the Inactive Ship Maintenance Facility in Philadelphia, Pennsylvania.

The *America* was originally scheduled to be sold as scrap, but there were hopes that the decommissioned *America* could be transformed into a museum, efforts that were eventually unsuccessful when the Navy announced early in 2005 that *America* would instead serve as a live-fire test and evaluation platform to aid the design of future aircraft carriers. There was opposition to the plan but, in a letter to those opposed to the plan, Vice Chief of Naval Operations Adm. John B. Nathman explained:

> *America* will make one final and vital contribution to our national defense, this time as a live-fire test and evaluation platform. *America*'s legacy will serve as a footprint in the design of future carriers—ships that will protect the sons, daughters, grandchildren and great-grandchildren of *America* veterans. We will conduct a variety of comprehensive tests above and below the waterline collecting data for use by naval architects and engineers in creating the nation's future carrier fleet. It is essential we make those ships as highly survivable as possible. When that mission is complete, the *America* will slip quietly beneath the sea. I know *America* has a very special place in your hearts, not only for the name, but also for your service aboard her. I ask that you understand why we selected this ship for this one last crucial mission and make note of the critical nature of her final service.

On 25 February 2005, a ceremony was held at the ship's pier in Philadelphia, attended by former crew members and various dignitaries. Their purpose was to offer a final salute to the USS *America* and men who served aboard her. As approximately three hundred former crewmembers gathered with their families, they listened as Board Members of the Carrier Veterans Association read a Congressional proclamation and former captain Kent Ewing gave a short speech before those crewmembers who wished to were invited to the podium to say a few words. The occasion concluded with a wreath laying ceremony.

On 19 April 2005, the *America* was towed down the Delaware and out to sea on her last voyage, for approximately four weeks of experiments in which various types of explosions, both surface and underwater, would simulate torpedoes, cruise missiles and small craft attacks. The ship was outfitted extensively with cameras and sensors to monitor and collect data which would be used to verify computer models. The tests would indicate how well carriers could be expected to survive battle damage, vital information in the planning of the next generation of carriers.[5]

Little information on the types of tests conducted, the results, or other information collected has been made available and most data has been classified by Naval Sea Systems Command.

On 14 May, with testing complete, the *America* was scuttled approximately 476 miles east of Charleston, South Carolina, in a controlled flooding caused by strategically placed scuttling charges. After a series of explosions below the ship's surface, the *America* settled gracefully on her keel, 16,800 feet below the surface of the ocean. On 20 November 2006, the government, as the result of a Freedom of Information (FOI) request by the USS *America*-Carrier Veterans Association, released the location of the sinking as 33.09.09N, 071.39.07W, around 250 miles (400 km) southeast of Cape Hatteras.[6]

At 84,000 tons, *America* is the largest warship to date ever to be sunk. She is not, however, the largest vessel to be sunk. That honor belongs to the supertanker *Seawise Giant*, which was sunk by Iraqi warplanes in the Strait of Hormuz during the Iran-Iraq War in the 1980s.

It is somewhat ironic that a vessel that came through several military engagements without ever being fired on by the enemy should finally succumb to "friendly fire." While many former crewmembers are unhappy with the fate of the *America*, they take comfort from the fact that she performed one last important service to her country.

Notes

1. McMichaels, William H. "USS *America* Stands Down," *Daily Press*, Hampton Roads, VA, 10 August 1996.

2. Ibid.

3. USS *America* Museum Foundation—http://ussamerica-museumfoundation.org/memoriam.html

4. U.S. Dept. of Defense—www.defense.gov/photos/newsphoto.aspx?newsphotoid=413

5. Lumpkin, John J. "Navy to Scuttle a Retired Carrier," Boston, MA, *Globe*, 6 March 2005.

6. Dujardin, Peter. "USS America's Sunken Location Revealed," *Daily Press*, Hampton Roads, VA, 20 November 2006.

USS *America* (CVA-66)
Joins the Fleet

In the mid–1950s, the U.S. Navy began the process of transitioning from the *Forrestal*-class aircraft carriers to the new *Kitty Hawk*–class super carrier when the keel was laid for the USS *Kitty Hawk* (CVA-63) on 27 December 1956, at the New York Shipping Corporation, Camden, New Jersey. She was commissioned 21 April 1961, at the Philadelphia Naval Shipyard, with Capt. William F. Bringle in command, and was named for the site where the Wright Brothers flew their first manned airplane.

The *Kitty Hawk* was followed by a second ship, the USS *Constellation* (CVA-64) built by New York Naval Shipyard, Brooklyn, New York, on 1 July 1956, and her keel was laid down 14 September 1957 at the New York Navy Yard. She was commissioned 27 October 1961, with Capt. T. J. Walker in command, and was named for the "new constellation of stars" on the flag of the new United States.

On 25 November 1960, a contract was awarded to the Newport News Shipbuilding and Dry Dock Corporation, Newport News, Virginia, to produce a third *Kitty Hawk*–class carrier (CVA-66) and her keel was laid on 9 January 1961. There was some discussion regarding building the USS *America* as an *Enterprise*-class nuclear carrier, but budget considerations resulted in her being conventionally powered.

In a letter from Secretary of the Navy, John B. Connally, to President John F. Kennedy dated 15 December 1961, the Secretary polled the President as to his choice from a list of potential names for the new carrier that included USS *Constitution*, USS *Alliance*, USS *America* and USS *Langley*, with brief backgrounds on each of the four. Also considered were USS *Congress* and USS *Williamsburg*. In a letter to the Navy Secretary dated 6 January 1962, the President selected the name USS *America* for the third *Kitty Hawk*–class carrier.[1]

She was launched on 1 February 1964, and commissioned on 23 January 1965. With a draft of thirty-eight feet and a beam of 248 feet, she stood as tall as a 23-story building with a flight deck of 4.57 acres. She had a top speed of 32 knots and a range of 12,000 miles. Including her aviation element, she carried a crew of over 5,000, with officers and enlisted gathered from all fifty states and three territories.[2]

It was a sunny Saturday afternoon on 23 January 1965, for the commissioning ceremony, and dignitaries included Dean Rusk, the Secretary of State; Paul Nitze, the Secretary of the Navy; Chief of Naval Operations (CNO) Adm. David L. McDonald; Adm. H.P. Smith, Commander-in-Chief (CIC) Atlantic Fleet; Vice Adm. John S. Thach, the Deputy Chief of Naval Operations (Air); and Virginia Governor Albertis S. Harrison, Jr. Following the playing of the National Anthem and the hoisting of the Ensign, Jack, and Commissioning Pennant, the new commanding officer, Capt. Lawrence Heyworth, Jr., approached the podium, read his orders, and formally took command of the fourth USS *America* (CV-66).[3]

Notes

1. John F. Kennedy Library, Boston Massachusetts. (http://www.jfklibrary.org/).
2. Heyworth Biography—Commissioning Pamphlet—USS *America*, Dept. of the Navy.
3. Ibid.

The Skippers: Profiles of Extraordinary Men

Capt. Lawrence Heyworth, Jr.
(January 1965–July 1966)

Lawrence Heyworth, Jr., was born in Chicago, Illinois, on 10 February 1921, to Lawrence and Marguerite Kallscheuer Heyworth. His father, a prosperous real estate developer arranged for his son to attend the prestigious Harvard School for Boys on Chicago's south side from 1926–1938. After a year at the University of Chicago, Heyworth was accepted by the U.S. Naval Academy at Annapolis as part of the Class of 1943. Because of the outbreak of World War II, and the needs of the service, the Class of 1943 would graduate early, in June 1942.

One of Heyworth's classmates and friend, James L. Holloway III, son of Admiral James L. Holloway, Jr., introduced him to his sister Jean Gordon Holloway, whom he married in 1946. Their two sons, Cmdr. Lawrence Heyworth III (USNA Class of 1970) and Lt. Cmdr. Gordon Heyworth served in the Navy, as did Lawrence Heyworth IV (USNA Class of 2005) who was the fourth generation to graduate from Annapolis.[1]

Immediately following graduation, Ensign Heyworth reported to the Submarine School at New London, Connecticut, and upon completion of training in September served as a member of a submarine relief crew at Pearl Harbor, Hawaii, until his assignment aboard the submarine USS *Finback* (SS-230) in December 1942.

The *Finback,* a *Gato*-class submarine, was almost as new to the Naval Service as Heyworth himself, having been commissioned on 31 January 1942, with Lt. Cmdr. Jesse Hull in command. Heyworth reported aboard just prior to departure on her third combat patrol which was 16 December 1942 through 6 February 1943, serving initially as an escort for a carrier task force.

During his twenty-six months aboard the *Finback*, Heyworth served as Asst. Communications Officer, Torpedo and Gunnery Officer, Diving Officer, Communications Officer, and finished his tour as Executive Officer. Heyworth would be aboard for nine of its twelve combat patrols, earning the ship thirteen Battle Stars and accounting for 59,383 tons of enemy shipping.[2]

Certainly his most memorable and historically significant event occurred on the *Finback*'s tenth combat patrol, when she departed Majuro in the Marshall Islands on 15 August 1944. Her mission was "lifeguard duty" in the vicinity of the Bonin Islands, a 200–300 mile area. As her then skipper, Cdr. Robert R. Williams recalled, "This was 1944. There were very few enemy targets left. So the main reason for our being on patrol was to act as lifeguards and pick up downed aviators."[3]

On the morning of 2 September 1944, four Grumman TBM 1-C Avenger torpedo bomber planes of Torpedo Squadron Fifty-One (VT-51) took off from the small carrier USS *San Jacinto* (CVL-30). Their target was a Japanese radio station located on the heavily fortified Chichi Jima Island, which was intercepting American radio traffic. Among the airmen was a twenty-year-old Lt. (jg) George Herbert Walker Bush, who at the time he earned his wings was the youngest naval aviator in the Navy.

Despite being hit by antiaircraft fire, and his plane catching fire, Bush pressed the attack, continuing his run and delivering his four 500-pound bomb payload. For his actions, he was awarded the Distinguished Flying Cross. The citation reads: "Leading one section of a four-plane division in a strike against a radio station, Lieutenant, Junior Grade, Bush pressed home an attack in the face of intense antiaircraft fire. Although his plane was hit and set afire at the beginning of his dive, he continued his plunge toward the target and succeeded in scoring damaging bomb hits before bailing out of the craft."

Unable to make it back to the *San Jacinto*, Bush piloted the aircraft out to sea and bailed out, as did one of his crewmen, but crewman's parachute failed to open and he fell into the sea. The other crewman, most likely dead, remained with the Avenger. Neither his gunner, Lt. (jg) William White, or Radioman Second Class John Delaney survived, nor it is known which crewman exited the plane. White, an intelligence officer, had replaced Ordnanceman Second Class Leo W. Nadeau, who flew with Bush on fifty-six of his fifty-eight combat missions.[4]

Bush, with a head injury, landed in the water, and inflated a rubber raft, but lost his water, rations, and paddles. Worse, the tide was carrying him

George Bush (kneeling, second from left) and other rescued airmen with some of the officers and men of USS *Finback,* September 1944 (George Bush Presidential Library and Museum).

toward Chichi Jima. Overhead, the other planes maintained watch and radioed the *Finback* with his position. Lt. Doug West dropped a medical kit, and the planes strafed a Japanese patrol boat that tried to capture him. At 11:56 a.m., the *Finback*, having carefully navigated several mines, surfaced and took the downed aviator on board. The moment was captured on 8MM film by Ens. Bill Edwards.[5]

Bush was onboard the following day for the rescue of Lt. (jg) James Beckman off the USS *Enterprise* (CV-6). Bush, as well as four other rescued airmen would remain aboard the *Finback* for thirty days, until the end of the patrol. Heyworth, now qualified for command of submarines, left the *Finback* in January 1945 to serve on the staff of the Commander Submarines, U.S. Pacific Fleet at Pearl Harbor. For his service aboard the *Finback* Heyworth was awarded two Bronze Stars with Combat "V" and a Navy Letter of Commendation with Combat "V."[6]

Following the war, Heyworth was accepted for flight training and reported to the Naval Air Training Command at Pensacola, Florida. He graduated, and was designated a naval aviator in late 1947, one of the few who were qualified to wear both gold aviator wings and the gold dolphins of the Submarine Service.

He was first assigned to Attack Squadron Two-E (VA2-E) at the Naval Air Station (NAS) Oceana, Virginia, from June to August 1948, then the squadron was designated as Anti-submarine Squadron Twenty-Two (VS-22) assigned aboard the escort carrier USS *Sicily* (CVE-118) flying the Grumman AF Guardian the Navy's first purpose-built anti-submarine warfare (ASW) carrier-based aircraft.[7]

Following North Korea's invasion of South Korea on 25 June 1950, an anti-submarine exercise was canceled, and the *Sicily* was ordered to the Far East in early July as the flagship of Carrier Division (CarDiv) 15.[8]

When the *Sicily* sailed on 4 July, Heyworth was no longer aboard, having been ordered to report for a six month test pilot training program at the Naval Air Test Center, Patuxent River, Maryland, in early July. A member of the fifth class of test pilots, he edged out classmate and future astronaut Alan Shepard to graduate top in his class. He remained at Patuxent until November 1952, and was among the first to land a Douglas F3D Skyknight jet fighter onto a carrier.[9]

From November 1952 until July 1953, Heyworth served as Flag Secretary and aide to Commander, Carrier Division Four aboard the attack carrier USS *Midway* (CVA-41). During his time aboard, the ship participated in NATO exercises in the North Sea, and later, during its Mediterranean cruise. In July, Heyworth was assigned as Executive Officer of Fighter Squadron Sixty-One (VF-61), the "Jolly Rogers" based aboard the modernized and recommissioned attack aircraft carrier USS *Lake Champlain* (CVA-39).[10]

Heyworth returned for a second assignment as a test pilot at Patuxent River in October 1955, and was the first naval aviator to fly the USAF F-104-A Starfighter, developed by the Lockheed Corporation as a "single-engine, high-performance, supersonic interceptor aircraft." Subsequently, he became the first Naval Aviator to join the "Double Supersonic Club" by flying twice the speed of sound.

After attending the Naval War College at Newport, Rhode Island, and graduating the Naval Warfare Course in 1958, he was temporarily assigned to a Replacement Air Group (RAG) for training in preparation of assuming command of Attack Squadron Eighty-One (VF-81) "Crusaders" which flew Grumman F9F-8 Cougars jet fighters off the attack aircraft carrier USS *Forrestal* (CVA-59), home ported at NAS Oceana. *Forrestal* operated primarily in the Mediterranean. Also on board were future astronauts Alan Shepard and Wally Schirra.[11]

In February 1959, Heyworth was called to Washington, D.C., to interview for selection into the Mercury Space Flight program. On 4 March

1959, the squadron transitioned to the Douglas A4D-2 Skyhawk ground attack aircraft and in July of that year VF-81 was re-designated Attack Squadron VA-81.

In November 1959, Heyworth was named Commander, Carrier Air Group Eight (CAG-8) aboard the *Forrestal*. In December 1960, Heyworth served a three-month tour as the *Forrestal's* Operations Officer before assuming the position of Executive Officer for the next year.[12]

Around March 1962, Heyworth was ordered to Washington, D.C., assigned to the staff of the Chief of Naval Operations-Air, where he remained until April 1963, when he assumed command of the fleet oiler USS *Pawcatuck* (AO-108) as part of the Sixth Fleet in the Mediterranean, his first command of a naval vessel. In May of 1964, Heyworth was selected as the prospective commanding officer of the USS *America* (CVA-66), the Navy's newest attack carrier. And on that Saturday afternoon in January, Heyworth became the first skipper of the USS *America*.

During his time, as the first in command on the new super carrier, Heyworth was responsible for getting the *America* operational, functioning smoothly and combat ready. Once outfitting of the ship was complete on 25 March, the ship got underway for local operations in the Virginia Capes. On 5 April, *America* conducted her first catapult launch/landing with the carrier's executive officer, Cdr. Kenneth B. Austin piloting a Douglas A-4C Skyhawk of VA-76. She conducted shakedown operations for the next two months in the Caribbean, concluding with her arrival at Guantanamo Bay, Cuba, on 23 June.

After a return to Norfolk, and a couple of short training cruises, *America* sailed on 30 November on a seven-month deployment to the Mediterranean with the Sixth Fleet. Although uneventful, she made port calls at Cannes, France; Genoa, Italy; Toulon, France; Athens, Greece; Istanbul, Turkey; Beirut, Lebanon; Valletta, Malta; Taranto, Italy; Palma, Mallorca, Spain; and Pollensa Bay, Spain.

From 28 February until 10 March 1966, *America* participated in a joint naval exercise with France, Fairgame IV which simulated a NATO response using conventional warfare against an aggressor invading a NATO ally. During this time, *America* competed against other carriers of the Atlantic Fleet to win the coveted Battle Efficiency Award, her first time in competition.

America returned to the Norfolk Naval Shipyard on 10 July, and shortly thereafter in a change of command ceremony, Heyworth turned over command of the carrier to Capt. Donald D. Engen.

In August 1966, Heyworth reported to Washington, D.C., as Executive

Capt. Don Engen (right) relieves Capt. Lawrence Heyworth as "Skipper" of CV-66 (official U.S. Navy photograph).

Assistant and Senior Aide to Adm. Horacio Rivero, the Vice Chief of Naval Operations.

Heyworth was appointed Commandant of Midshipman on his return to Annapolis, on 18 July 1967, and served briefly as its forty-fifth Superintendent (22 June–20 July 1968) acting temporarily until Vice Adm. James F. Calvert, a fellow graduate of the USNA Class of 1943, could assume the position, making Heyworth's twenty-eight-day tenure the briefest of the Academy's sixty-one Superintendents.[13]

On 7 December 1969, Heyworth, newly promoted to Rear Admiral, was ordered to NAS Jacksonville, Florida, as Commander Fleet Air, responsible for operations in the southwest United States and the Caribbean, his actions earning him the award of a Legion of Merit.

In June 1971, he finished his career as Deputy Chief of Staff for Military Assistance, Logistics and Administration to the Commander in Chief—Pacific based in Honolulu, Hawaii, until his retirement on 1 July 1973.

Captain Heyworth as Commandant, U.S. Naval Academy, circa 1967 (courtesy Heyworth family).

He stayed active in his thirty-year retirement, and was invited with his shipmates to the inauguration of President George H.W. Bush in January 1989, after which he presented the President with a golf shirt commemorating his time aboard the *Finback*. He passed away at his Virginia Beach home on 4 May 2003, and was buried in a private ceremony at the Naval Academy.[14]

Notes

1. Burgess, Colin. *Selecting the Mercury Seven—The Search for America's First Astronauts*. NY Springer-Praxis Books, 2011.
2. Bauer, K. Jack; Roberts, Stephen S. *Register of Ships of the U.S. Navy, 1775–1990: Major Combatants*. Westport, Connecticut: Greenwood Press, 1991.
3. Christmann, Timothy J. "Vice President Bush recalls World War Two experience as 'sobering.'" *Naval Aviation News*, March-April, 1985.
4. Ibid.
5. http://www.youtube.com/watch?v=om4u_DxyJxE&feature=related
6. Biography—Rear Adm. Lawrence Heyworth, Jr.—Naval History Division, 2 October 1973.

7. Heyworth Biography—*Commissioning Pamphlet—USS America*, Dept. of the Navy.

8. Mooney, James L. *Dictionary of American Naval Fighting Ships*, U.S. Navy History Division—Volume VI, 1976.

9. Burgess, Colin. *Selecting the Mercury Seven—The Search for America's First Astronauts*. NY Springer-Praxis Books, 2011.

10. Biography—Rear Adm. Lawrence Heyworth, Jr.—Naval History Division 2 October 1973.

11. Burgess, Colin. *Selecting the Mercury Seven—The Search for America's First Astronauts*. NY Springer-Praxis Books, 2011.

12. Biography—Rear Adm. Lawrence Heyworth, Jr.—Naval History Division 2 October 1973.

13. United States Naval Academy www.usna.edu/

14. Interview with Gordon Heyworth, 10 July 2012.

Capt. Donald D. Engen
(July 1966–July 1967)

In the fourth grade I announced to my parents that I wanted to be a naval officer and go to sea.—Donald D. Engen[1]

Donald Davenport Engen was born in Pomona, California, on 28 May 1924, son of Sydney M. and Dorothy (Davenport) Engen. His goal while in school was eventually to be accepted by the U.S. Naval Academy. During his elementary and high school education, he was taken to various local airfields (Burbank, Mines, etc.) by his parents and grandparents to watch air races and stunt flyers. Though fascinated by the aerial events he didn't at the time connect flying with becoming a naval officer.

He graduated from a Pasadena high school in May 1941, and then set his sights on getting an appointment to the Academy from Carl Hinshaw, a Califor-

Capt. Don Engen (official U.S. Navy photograph).

nia Republican congressman. He subsequently took academic merit examinations for entrance into the service academies and awaited the results. In the interim he attended a Pasadena Junior College where he met Mary Baker his future wife. She was sixteen and he was a year older.

Five days after the Japanese attack on Pearl Harbor he was notified by Congressman Hinshaw that he had been awarded a third alternate appointment to the Academy. Because of the war, Engen was convinced that he would be accepted and took entrance examinations in February 1942 at the Naval Reserve Armory in Los Angeles.

His dream appeared dashed when he was informed in April that he had failed the chemistry test in the entrance examinations and as a result could not enter the Naval Academy. However, because the Navy had lowered the age from twenty-one to eighteen for naval aviation and reduced the academic requirements from two years to a high school diploma, he found a new pathway to a naval commission. On his eighteenth birthday with a written note of permission from his parents he enlisted as a seaman second class in the Naval Aviation Cadet (NAVCAD) Program. Breezing through the various physical, aptitude and final officer screening tests at a Navy recruiting station he joined the Navy's NAVCAD Program on 9 June 1942. He was ordered to Civilian Pilot Training (CPT at the time was part of the initial training process for Army and Navy would-be aviators). Hundreds of colleges and universities offered CPT programs. Engen reported for two weeks of ground school training at Pasadena Junior College and then was bused to Baker, California, for flight training in J3 Piper Cubs. When not flying, he and his classmates underwent physical fitness training. Engen soloed in August 1942 after seven hours and forty-five minutes of flight instruction. He qualified for a private pilot's license after 36 hours of flying. He had made the "cut" and was sent to the naval preflight school at St. Mary's College near Oakland in September 1942.

Three other Navy preflight schools had been established. During the war the four schools would turn out 5,000 Naval Aviation Cadets every three months. In addition to the academic program, Cadets had to go through strenuous physical training. Cadets were formed into battalions. They marched in platoons, then companies, and then battalions. They were quarantined for four weeks in the pre-flight program and were allowed a six-hour liberty every other weekend. Cadet's pay at the time was $75 per month, paid on the fifth of every month. In addition to ground school, Cadets daily did fifteen minutes of calisthenics, one hour of team sports, such as football, soccer, combat track or other body contact sports then one hour of individual sports, e.g., boxing, wrestling, run an obstacle course or strenuous swimming. Cadets marched to all events. After dinner they returned to their barracks for two hours of individual study after which they were allow thirty minutes of free time to write letters home, read, etc. Each cadet was given a $10,000 U.S. National Life insurance policy with their parents as beneficiaries. Cadets could not marry until they received their wings and commission as an ensign at the end of their flight training. (co-author Wise went through flight training in 1952 and not much had changed in the Pre-Flight program routine except that the hub of Naval aviation training had been moved to Pensacola, Florida). In the 1950s Pre-flight training was done at Naval Air Station, Pensacola, Florida and basic flight training was conducted at outlying fields, Whiting, Saufley, Corry and Barin. Carrier qualifications were conducted on World War II small carrier decks in the Gulf of Mexico.

In October 1942 the cadets at St. Mary's College learned that because of the heavy losses of Navy pilots in the fleet, their training would be accel-erated and they would earn their wings in six to nine months. Three hun-dred cadets were undergoing training and told that their graduation date was set for 24 November 1942. However, some 70 (which included Engen) of the 300 were selected to go to the Naval Reserve Aviation Base at Los Alamitos, California. The others were sent to elimination (E) bases (estab-lished to weed out those who could not adapt to flying because of air sick-ness or lack of coordination).

Arriving at Los Alamitos in early December, Engen saw rows of Navy SNV training aircraft on the airfield. Manufactured by the Vultee Aviation Manufacturing Company the BT-13 "Vultee Vibrator" (nicknamed by pilots) was the mainstay of training aircraft for the U.S. Army Air Corps and the Navy from 1939 to 1944. There were 11,537 Vultees built to meet the needs of American military aviation training. Allied student pilots also trained in the U.S. learning their basic flying skills in these aircraft. In addition to the Vultee trainers there were some 40 bright yellow N2S and N3N Navy biplanes lined up near a lone hangar. Engen received more training which included Morse code, dead reckoning and celestial navigation.

Engen completed primary training in February 1943 and headed for further training at Corpus Christi, Texas. He initially flew SNVs (a variant of the Vultee aircraft), requesting that he be selected to fly dive bombers. He flew instrument training flights in the back seat of SNJ-3s and -4s while under a canvas hood and continued his training until ordered to Naval Air Station, Kingsville, Texas, which was the advanced training base for fighters and dive bombers. Engen completed advanced training and was designated a Naval Aviator on 9 June 1943. Among his graduation group were pilots of all training disciplines. One of those was George Herbert Walker Bush. Engen was then ordered to Scout Bombing Squadron Three (VSB-3) at Naval Air Station Daytona Beach, Florida, for operational training.

Engen and other Officer students began their advanced training by practicing field carrier landings flying SNJ-3/4 Texans at the nearby Naval Auxiliary Air Station (NAAS) Banana River. Once the Landing Signal Officer (LSO) was satisfied with the performance of the students they were switched into flying battle-worn SBD Douglas Dauntless dive bombers. After the group perfected bombing ground targets using practice bombs, they progressed to dive bombing a target boat that cruised on Lake George, west of Daytona Beach.

On 25 July 1943, Engen was told he would be ordered to join a Pacific Fleet squadron. The next month he took a train to Chicago en route to NAS Glenview, an air station some 30 miles north of the windy city. After additional field carrier landing training he flew to the paddle wheel steamer (converted to an aircraft carrier) USS *Sable* (IX-81) sailing on Lake Michigan and after eight landings was carrier qualified. He returned to Pasadena, and got engaged to Mary Baker (she was eighteen and Engen was nineteen). He then departed for NAS North Island and joined Air Group Nineteen, reporting to Bombing Squadron Nineteen at NAS Los Alamitos. The Air Group consisted of Bombing Squadron Nineteen (VB-19) Helldivers, Fighter Squadron Nineteen (VF-19) Hellcats and Torpedo Bomber Squadron Nineteen (VT-19) Avengers. Amidst the intensity of preparing for overseas duty and joining the war, the engaged couple eloped to Yuma, Arizona, on 23 September. In January 1944 VB-19 pilots flew to NAS North Island and boarded the USS *Altamaha* (CVE-18), an escort jeep carrier, for carrier qualifications. After completing this phase the Air Group was ordered to NAS Alameda and loaded aboard the USS *Lexington* (CV-16). The ship moored next at Ford Island in Hawaii and offloaded Air Group personnel; the *Lexington* continued westward to join in island campaigns. More training was conducted by the Air Group flying out of NAS Kahului, Maui, as they awaited deployment to the Pacific combat area. In May 1944 VB-19 received the first of the Navy's newest dive bomber, the SB2C-3 Helldiver. By the end of the month the squadron had its full complement of 36 aircraft. Prior to this the pilots had trained in SBD and older model SB2Cs aircraft. The pilots found that the new aircraft with all its modifications was a delight to fly. In early June Air Group pilots carrier qualified on the USS *Franklin*

(CV-13) and then went on board the USS *Intrepid* (CV-11) for transport to the Western Pacific. It was Air Group Nineteen's turn to join the war.

The *Intrepid* arrived at Eniwetok Atoll on 30 June. Ships of Task Force Fifty Eight Point Two (TF) 58.2 were already anchored in the Atoll lagoon. Other TF 58 combatants were still supporting the invasion of Saipan or were en route from the battle of the Philippine Sea. Though the battle was a success, the task force lost 150 planes and many pilots. Air Group Sixteen aboard the *Lexington* had taken many losses and needed to be reconstituted. VF-19 F6F Hellcats, VB-19 Helldivers and VT-19 Avengers of Air Group Nineteen were to replace the battered Air Group.

On 1 July, Air Group aircraft were catapulted from the *Intrepid* while the ship was anchored and landed on the atoll's coral strip for further transfer to the *Lexington*. Admiral Raymond Spruance was commander of the Fifth Fleet in the USS *Indianapolis* (CA-35). Vice Admiral Marc Mitscher was commander of TF Fifty Eight (CTF-58) in *Lexington*, and Rear Admiral Frederick Sherman was commander of Task Group Fifty Eight Point Three (TG-58.3) in USS *Essex*. Four days later TG 58.3 steamed into Eniwetok's lagoon, having participated in the Saipan and Philippine engagements and Air Group Nineteen saw their first view of *Lexington* since the previous February as the ship anchored in carrier row. Dubbed the "Blue Ghost" by Tokyo Rose, the *Lexington* was the only *Essex*-class carrier painted blue grey rather than the usual zigzag camouflage design on the other carriers. The *Lexington* and most of the Fifth Fleet sortied from the Atoll on 14 July 1944, and supported the invasion of Guam for the remainder of that month. Task Groups were split from the main force to attack other Japanese held islands. Engen sank his first ship in the Palau group, a 1,000-ton coastal freighter. On 4 August, Engen and 17 VB-19 dive bombers attacked ships in Iwo Jima harbor. His division of six aircraft were the last element in the attack and they hit and sank a Japanese destroyer.

While waiting to be launched to attack Palau, Engen noticed Vice Admiral Mitscher sitting on the inboard side of his open flag bridge in a pedestal chair, alone, facing aft. He sat there for almost every launch and recovery, with his chin cupped in his right hand, his expression and position never changing. He was always just there. He was revered by pilots and crewmen alike.

The island of Chichi Jima, an island north of Iwo Jima, was attacked on 5 August by VB-19 bombers and several of Engen's shipmates were shot down. The island's air defense fire was more intense then encountered at Iwo Jima. (See James Bradley's book *Flyboys* to learn more about Chichi Jima.)

On 26 August Admiral Halsey assumed the fleet command from Admiral Spruance, and the Fifth Fleet became the Third Fleet. That meant Vice Admiral Mitscher became CTF 38, and Rear Admiral Frederick Sherman became CTG 38.3. In Engen's task group the carriers continued to be *Lexington*, *Essex*, *Langley* and *Princeton*. The entire Task Force of four Task Groups weighed anchor and moved northwestward to do battle with Japanese held islands and liberate the Philippines. TF-38's four task groups, each included four aircraft carriers, battleships, cruisers, destroyers and support ships. En route TG Thirty Eight Point Three moved into position to support U.S. ground forces invading the island of Peleliu which proved to be a vicious campaign. Fuel and ammunition depots, shore installations and aircraft on the island were destroyed and left burning, however, the Japanese anti-aircraft fire was fierce as the entrenched Japanese fought desperately to hold on to Peleliu. On 9 September 1944, TG 38.3 aircraft struck targets on Mindanao, the southernmost island in the Philippines, resistance was light but when the air group attacked the Visayan and the Central Philippines, Japanese fighters and bombers were abundant and aggressive. VB-19 sunk numerous enemy ships and VF-19 had a field day shooting down Japanese aircraft, in fact, even one of Engen's squadron mates, flying his SB2C-3, shot down an enemy Zero.[2]

The *Lexington* moved north along the Philippine chain and enemy air defenses were intense, especially around Manila. The Japanese took heavy losses in aircraft, freighters, oilers and troop ships. To protect American Philippine invading forces, three task groups moved north to attack Okinawa. Hundreds of Japanese aircraft were shot down and TG 38.3 bombers and torpedo planes sunk some fifty ships. Within a few days the task groups turned south and attacked Formosa and the Pescadores. Since early September the task groups had been under heavy attack by land-based Japanese aircraft.

Through intelligence, Task Group commanders knew that the Japanese had deployed naval combatants to oppose the U.S. invasion of Leyte. On 24–25 October, the U.S. fleet scoured the seas around the Philippine Islands in search of enemy forces. On the 25th it found a Japanese surface force (five battleships which included the super battleship *Musashi*, twelve cruisers and fifteen destroyers sailing toward the Leyte Gulf via the South China Sea, the Sibuyan Sea and the San Bernardino Strait. A second enemy force consisting of two battleships, a cruiser and four destroyers was sighted moving east through the Sulu Sea. It was to join up with the main South China Sea battle force in the San Bernardino Strait to effect a north/south pincer attack on the American amphibious and support ships lying off the beachhead. At the same time the Japanese planned a ruse to draw Task Force 38.3 away from the Gulf area by sending a small carrier group south in open water to feint an attack on the American naval forces in the Gulf. The Task Force 38.3 commander Admiral "Bull" Halsey elected to attack the Northern force, a move that would later prove controversial. Engen flew in the first strike on the Southern forces. In the ensuing day long battle, four enemy battleships and a cruiser were heavily damaged and the *Musashi* was sunk. As the Japanese forces retreated, the Northern Japanese carrier force which included the carriers *Zuikaku, Chitose, Chiyoda* and *Zuiho* in company with two battleships, three cruisers and eight destroyers was attacked by TF 38.3 aircraft. In the ensuing battle the Japanese launched 76 planes against TF 38.3 ships. Most were shot down since the enemy aviators were poorly trained and those who survived eventually landed on Luzon airfields. The Northern force lost three of its four carriers, *Zuikaku, Chitose* and *Chiyoda* and several of their escorting ships.[3] Engen who participated in the bombing of the *Zuikaku* was awarded the Navy Cross for his action during the battle, his citation for the award was as follows:

> For extraordinary heroism … in operations against enemy Japanese forces during the Battle for Leyte Gulf, 25 October 1944. Courageous and skillful in the face of enemy air opposition and extremely intense and continuous fire from hostile anti-aircraft batteries, (he) boldly pressed home a hazardous dive-bombing attack on a Japanese aircraft carrier, and, accurately placing his bomb scored a direct hit upon his target, despite its desperate evasive tactics. A superb and intrepid airman, he contributed directly to the sinking of the enemy aircraft carrier and played a gallant part in strenuous aerial operations during this critical period of the Pacific War....

Engen also received the Air Medal for operations against Japanese forces in the Marianas, Palau, Kazan, Bonin and Philippine Islands. He was later awarded the Distinguished Flying Cross for heroism and extraordinary achievement in the vicinity of the Philippine Islands on 5 November 1944.[4]

Forty-two years later Engen had cause to remember the sinking of the Japanese carrier when President Ronald Reagan appointed him administrator of the Federal Aviation Administration (FAA) in 1984. In 1986 Engen was introduced through a vice president of McDonnell Douglas to a Mr. Kadota, the president for operations of a new Japanese airline that had just ordered a large number of DC-10 and MD-80 airplanes. They met at the Congressional Press club in Washington one evening. The men talked through an interpreter. Engen learned that Kadota had been a "kamikaze" pilot during World War II and that he was interested to know what Engen did in the war. Engen answered that he was in the U.S. Navy. Kadota asked pointedly what Engen did during the war. He answered that he was a Navy pilot and that he and others had sunk an aircraft carrier, the *Zuikaku*. Kadota appeared surprised and answered that the *Zuikaku* was his ship. Engen asked, "How long were you the water?" Kadota answered, "five days" and they both laughed. Over the years they formed a bond. Engen had helped save his life since Kadota had never completed his World War II suicide mission.[5]

During the October battles the *Lexington* had expended most of its ammunition and had to leave the line and move westward to rearm, refuel, and reprovision. Air Group Nineteen had lost many pilots and aircraft. The ship returned to the line on 5 November 1944, and joined in to do battle with the remnants of the Japanese fleet. An enemy cruiser had been reported in Manila Bay. Strike groups from four carriers flew en masse to destroy the ships. Engen was among those who dived on the cruiser *Nachi* that took direct hits from Helldivers and torpedo planes. The cruiser broke into three pieces and sank. Upon his return to the ship, he was ordered to report to the flag bridge to recount the loss of VB-19's skipper during the attack on the *Nachi*. As he went through the ship's island aft of the medical station he noticed stacks of wire basket litters with bodies in them. The ship had been struck by a "kamikaze" aircraft an hour before. On that day VB-19 lost two aircraft, eight officers and two enlisted men and another five officers killed. *Lexington* lost 46 killed and 146 wounded to enemy dive bombers.

The following day, *Lexington* headed for the fleet anchorage at Ulithi. During the past five months of combat VB-19 was practically decimated by the losses of pilots, airmen and aircraft. It was decided that rather than reconstitute Air Group Nineteen that it would be replaced by a new air group. The war was essentially over for the battered air group. Air Group Twenty off *Enterprise* relieved Air Group Nineteen on *Lexington* and on 23 November the *Enterprise* transported Engen's group to Hawaii.[6]

Bombing Squadron Nineteen had an impressive record during its five months in battle. Its combat targets included Guam, Saipan, Chichi Jima, Iwo Jima, Haha Jima, Peleliu, Mindinao, Cebu, Leyte, Mactan, Coron, Surigao, Luzon, Negros and Okinawa. Sorties flown totaled 1,364. Naval ships sunk: two Aircraft carriers, one Heavy Cruiser, one Destroyer Escort, two Troop Ships, one Submarine Tender. Merchant Ships Sunk: eight Tankers, twenty-one Cargo and miscellaneous ships. Naval Ships Damaged: one Aircraft Carrier, three Battleships, one Cruiser, three Destroyers, two Minelayers. Merchant Ships Damaged: fourteen Tankers, fifty-three Cargo and miscellaneous ships. Airfields Struck: twenty-eight. Ship and Harbor Facilities: ten. Industrial and Military Targets: 301. Aircraft Destroyed: In the Air—ten, On the Ground—105. Probable in the Air—one. Damaged, on the Ground—seventeen. Individual Awards Presented: thirty-four Navy Crosses, three Silver Stars, sixty Distinguished Flying Crosses.[7]

VB-Nineteen personnel were transported to San Diego aboard the USS *Long Island* (CVE-1) and were given a thirty-one day leave. Engen was ordered to join a new squadron, Bombing-Fighting Nineteen (VBF-19) which was assigned F6F Hellcats and F4U Corsairs. VF-19 received the first F8F-1 Bearcats much to the envy of Engen and his bombing squadron mates. VBF-19 trained for the coming invasion of Japan. Transported to Hawaii for further training and deployment, the squadron heard that atomic bombs had been dropped on Hiroshima and Nagasaki in early August 1945. Much to the elation of all Americans, the war was suddenly over. Very soon thereafter pilots began to leave the services for civilian life. Engen applied for a regular commission (he was still a reserve officer) but more deployments and time away from his family finally convinced him to return to civilian life and he was released from active naval service on 1 February 1946. However, he continued to fly as a reserve pilot in VBF-716 at the Naval Air Reserve at Los Alamitos, California.

Engen applied to be a pilot with United Airlines but found that they were mostly hiring ex-military pilots with multi-engine experience. He did a stint at the United Airlines reservation office in Long Beach. Tired of the bland job he later worked as a junior engineer at a Consolidated Vultee plant hoping eventually to become a company test pilot. He missed flying and decided to return to active duty in the Navy.[8]

Engen once again applied for a regular commission, was accepted and returned to active duty in August 1946. In October he reported as Project Pilot with the Pilotless Aircraft Unit, Chincoteague, Virginia. He remained there until January 1947, after which he had similar duty at the Naval Air Missile Test Center, Point Mugu, California, the latter offered him to fly twenty different kinds of aircraft. At Mugu, Engen checked out in twin and four-engine aircraft. He particularly liked to fly the North American B-25 Billy Mitchell. While in those assignments he was a pioneer in the development of missiles. From June 1947 to September 1948 he was a student (five term college program) at the University of California. Following his schooling Engen reported to Fighter Squadron Two Hundred Twelve (VF-212) part of Carrier Air Group Twenty One, which was a three squadron group at NAS Sand Point in Seattle, Washington. The air group consisted of VF-211 that flew F6F-5s Hellcats, VF-212 F6F-5Ns (Hellcat night fighters) and VT-213 Avenger torpedo bombers. Engen had completed several weeks of antisubmarine warfare and radar training at NAS Ream Field before reporting to VF-212. He was made the Operations Officer since he was the only Lieutenant in the eighteen plane squadron (the CO and XO were Lieutenant Commanders and the rest of the pilots were Lieutenants Junior Grade, Ensigns and midshipmen).[9]

Engen was next ordered to San Diego and assigned to VF-52, the Navy's only jet transition squadron at the time where he trained in the P-80 Shooting Star. Following transition training he was ordered to VF-51 in Air Group Five, the first jet squadron in the Navy which flew the FJ Fury. The FJ-1s were replaced by F9F-3 Panther jet fighters in 1949 and squadron pilots carrier qualified on board the USS *Boxer* (CV-21) in September of that year. During training in Panthers, the Navy perfected Jet aircraft instrument approach procedures for both land and carrier landings. In mid–April 1950, VF-51 loaded on board the USS *Valley Forge* (CVA-45) and prepared to be the first jet air group to deploy to the western Pacific.

By June the *Valley Forge* had joined Task Force 77. Together with aircraft from HMS *Triumph*, Air Group Five fighters and attack planes made the initial United Nations air strikes on North Korea. On 3 July 1950, Engen, as section leader, flew in the first offensive mission against the airfield in P'yongyang, North Korea, and laid down flak suppression fire before the attack element arrived to strafe and bomb the airfield. A few North Korean Yak–9 prop driven fighters were in the air and they were quickly shot down. With air dominance, the Panthers joined the strike forces and attacked enemy aircraft on the ground, transportation facilities, ships and power stations. The North Korean countryside seemed to be oblivious to the war's beginning. Not so with the North Korean army that eventually fought its way south to Pusan.

Enemy ground fire became more accurate and losses in aircraft mounted. Operations to halt North Korean resupply routes continued and as General MacArthur planned his September invasion of Inch'on to cut off the North Korean army south of Seoul, the *Valley Forge* moved into the Yellow Sea to support the operation. On the 4th of the month, *Valley Forge* detected a bogey moving south down the Yellow Sea headed for the carrier. Four Corsairs were launched to intercept the oncoming threat. The bogey was identified as a Soviet twin-engine Tupelov bomber, a Tu-2, with Soviet markings. As one of the Corsairs flew past the bomber, its tail gunner opened fire. Another Corsair returned 20 mm fire and the Soviet aircraft was hit causing it to start on fire. The bomber dove toward the water and crashed near an American destroyer which was screening the force. One survivor was picked up by the ship but promptly died; he was identified as the pilot. Air Group Five had just shot down a Soviet bomber! The body of the Soviet pilot was transported to the fleet flag ship and interred in the refrigerated meat locker. Washington and Moscow exchanged views, messages flew back and forth, time passed. The body was transferred to the *Valley Forge* and eventually ended up in a refrigerated facility in Sasebo, Japan. The Soviets would never admit that one of its aircraft had been flying over the Yellow Sea, let alone that it had been near the U.S. Task Force. The incident just faded away. The fate of the body was never known.

The invasion of Inch'on went down in history as a classic operation on 15 September. Over two hundred ships were involved in the landing and the Marines and Army stormed ashore that same day to cut the enemy supply lines across Korea. The U.S. and South Korean forces broke out of the Pusan perimeter and more than one-half of the North Koreans were killed or captured.

The *Valley Forge* returned to combat after a short reprieve in Sasebo, Japan. Air operations soon included forays against targets along the Manchurian and Soviet borders. The *Valley Forge* again visited Sasebo on 29 October. Because of the lack of information about Air Group pilots missing in action, Engen and another squadron mate were sent to Korea to learn what they could about the missing. At Seoul they made contact with the Fifth Air Force escape and evasion unit which was headquartered with the Army graves registration team. They were able to identify five Air Group Five pilots who had been killed in action. The pilots had been buried at their crash sites. Nine additional pilots would remain missing in action. Their mission accomplished, they grabbed a ride on a C-54 transport which had to unload carbine ammunition for the front lines before taking wounded aboard for a return to Japan. Upon landing, Engen saw that military personnel were moving south in a hurry; there was mass confusion everywhere. There was frantic talk about charging wild Chinese troops riding shaggy ponies blowing bugles as they crossed into Korea. The Chinese had entered the war the previous night. Needless to say Engen and his mate found themselves in a precarious position. They helped load the wounded, stayed onboard and arrived back in Sasebo on 4 November. The *Valley Forge* sailed for the war zone the following morning. Air Group Five was ordered to attack the rail bridges across the Yalu River. This was particularly difficult for the attacking aircraft since they were strictly forbidden to cross over into Manchuria. The anti-aircraft fire was heavy and a few MiGs came out; however, Engen's division never saw them. The Air Group had settled into a routine when the *Valley Forge* suddenly was ordered to Yokosuka, Japan, and then to San Diego. The ship returned to Korea after a short stay and Air Group Five received a new complement of pilots, (customary when an air group had been on a long cruise); among the new pilots was Ensign Neil Armstrong (who later would be first to step on the moon). Engen was awarded a second and third Air Medal for his Korean service. He was also entitled to wear the ribbon for and facsimile of the Navy Unit Commendation awarded to the USS *Valley Forge*.[10]

Many of the old Air Group pilots received orders for new duty stations. Engen was ordered to attend the U.S. Naval General Line School at Monterey, California. He attended General Line School between January and December 1951, when he became Flight Test Officer in the Office of the

VF-21 Ready Room, USS *Forrestal*, January 1956. Briefing Secretary of the Navy C.S. Thomas. Left to right: Lt.(jg) T. J. Cassidy, Capt. John Wolmers USAF, Sec. Thomas, Lt. Cdr. Joe Humes, Lt. Cdr. Don Engen (official U.S. Navy photograph).

Cdr. Don Engen boarding F-4H1 Number 1 at Edwards AFB for an assault on the World Altitude record—September 1959 (official U.S. Navy photograph).

Bureau of Aeronautics Representative, Dallas, Texas. As an Exchange Officer, he attended the Empire Test Pilots School, Farnborough, England, for a year, December 1952-December 1953, and in January joined Experimental Squadron Three as project Pilot and Type Leader and was engaged in air refueling and new fighter aircraft projects. In July 1955 he was assigned to Fighter Squadron One Hundred Twenty-One as Executive Officer and from August 1957 to October 1959 was attached to the Naval Air Test Center, Patuxent River, Maryland.

Engen was then ordered to day-night Fighter Squadron Twenty One as the Executive Officer home based at NAS Oceana, Virginia. The squadron was composed of FJ-3/3M Fury jet fighters (Navy version of the USAF F-86 Sabre jets). From June 1957 to September 1959, Engen was assigned to the Carrier Branch at the Naval Air Test Center (NATC) at Patuxent River and then commanded Fighter Squadron Twenty One flying the F3H-2 all weather Demon. Detached from VF-21 in October 1961, he assumed command of Carrier Air Group Eleven in January 1962. A year later he was assigned to the USS *Coral Sea* (CVA-43) as Operations Officer. Selected for deep draft assignment, he commanded the USS *Mount Katmai* (AE-16) which participated in operations off Vietnam. In August 1965, he reported for instruction at the Naval War College, Newport, Rhode Island, after which he was told that he would be given command of the nation's largest and newest carrier, the USS *America* (CVA-66). On 20 July 1966, before the assembled crew Captain Engen relieved Captain Lawrence Heyworth, Jr., and reported his assumption of command to Rear Adm. J.O. Cobb, Commander of Carrier Division Two.[11]

After completing its yard period, dock and sea trials, and refresher training at Guantanamo, Cuba, the ship returned to Norfolk where the Commander of Carrier Division Four, Rear Adm. Dick H. (Tex) Guinn and his staff embarked. In late November Air Wing Six aircraft were loaded on board and *America* departed Norfolk to participate in an Atlantic Fleet exercise, LANTFLEX 66. Following a successful Operational Readiness Inspection, *America* deployed to the Mediterranean and the U.S. Sixth Fleet on 10 January 1967, in the midst of the Cold War and a Middle East Crisis.

As the carrier passed the Azores Islands, two Soviet Bear four-engine turboprop maritime patrol aircraft flew around the northern tip of Norway into the Atlantic flying toward the *America*. During this time it was routine for the Soviets to overfly America carriers as they entered the Mediterranean, especially those that had come out of a yard period. They were reconnaissance aircraft, electronic and photo collectors. The aircraft were detected hundreds of miles away and were intercepted by F4B Phantoms from VF-33 and VF-102 and escorted as they flew around the ship at 1,000 feet eventually departing northward. Also, two Soviet AGI ships (small Soviet intelligence gathering ships) awaited the arrival of the *America* as the carrier approached Gibraltar. After relieving the USS *Independence* (CVA-62) in the Bay of Pollenensa and the turnover of CARDIV commanders, *America* now as a member of the Sixth Fleet conducted national and NATO operations. Using fleet anchorages to conserve fuel, the ship early in its deployment stayed mostly in the central or northwestern part of the Mediterranean. In-port periods in allied countries lasted four to seven days while at sea Engen pressed for the maximum in flight operations. During mid–April 1967 America and its task group was joined by the USS *Saratoga* (CVA-60) and its support ships in conducting a nine day NATO naval exercise in the Ionian Sea called Operation Poopdeck. During the exercise Black Sea-based Soviet naval combatants, mostly turbine-powered guided missile cruisers, entered the Mediterranean and attempted to create an incident at sea by their aggressive and obstructive operations. In May of that year, mounting intelligence indicated that tension between Israel and surrounding Arab countries was reaching a serious stage. The two TF 60 carrier groups (*America* and *Saratoga*) were positioned south of Crete, put on alert and prepared for national tasking, although no one knew what that meant. On 29 May, newsmen began arriving by *America*'s C-1A (utility aircraft that carried passengers and mail to and from the ship). The three major networks (which included Bill Gill of ABC and Bob Goralski of NBC), the wire services and a number of news publications were represented. Rear Admiral Geis, the new CARDIV commander had been the Navy's Chief of Information for the CNO and was empathetic to their needs, which they much appreciated.

On 5 June, the Arabs and Israelis went to war and the Sixth Fleet task force carrier groups conducted a general quarters drill. Once completed, the ships remained in a high state of readiness. More Soviet ships entered the Mediterranean and one particular Soviet guided missile destroyer (DDG) became a nuisance during flight operations. Admiral Geis ordered a destroyer screen, a DDG, to take on the role of shouldering the Soviet ship aside when it approached too closely to *America*. While this activity continued above, an underwater sonar contact was made by a task force destroyer with a submarine, not friendly. The ship maintained contact together with an ASW helicopter. On 7 June, Combat Information Center (CIC) reported to the bridge of the *America* that a U.S. ship named *Liberty* had been attacked by naval motor torpedo boats and aircraft. Engen had no knowledge of such a ship and later found that the navy was running two lines of authority, fleet operations and covert intelligence gathering ships. Neither was aware of what the other one was doing. The *America* launched four A-4Cs along with F-4B escorts. The flight leader announced on the departure radio frequency, "We're on the way. Who is the enemy?"

Within minutes President Johnson was in radio contact with Admiral Geis directing him to recall the aircraft. He told Admiral Geis that the Israelis admitted that they had attacked the ship thinking it was an Arab intelligence ship. The *Liberty* was ordered to steam north while two task force destroyers moved south to escort the battered ship. Sixth Fleet commander Vice Admiral Martin issued a public denial that the U.S. was supporting the Israeli forces. Since the Soviet ships were listening to communications between TF-60 ships and aircraft, they knew what the situation was. The two destroyers rendezvoused with the *Liberty* at 6:00 a.m.

on 9 June, and transferred medical personnel to the *Liberty* to assist in treating the wounded. At 10:30 a.m. two *America* helicopters rendezvoused over the *Liberty* and began transferring the more seriously wounded to the *America*. At 11:30 a.m. Engen brought the *America* within two hundred yards of the *Liberty* and put boats in the water to facilitate damage assessment and transfer of the dead. Thirty-four *Liberty* crew members lost their lives and seventy five were wounded, fifteen seriously. (Engen in his book, *Wings and Warriors, My Life as a Naval Aviator*, suggests that for those interested in the full story, the most scholarly and factual treatise they should read is the doctoral thesis of Rear Adm. Jay Crystol, USNR (Ret.).)

Following the *Liberty* incident, the *America* returned to its routine operations. Engen left the ship before it returned to the United States. He had received orders to report to Washington, D.C., to attend George Washington University to complete his long-sought baccalaureate degree before reporting to the staff of CNO in the Pentagon.

In July 1967 Capt. Frederick C. "Fox" Turner, USN, relieved Captain Engen while the ship was anchored at Valletta, Malta.[12]

In September 1967 Engen received a Bachelor of Science degree in

America's crew "man the rail" to see first-hand the bullet-ridden, torpedo scarred USS *Liberty* while the USS *Little Rock* passes alongside to inspect damage—June 1967 (official U.S. Navy photograph).

Business Administration. Assigned in September 1968 to the Office of the Chief of Naval Operations, he headed the Aviation Plans Branch until February 1970, then served as Assistant Director of Strategic Plans Branch and from August of that year as Director for which he was awarded the Legion of Merit.

In July 1971 Engen assumed command of Carrier Division Four and "for exceptionally meritorious conduct ... from 9 March to 23 July 1972, as Commander Task Force Sixty/Commander Task Force Five Hundred Two and Commander Carrier Division Four," he was awarded a Gold Star in lieu of the Second Legion of Merit. In June 1973 Engen became Deputy Commander in Chief, U.S. Naval Forces, Europe and Chief of Staff and Aide to the Commander in Chief, U.S. Naval Forces, Europe. His final tour before his retirement in 1978, was as Deputy Commander in Chief, U.S. Atlantic Command and U.S. Atlantic Fleet.

Military Awards: Navy Cross, two Legion of Merit Medals, the Distinguished Flying Cross, Air Medal with two Gold Stars, the China/Korean/United Nations/Vietnam Service Medals and numerous campaign ribbons, unit and personal citations.[13]

After retirement Engen became the general manager of the Piper Aircraft Corporation plant in Lakeland, Florida, after which he returned to Washington to assist an old friend and former chief of the Center for Naval Analysis in his war-gaming efforts. In 1982 President Ronald Reagan appointed him to be a member of the National Transportation Safety Board (NTSB) and then in 1984 the President appointed him to be administrator of the Federal Aviation Administration (FAA). In 1987 Engen created a renewed Aircraft Owners and Pilots Association Air Safety Foundation. He next accepted the Dewitt Ramsey chair for naval aviation at the Smithsonian Institution's National Air and Space Museum in Washington, D.C. In 1996 the Secretary of the Smithsonian Institution named him to be the Director of the National Air and Space Museum.[14]

During his years in public service and later, he received many awards, among them the Society of Experimental Test Pilots' Doolittle Award for Technical Management (1984), the National Achievement in Aviation Award from the Aero Club of Washington (1988) and the National Aeronautics Association's Elder Statesman of Aviation. The Soviet Union awarded him the Yuri Gagarin Gold Air and Space Medal in 1992, for his lifetime of work in aviation, and in 1998 the National Association of Aviation Officials awarded him their Honorary State Aviation Official award.

In his book, *Wings and Warriors*, he mentions his incurable aviation addiction and continued glider flying in the skies over Nevada. In July 1999, tragedy struck while he flew a motorized glider with his friend and long time pilot, William Ivans. Their glider crashed near Minden, Nevada, and both men were killed. Engen had been a pilot for fifty-seven years and had flown more than 7,500 hours in all types of aircraft, including his favorite, the glider. Both he and his wife Mary, who died in 2006, are buried together at Arlington National Cemetery. On Admiral Engen and his wife's tombstone at Arlington are the words, "GONE FLYING."[15]

Note: Coauthor Jim Wise served as ship's Intelligence Office aboard USS *America* during Captain Engen's entire tour as Commanding Officer, and remembered that "He was without peer as a naval officer and aviator. Intellectual, humble and soft spoken, he was greatly admired and respected by all who served with him. In fact, when the ship was anchored in Valletta Harbor, Malta, before his change of command, crewmen slipped notes under the door of his in-port cabin voicing their admiration of him. Some requested a change of duty so they could continue to serve with him."

Flying the FJ-3 with VF-21 in the Words of Vice Admiral Donald D. Engen, USN (Ret.)

"I first flew the FJ-3 when I was assigned to VX-3 at NAS Atlantic City. The FJ-3 was built by North American in Columbus, Ohio, and all the production aircraft were picked up at Columbus to be delivered to the different squadrons. VX-3 received its FJ-3s before the fleet, and developed tactics with the Sidewinder air-to-air missile. The FJ-3 with its J-65 engine was very nimble, an absolute delight to fly because it had what I believe was the perfect harmonization of the controls, e.g., ailerons, elevators and rudders.

"The initial FJ-3s had a vile operating room green cockpit. I never understood why anyone would use such an unusual color. Other than that, however, the aircraft was a very sensibly laid-out airplane. The pilot was comfortably seated with good, around-the-clock visibility. The controls were well placed, too.

"Its control harmonization allowed the Fury to be a wonderful aerobatic aircraft. Early on, I developed a number of maneuvers which suited my aerobatic desires, including an Immelman on takeoff. When a plane was clean, without its wing tanks, you could take off, and if you had 210 knots as you crossed over the end of the runway—and you usually did—you could immediately pull up into an Immelman, with about 3.2 Gs in the initial stages, go over the top at 2,800 feet, with 124–5 KIAS, ample enough at that light weight to climb away. It was a very spectacular maneuver.

"I left VX-3 and went to VF-21 as Executive Officer. VF-21 was transitioning from F9F-6s to FJ-3s, and my experience would help the squadron. During our training, we made our initial carrier quals on the new aircraft carrier USS *Forrestal* (CVA-59), and deployed to Guantanamo Bay, Cuba. There were several good pilots in the squadron, and I picked three, Capt. John Wollmers (a USAF exchange pilot), Lt. (jg) Tom Cassidy (later rear admiral) and Lt. Cdr. M.D. Short, to be part of an aerobatic team which we called 'The Gray Ghosts.'

"We developed our routine at Gitmo and put on a respectable show. One of our maneuvers was a double–Immelman. This vertical maneuver was possible provided we accelerated to 560 knots at low altitude—50–100 feet—and we'd begin to pull up until the first Immelman was completed at 5,800 feet. As long as we had 235 knots, there was ample speed to continue on to a second Immelman in a four-plane diamond. We raised a lot of interest and performed before the Secretary of the Navy, and in an international competition during a deployment to the Far East, in Australia, the Philippines, and Hong Kong.

"VF-21 sharpened its skills in gunnery, day and night intercepts, and developed into quite a formidable squadron. When we returned from Guantanamo, our pilots were well versed in the FJ-3. We subsequently deployed to the Far East under Cdr. Ralph Werner (he made the first landing on the *Forrestal* in a VF-21 FJ-3 on 4 January 1956) with a stop in Sidney, Australia, then an eight month deployment in the Western Pacific.

"We generally flew with our wing tanks. Occasionally, we removed them to fly intercept missions in the clean configuration. But in this configuration, the Fury had very short legs, maybe 3,800 pounds of internal fuel. This made for a short 45-minute cycle, and the ship had difficulty performing its normal launch cycles, normally 1½ hours.

"We never dropped our tanks because they cost as much as a Cadillac at that time, apiece. Of course, in an emergency, they could have been jettisoned.

"During this deployment the squadron had an inadvertent mixup in the types of hydraulic fluid for the aircraft. The entire squadron—sixteen aircraft—was contaminated with red hydraulic oil, when they required a water-based hydraulic fluid called Skydrol, which also happened to be a very good paint remover! Because of the mixup, part of VF-21 went ashore at NAS Atsugi, Japan, for maintenance. The other part remained on the ship with what serviceable aircraft remained.

"Although the FJ-3 was a day fighter, we also flew it at night, albeit the intercept procedures required visual sighting. We had dogfights in the clear moonlight at 35,000 feet. I had several years' experience in night fighting and I would occasionally turn out our lights and fight using contrails and the light of the moon.

"One night, I succeeded in getting on someone's tail. And, wanting him to know I was there, I got behind him at 35,000 feet, and dropped my landing gear. The Fury's landing light was on the nose wheel, which was very unusual since most carrier aircraft did not have landing lights. So, I dropped my landing gear behind this other FJ, turned on my landing light, and 'shot' him down.

"Of all the aircraft I have flown, except perhaps the Crusader III, the Fury was the most 'fun' airplane. The FJ-3 was nimble and fun to fly around the carrier. You had precise speed control in the pattern. The mid–50s was the transitional period from the human-directed 'Paddles' approach to the mirror approach, which I had tested in England in Sea Vampires on board HMS *Illustrious* during an exchange tour at The Empire Test Pilot School. Sometimes the carriers we flew from had a mirror, and sometimes, they used LSOs. Regardless of the system, the FJ-3 was very stable, and you could fly it within 2–3 knots of your desired airspeed. It responded well to wave-offs. All you had to do was pick up the gear, milk up the flaps, and the air-craft would handily fly away. Coming aboard was easy, and I believe you could pick the wire you wanted to catch.

"However, the FJ-3 was not without its problems, not all of its own making. In late 1955, Lt. Cdr. Joe Humes, the Ops Officer for VF-21, while recovering aboard *Forrestal*, just ahead of me, had a wire part. The cable wrapped around his tailhook, snapping his Fury inverted on the deck. Joe was killed instantly. His Fury slid up the deck and off into the water and disappeared.

"People from Patuxent came out to investigate, and Lt. Cdr. Bill Nichols was the test pilot flying with the Flight Test Division, for the Fury's carrier suitability. He duplicated the mishap, so well, unfortunately, that Bill, too, was killed when a wire parted. Now we had lost two pilots without knowing the reason.

"We later found that the wedged fitting on the crossdeck pendant was striking the new steel deck in a way which caused it to fracture. Today, on any carrier, you will see a rubber insert in the deck by each pendant. When the wire is first engaged by a plane's hook, it will first strike this rubber insert, preventing the forced wedged fitting from breaking.

"Once, after my tour with VF-21, when I was assigned to NAS Patuxent, I was flying an FJ-3, investigating vertical entries into the fully developed inverted spin. I got as much speed as I could at 25,000 feet, something like Mach 0.86, and with intent, pulled to the vertical. As my airspeed bled off, I planned to put in full forward stick and full right rudder. When the airplane departed, it should have spun inverted, but nothing happened. The airplane continued to zero airspeed, then tumbled, nose over tail, twice before it entered a fully developed, inverted spin. After the desired five turns, I recovered. My chase plane was orbiting overhead. I called him. 'Did you see that?' 'Yeah,' the chase pilot replied. 'Do it again!'

"During the fleet introduction of the FJ-3 in the 1954–55 timeframe, we made many trips to Columbus. We worked with Jim Pearce, the chief test pilot for Columbus, and Dick Wenzell, the company chief test pilot, instrumental in bringing about the Fury's great flying qualities.

"The Fury was very flexible and you could do many things with it because it was so aerodynamically clean. The wings would twist and there was a slight tendency for one wing to drop as you went transonic. The right wing would drop slightly, which was annoying. You had to hold in left aileron to fly straight.

"I developed a procedure for changing the set of the wings. It wasn't always the right wing. I think it might have been a quirk in the aircraft's manufacture, or perhaps in the hamfistedness of the pilots. As you reached this transonic range, if you laid the stick over promptly to the right, and rolled the aircraft, you could change the set of the wing slightly. The next time the plane went through the transonic range, it might do so without either wing dropping, or perhaps the left wing would drop. You could develop an airplane which went transonic smoothly.

"One of the FJ-3's shortcomings was the engine. It had a total-discharge-of-oil system which atomized the internal oil and sprayed it over the engine bearings. This oil spray was vented overboard in a fine mist which could also affect the paint. But the major problem was that if the oil spray was interrupted, the engine could seize. During the development cycle in the 1956–57 timeframe, we did lose a number of engines to oil starvation. Engines seized, and the pilots had to set up flameout approaches. Generally speaking, the pilots recovered and did not eject, a credit to them. Later, procedures recommended ejecting.

"The FJ-3's nimbleness, its thrust-to-weight ratio, and its ability to fly at high altitudes made it easy to achieve supersonic flight. This was generally accomplished in a dive, after a split 'ees' at altitude, aiming the airplane at a target on the ground. The sonic boom would come off the aircraft as we pulled out. We developed some accuracy in aiming the boom at some point on the ground.

"You shouldn't think we pilots did happy-go-lucky, or strange things. This only indicated how the plane was developed and flown by some people. Hours were spent in training in precision flying, gunnery, and interception. It was a good combat aircraft.

"The J-65 engine was one of the weak links in the FJ-3, particularly because of the previously mentioned oil problems. All the pilots were very concerned and we spent a lot of time in 1955–56 practicing flameout approaches. I never had an engine fail, but several of my squadron mates did, and they were able to return. One day in 1955, when I had climbed to 53,500 feet, in an FJ-3 without drop tanks, I shut down the engine and glided to 20,000 feet in sixteen minutes. I relit the engine and returned.

"The FJ-3 was a true fighter. It had four 20 mm cannon in the nose. We practiced gunnery at 35,000 feet and 18–20,000 feet. VF-21 achieved a moderate success in gunnery. While the cannon was considered the main armament, we also carried Sidewinders. The FJ-3 was considered a dedicated air-to-air combat aircraft and was not configured for close air support, or bombing" (1987 interview of Vice Adm. Donald D. Engen, USN [Ret.] by aviation writer and historian Peter B. Mersky).

Notes

1. Engen, Donald D. *Wings and Warriors*, Washington, DC: Smithsonian, 1997.
2. Ibid.
3. Potter, E.B. *Sea Power: A Naval History*, Annapolis, MD: Naval Institute Press, 1981.
4. Official Biography of Vice Adm. Donald D. Engen, USN, Naval History Division, Washington, DC.
5. Engen, Donald D. *Wings and Warriors,* Washington, DC: Smithsonian, 1997.
6. Ibid.
7. VB-19 Bombing Nineteen, Stats, stories and songs of a squadron from the carrier USS *Lexington.* http://www.emersonguys.com/bill/vb19.htm.
8. Engen, Donald D. *Wings and Warriors*, Washington, DC: Smithsonian, 1997.
9. Ibid.
10. Engen, Donald D. *Wings and Warriors*, Washington, DC: Smithsonian, 1997.
11. Official Biography of Vice Admiral Donald D. Engen, USN, Naval History Division, Washington, DC.
12. Engen, Donald D. *Wings and Warriors*, Washington, DC: Smithsonian, 1997.

13. Official Biography of Vice Admiral Donald D. Engen, USN, Naval History Division, Washington, DC.

14. Engen, Donald D. *Wings and Warriors,* Washington, DC: Smithsonian, 1997.

15. Smithsonian Institute press release, 14 July 1999: "National Air and Space Museum Director Donald Engen Dies in Glider Accident."

Capt. Frederick C. Turner
(July 1967–October 1968)

"The Sixth Fleet will be able to meet its commitments in support of national policy without home-porting in Athens."—Admiral Turner, Commander Sixth Fleet, commenting after Greece, angry that the U.S. did not do more to prevent the 1974 Turkish invasion of Cyprus, withdrew its permission for the fleet to use the harbor at Elefsis, Cyprus, May 1975.

Vice Admiral Frederick Charles "Fox" Turner, USN (Ret.), summarizes his significant naval career events as follows:

1. F2H "Banshee" project test pilot at Tactical Test Division. During B-36 and Navy flap, took pictures of Washington, D.C., from 51, 000 feet. Raced the sun (for 1950 issue of *Life* magazine) from coast to coast. The sun won!

2. Student in the first test pilot class at Patuxent River, Maryland.

3. Graduated No. 2 in class at Empire Test Pilots School, Farnborough, England.

4. Led the AirLant Introduction Program for the F7U-3 Cutlass. Formed a Cutlass flight demonstration team, "The Dandy Ganders." Performed over the USS *Forrestal* when she was commissioned.

5. Demonstrated the F8U-1 on the French carrier *Clemenceau.* Went to Paris and helped sell the F8U to the French navy.

6. Led the first TA4-J introductory formation flight into the Advanced Training Command in Corpus Christi, Texas.

7. In the Pentagon, was the Navy sponsor for the F/A-18.

8. Was the last Navy World War II carrier pilot to leave duty: July 1979.[1]

"Fox" Turner was born in Boston, Massachusetts, on 13 June 1923, son of Charles J. and Margaret (Enright) Turner. He enlisted in the U.S. Navy on 28 July 1942, and in January 1943 was appointed Naval Aviation Cadet (NAVCAD), U.S. Naval Reserve. After flight training, he was designated a Naval Aviator, 21 December 1943, and commissioned Ensign, USNR, to date from 1 December that year. He subsequently advanced in rank to Vice Admiral, having transferred from the Naval Reserve to the U.S. Navy on 15 August 1946.

After receiving his Wings, he had operational training in F6F aircraft before being assigned to Fighting Squadron Eighty-Two in April 1944. "For heroism and extraordinary achievement … as pilot of a Fighter Plane in Fighting Squadron Eighty-Two, attached to the USS *Bennington*, during operations against enemy Japanese forces…" from 16 February to 19 May 1945, he was awarded the Distinguished Flying Cross and Air Medal, Gold stars in lieu of the Second and Third similar awards. During this period, Lieutenant, Junior Grade, Turner completed twenty missions and "…contributed materially to the infliction of extensive damage on enemy shipping, airfields and installations…." He was next assigned as Operations Officer of Fighter Squadron Seventeen-A, the first Navy Jet squadron.

In November 1947 he reported for test pilot training at the Tactical Test Division, Naval Air Test Center (NATC), Patuxent River, Maryland, and remained after graduation as Project Officer in Charge of Tactical Evaluation of the F2H, Banshee, until December 1949. He then traveled to England, where he was an Exchange Student at the Empire Test Pilot School, Farnborough. Graduated in December 1950, he next joined Experimental Squadron Three as Project Officer. As such, he was Naval Liaison Officer to the Armed Services weapons evaluation tests at Fort Bragg, North Carolina. One year later he was detached to attend the University of Pennsylvania at Philadelphia, and in August 1953 he reported as a student (General Line) at the Naval Postgraduate School, Monterey, California.

Capt. Frederick C. Turner (official U.S. Navy photograph).

From March 1954 until October 1956 he served as Administrative, Operations and Executive Officer of Fighter Squadron Eighty-Three, an F7U Cutlass squadron, after which he had duty in connection with air readiness on the Staff of the Commander in Chief, U.S. Atlantic Fleet. In July 1958 he reported for instruction at the Armed Forces Staff College, Norfolk, Virginia, and upon completion of the course there in February 1959, was assigned as Operational Planning Officer, in the Bureau of Naval Personnel, Navy Department, Washington, D.C., where he remained until May 1961. While there he studied at the University of Maryland, at College Park, from which he received the degree of Bachelor of Science in 1961.

After a brief tour of duty with Fighter Squadron One Hundred Seventy-Four, he assumed command in October 1961, of Fighter Squadron Thirty-Two. He was detached from that command in May 1962 and after two months instruction with Carrier Air Group Four, reported in July as Commander Carrier Air Group Three. During the year August 1963 to August 1964, he attended the Industrial College of the Armed Forces, Washington, D.C., and received a Master of Science degree in Business Administration from George Washington University.

He next served on the staff of Commander Carrier Division Six. In November he became Commanding Officer of the USS *Sandoval* (APA-194). *Sandoval* was awarded the "E" for battle efficiency while under his command. In May 1967 he was detached to join the Staff of Commander Naval Air Force, Atlantic Fleet. On 31 July 1967, he assumed command of the USS *America* (CVA-66), which operated in waters off Vietnam. He was awarded the Legion of Merit "for exceptionally meritorious conduct in the performance of outstanding service as Commanding Officer of the USS *America* ... conducting combat operations against the enemy in North Vietnam...." The USS *America* was awarded the Navy Unit Commendation, the Navy "E" for battle efficiency and the Admiral Flatley Memorial Award for outstanding achievement in accident prevention, while under his command.

On 7 June 1968, he was selected for promotion to Rear Admiral. On 30 October 1968, he became Chief of Naval Air Advanced Training at Corpus Christi, Texas, and "for exceptionally meritorious service ... from October 1968 to August 1970..." was awarded a Gold Star in lieu of a second Legion of Merit. In August 1970 he reported as Assistant Chief of Naval Personnel for Personnel Control, Navy Department and was awarded a Gold Star in lieu of the Third Legion of Merit "for exceptionally meritorious conduct..." in that capacity from August 1970 to March 1972. In May 1972 he assumed command of Carrier Division Two (later redesignated Carrier Group). He was awarded a Gold Star in lieu of the Fourth Legion of Merit "for exceptionally meritorious conduct ... as Commander Task Force Sixty and Commander Carrier Group Two while permanently deployed with the United States Sixth Fleet from July 1972 to May 1974...." In August 1974 he was designated Commander Sixth Fleet. From September 1976 to July 1979 he was Deputy CNO (Air Warfare). He retired from the Navy on 1 July 1979. Following his retirement he worked for Teledyne Technologies, Inc., and two French companies (He was fluent in the French language).

In addition to the Legion of Merit with three Gold Stars, the Distinguished Flying Cross and the Air Medal with two Gold Stars, Rear Admiral Turner has the American Campaign Medal; Asiatic-Pacific Campaign Medal with two stars, World War II Victory Medal; Navy Occupation Service Medal, Asia Clasp; National Defense Service Medal with bronze star; Armed Forces Expeditionary Medal (Cuba); and the Vietnam Service Medal with bronze star. He also has the National Order of Vietnam Fifth Class, the Republic of Vietnam Gallantry Cross with Palm, and the Republic of Vietnam Campaign Medal with Device.[2]

"Top Flyer Retires"

When Vice Admiral Turner closed out thirty-seven years of naval service on 1 July 1979, his retirement ceremony was held at the historic Washington Navy Yard in the nation's capital. Leutze Park was the scene—a neatly manicured rectangle of green situated amidst vintage cannons and stately officer quarters painted a bright white.

The Navy Band was there in its blue coats as was the crack ceremonial guard in freshly pressed uniforms. A contingent of friends and guests in their best summer suits and dresses occupied seats which were comfortably close to the podium. The official party consisted of the Chief of Naval Operations, Adm. Thomas B. Hayward; Commandant, Naval District Washington, Rear Adm. Karl J. Bernstein; and the principal of the hour, Vice Admiral Turner.

It was an elegant but relaxed affair and although it was only one of hundreds which are held at Leutze Park, air stations, and aboard ships throughout the fleet each year, this ceremony had a character all its own. For a few moments, all attention was focused on a man who, as DCNO (Air Warfare), was stepping down as Naval Aviation's "top" aviator. Of special significance was the fact that Vice Admiral Turner was the only officer on active duty to have flown combat missions from aircraft carriers in World War II.

Members of his family, including Pamela, a Lieutenant junior grade who "will carry on after me," looked on from the front row as Admiral Hayward made his remarks and then introduced his colleague who was retiring.

"I tried to join the Navy right after Pearl Harbor," Vice Admiral Turner began, "but my father put a stop to it. He figured I didn't really know what I was up to. I found some recruiting brochures about Naval Aviation and surreptitiously displayed them around the house. He eventually looked at them and told me, 'Now this looks like a good outfit, why don't you try it.' My ploy worked and by 1944 I was flying Hellcats in the Pacific."

Vice Admiral Turner commented that a formation fly-by would certainly accentuate the day's proceedings but quickly added that fuel and related problems precluded such activities. Instead, he asked the audience to put their imaginations to work while he articulated a magnificent, albeit "invisible," sequence of fly-bys.

Gesturing toward the upper heights, the admiral introduced Hellcats from VF-82 and Bennington, Banshees from VF-17A, a variety of flying machines from the test center at Patuxent River, and another batch from England's Empire Test Pilot School and U.S. based VX-3.

Winging by next were Crusaders from VFs 83 and 32 (he commanded the latter), and a flock of birds from Carrier Air Group Three which he once guided as CAG. In a sail-by, USS *Sandoval* loomed proudly on the horizon followed by USS *America*, ships which he had skippered. There were more airplanes, this time from the training command which he headed, and a powerful armada of Sixth Fleet warships which he commanded before taking on Air Warfare duties in the Pentagon. The imaginary dramatics were a nice touch. Influenced by his Mediterranean experience with the Sixth Fleet, the admiral then addressed friends representing the Greek, French and Italian military. With impressive fluency, he spoke in each of their respective languages. This was even a nicer touch.

Finally, he expressed gratitude to "Red," for she preserved in the arduous pattern of Navy wives who waited for their husbands and, when they could, followed them far and wide across the country and around the world. There were a lot of duty stations over nearly four decades of service life and a cumbersome parade of moving bands.

"I would receive orders," said the admiral, "and tell Red about the new assignment. Invariably, she would ask 'Where?' And I'd tell her. Then she would inquire, 'Where's that?' And I'd tell her. There was a brief pause and then she would say, 'O.K., let's go!'"

In closing he referred to retirement as a form of new assignment and paraphrased the ritual which had been a part of their lives through the years. He said, "I'll anticipate Red's comment one last time and say, 'O.K., let's go!'" Perhaps the nicest touch of all.

There was an unexpected but pleasant disruption at the end of the ceremony. The troops had marched off the rectangle and people had risen from their seats.

Capt. James W. Conte, senior chaplain at the Naval Academy, who shared the platform with the admirals, commandeered the microphone.

"Would everyone please hold it a moment," he requested. "I have something to add!" At which point he presented Vice Admiral Turner, who is Catholic, a leather-bound portfolio containing a special papal blessing.

"When the time comes, Admiral," said the chaplain, with the right combination of amusement and sincerity, "hand this to Saint Peter. It might help you get in."

There was applause and people were soon in motion again, making a short walk toward the Anacostia River and the Naval Museum where refreshments were waiting.

Interspersed among the paintings, artifacts and the Museum's imposing nineteen-foot high centerpiece, the fifty-three-year-old fighting top from the USS *Constitution*, were poster-size photographs of the principal of the day. They are presented here not for aggrandizement but to reflect that certain special nature of the professional life of a Naval Aviator.[3]

Notes

1. Internet/Google: PDF Vice Adm. Frederick C. "Fox" Turner, USN (Ret.)
2. Official Biography of Vice Adm. Frederick C. "Fox" Turner, USN (Ret.), Navy History and Heritage Command, Washington, D.C.
3. Commander Rosario Rausa, October 1979 issue of *Naval Aviation News*, Navy Department, Washington, D.C.

Capt. Richard E. Rumble
(October 1968–December 1969)

"The performance and professionalism of all hands was flawless."— Capt. Richard Rumble commenting on the USS *America* crew's performance during combat operations in Vietnam.

On 24 March 1945, the heavy cruiser USS *Salt Lake City* (CA-25) lay off shore of the island of Okinawa, Japanese territory approximately 400 miles south of the main islands of Japan, and began a bombardment of the island that would continue unabated, day and night, for the next 66 days. The island was being seized for use as an air base during the upcoming invasion of Japan.[1]

Known unofficially as "Old Swayback" or the "Swayback Maru," the *Salt Lake City* was a *Pensacola*-class cruiser commissioned in 1929 and thus was the oldest heavy cruiser in the fleet. As such, she was considered the most expendable and was in almost continuous operation throughout the war, ultimately fighting in 31 Pacific war engagements, more than any other ship in the fleet.

The *Salt Lake City* was at sea escorting the USS *Enterprise* (CV-6) back to Pearl Harbor from Wake Island on 7 December 1941, when the Japanese attacked, but is credited with firing the first shots at Japanese held territory. Part of a Task Force, commanded by Adm. William F. Halsey, attacking a major Japanese base on the Wotje Atoll, Marshall Islands, on 1 February 1942, the *Salt Lake City* opened fire seconds before the other ships making her shells the first U.S. Naval ordnance to land on Japanese territory. The raid resulted in heavy damage, including fifteen Japanese vessels sunk and numerous barracks, hangars and planes on fire.[2]

After escorting the naval force that carried the bombers for the Doolittle Raid on Tokyo in April 1942, the *Salt Lake City* helped cover the landings at Guadalcanal, saw action at the Battles of Coral Sea, Savo Island, and Cape Esperance, and also operated in the Aleutians. She supported the invasion at Tarawa in November 1943, harassed and bombarded many Jap-held islands including Wotje, Taroa, Kwajalein, Majuro, Palau Yap, Ulithi and Woleai throughout March and April 1944.

Returning from the Aleutians, while at Pearl Harbor undergoing minor repairs, the *Salt Lake City* took on new crewmembers. Among them was a brand new officer, Ensign R. Rumble, Annapolis Class of 1945, who reported aboard in August as Assistant Navigator. Rumble later recalled, "Almost immediately upon reporting on board, the six of us were introduced, counseled and given our assignments by the XO (a USNA grad but a recalled Naval Reservist). I was assigned as Assistant Navigator. Why, I don't know. He stressed the fact that we, as Naval Academy graduates, represented about ten per cent of the wardroom officer complement and that with our education and training we were expected to be models of what a naval officer should be."

The ship continued on to Mare Island Navy Yard, California, arriving on 7 May, and remained under repair until 22 June 1944, then operated in San Francisco Bay for shakedown trials and gunnery practice, and to take on new crew. By the time the *Salt Lake City* lay off of Okinawa in March 1945, Rumble was a veteran having endured the severe weather of the Aleutians, participated with the USS *Pensacola* (CA-24) and USS *Monterey* (CVL-26) in the attack on Wake Island on 3 September 1944, and the second Battle of the Philippine Sea in October. In November through January 1945, Rumble watched as enemy positions on Iwo Jima, Chichi Jima and Haha Jima came under the fire of the cruiser's 8-inch and 5-inch guns. "*Salt Lake City*'s major contribution," Rumble later wrote, "was to provide gunfire support for amphibious operations as well as Cruiser Task Group 'hit and run' raids along the Jima archipelago prior to the forthcoming landing and occupation of Iwo Jima."

Those days, as the *Salt Lake City* lay off of Okinawa, and as Japanese Kamikazes buzzed menacingly in the dark skies above as the fleet fought furiously to secure the island for use as an airfield, Rumble, a surface officer, most certainly must have mused on the growing role of combat aviation in future wars. Unlike the majority of officers that would command the *America*, Rumble, although interested in aviation from an early age, did not begin his naval career as an aviator.

"I was interested in aviation from the time I was in Junior High, living in Coronado with two young naval aviators, Tommy Booth and Sheik Sutherland, and their families living next door. They were carrier flyers and frequently took me with them when they had occasion to run out to the NAS or go aboard their homeported carrier." Both went on to become Admirals.[3]

Richard Edwards Rumble was born in San Diego, California, on 26 October 1922, son of Rear Adm. Cyril and Eileen Rumble. His father, a student at the University of Washington when the United States entered World War I, went with his fraternity to a Navy recruiter and enlisted en masse. Invited to enroll in the newly established officer-training program following the end of the war, he earned a commission as an ensign and retired as a Rear Admiral shortly after World War II.

His father was in command of the light cruiser USS *Concord* (CL-10) on 12 August 1945, when, as the flagship of Task Force Ninety Two, the ship shelled Paramushir, one of the Kurile Islands in the northwest Pacific, arguably the last salvo of World War II. "His ship fired the last shot in World War II. I'm not sure my father was aware or took any pride in this historical fact. Notwithstanding, some of his enthusiastic crewmembers reminded me of this singular accomplishment during a USS *Concord* Reunion."[4]

Rumble enlisted in the U.S. Navy Reserve on 1 April 1940, while still attending high school in Long Beach, California, hoping it would improve his chances to win an appointment to the U.S. Naval Academy. Part of a Navy family that frequently relocated, he had no real "home" state. "The only opportunity known to me at the time for my entrance in the USNA was a competitive presidential appointment. These appointments were limited to 15 from all applicants from the sons of military personnel. To improve my chances for an appointment, I enlisted in the Naval Reserve.... In this arena, 100 competitive appointments were available. I actually was awarded both; one of the Presidential and one of the Naval Reserve Appointments. Later, the Presidential appointment was withdrawn."[5]

Rumble entered the U.S. Naval Academy, Annapolis, Maryland, on 3 July 1941, and graduated with the Class of 1945 on 7 June 1944 (accelerated

Lt.(jg) Richard Rumble greeting his father, Capt. Cyril Rumble aboard the USS *Concord* in Adak, Alaska, August 1945 (courtesy Richard Rumble).

course due to World War II), he was commissioned Ensign and upon graduation in 1944, he reported on board the USS *Salt Lake City* (CA-25).

During operations off Okinawa, the *Salt Lake City* would expend 9,070
eight-inch shells, 14, 225 five-inch shells, 5,770 40 mm and 1,711 20 mm
shells. She operated off Okinawa until 28 May 1945, without a single loss
of life. After sailing to Leyte on 31 May for rest and repairs, the ship returned
to Okinawa on 6 July for duty covering mine-sweeping and patrolling the
East China Sea.

Shortly after the operation at Iwo Jima, Rumble and a buddy, Joe Bolger, applied for flight training and were subsequently detached from the
USS *Salt Lake City* at Attu, in the Aleutian Islands on 31 August 1945, Rumble and Bolger were sent to the States for flight training, while the ship was
ordered to Japan for the surrender ceremonies and to cover the occupation
of Ominato Naval Base, Northern Honshu, Japan.[6]

"I couldn't believe the sincere but negative counseling we both received
from the Department Heads and XO to the fact that there was no future in
naval aviation. In any event, our requests went out, and in early August, we
received our orders."

Rumble underwent primary flight training in Dallas, Texas, then basic
flight training at Corpus Christi before reporting to the Naval Air Station,
Pensacola, Florida, for gunnery, tactics and carrier qualification. He completed advanced training at NAS Banana River, Florida, and on 5 March
1947, he was designated a Naval Aviator. In August of that year, he joined
Fighter Squadron Nineteen (VF-19A) "Satan's Kittens," which was re-
designated VF-191 on 24 August 1948.

As part of Air Wing Nineteen (CVG-19) aboard the USS *Boxer* (CV-
21) the squadron was in the process of transitioning from the Grumman
F6F Hellcat to the Grumman F8F Bearcat (affectionately called "Bear").
Most of the time was spent training reservists on peacetime patrols of the
California coast. The *Boxer* did achieve distinction when on 10 March 1948,
an FJ-1 Fury fighter jet launched from her deck, the first launch of a jet aircraft from a carrier. For the remainder of 1948 and 1949, *Boxer* participated
in numerous battle drills and acted as a training carrier for jet aircraft
pilots.[7]

"The three years in VF-191 were a mix of deployments; up and down
the West Coast, the Hawaiian Islands, the Philippines, Korea and Hong
Kong. Our last cruise in Westpac ended just before the Communist invasion
of Korea," Rumble recalled. "Thus ended my first at sea tour as a naval aviator and, as it came to pass, a bachelor."[8]

In July 1950, Rumble was assigned to the Naval Air Test Center, Patuxent River, Maryland, where he was trained as a test pilot, saw duty in connection with armament tests, served as Aide to the Commander, Naval Air Test Center and served on the Staff. "My first jet flights were a handbook read the night before, then a flight the next day, in each of the stable of jets at the school." It was during this time that he met, and subsequently married his wife, Bernice.

He remained on staff until February 1953, when he was assigned to Fighter Squadron One Hundred Seventy Three (VF-173) "Jesters," flying the Grumman F9F-6 Cougar out of Jacksonville, Florida. The squadron embarked on a world cruise aboard the USS *Wasp* (CVA-18) on 16 September 1953, as part of Carrier Air Group Seventeen (CVG-17). The ship departed Norfolk, and conducted NATO exercises in the North Atlantic, then moved south through the Mediterranean and Suez Canal before joining Task Force 71 for operations in the Western Pacific. The ship hosted Nationalist Chinese President Chiang Kai-shek on 10 January 1954, followed by an air show put on by the air group. *Wasp* also hosted Philippine President Ramon Magsaysay on 12 March, before docking at its new home in San Diego on 1 May 1954, while the squadron departed, flying back to Jacksonville.[9]

Departing the squadron in September 1954 he was assigned as Assistant Air Group Training Officer on the Staff of Commander Naval Air Force, Atlantic Fleet. "This split sea/shore assignment proved to be a rewarding experience … I was indoctrinated into the 'why' and 'wherefore's' of a large operating staff." Rumble remained at Virginia Beach until March 1956 when he accepted a position as Flight Test Officer in the office of the Bureau of Aeronautics Representative, North American Aviation, Inc., Columbus, Ohio. "In my position … I had to be very careful to avoid the undue contractor pressure to accept production aircraft not fully ready in order to meet contractor promised delivery schedules."[10]

From August 1958 until January 1959, Rumble attended classes at the Armed Forces Staff College, Norfolk, Virginia, following which he reported as Executive Officer of Attack Squadron Eighty One (VA-81) "Crusaders" at NAS Oceana, flying the A-4B Skyhawk. On 9 November 1960, Commander Rumble assumed command of the squadron. The squadron deployed to the Mediterranean on 9 February 1961, as part of Carrier Air Group Eight (CVG-8) aboard the USS *Forrestal* (CVA-59).

In January 1962 he joined the USS *Independence* (CVA-62) as a department head, just as it was returning to Norfolk from a deployment. "While I had carrier experience, I knew little about the fine points of scheduling and integration of air operations with the myriad of ship functions. What fun and what a learning experience under a very sharp and demanding CO."

In August 1962 he became Commander Carrier Air Group Ten (CVG-10). The wing was based at Cecil Field, Jacksonville, Florida, and embarked in USS *Shangri-La* (CVA-38), a World War II–era *Essex*-class carrier. Following an extensive overhaul at the New York Naval Shipyard, the ship deployed on 1 October 1963, on a Mediterranean cruise, with port calls in France, Italy, Greece and Turkey, before returning to her home port at Mayport, Florida, on 23 May 1964. During the cruise, on 23 December 1963, CVG-10 was redesignated Carrier Air Wing Ten (CVW-10).

Shortly after returning from the deployment, Rumble was assigned to duty with a preliminary Joint Planning Staff, created by Secretary of Defense Robert McNamara. Joint Task Group Two was a joint-service effort toward developing tactics for responding to and evading ground to air missiles. "There was an Air Force General, an Army Brigadier General, a Navy Admiral, with a Marine Colonel as Chief of Staff. It was mostly a political contest between the Air Force, Army and the Weapons System Evaluation people, with the Navy ambivalently positioned on the sidelines." Initially headquartered in Washington, D.C., Rumble elected to remain in the Capital following the decision to move the task group to Albuquerque, New Mexico, once the initial planning phase was complete, and he took an assignment as Rating Manager and Program Manager for Aircraft Weapons System, Personnel Program Management Division, Bureau of Naval Personnel, Navy Department in Washington, D.C., reporting on 23 December 1964. On 1 July 1965, Rumble was promoted to Captain.

On 25 February 1966, Rumble reported for instruction at the National War College, Washington, D.C., and earned a degree in International Affairs from George Washington University. While at the War College, he learned his next at-sea assignment would be command of a deep draft vessel, followed, hopefully, by the command of a carrier.

On 25 May 1967, he assumed command of the USS *Marias* (AO-57) a fleet oiler out of Norfolk. A little more than a year later, on 4 October 1968, Rumble took command of the USS *America* while at sea at Yankee Station, off the coast of Vietnam, relieving Capt. Frederick "Fox" Turner. Rumble recalled, "We were on the line for 38 days with the night flying cycle. Having written a paper advocating blockade of North Vietnam for my Master's thesis, it was disconcerting for me to sit there on the bridge during our night ops and observe the endless passage of Communist ships obviously bound for ports in Vietnam that should have been our targets rather than what we were doing; sowing the countryside of North Vietnam with ordnance."[11]

It was the ship's first tour of duty with the Seventh Fleet, off Vietnam. During her total 112 days on station, her aircraft targeted roads, bridges and other strategic targets. It was *America's* first combat cruise, and it was not without cost. CVW-6 lost ten men to enemy action, five killed-in-action (KIA) and five prisoners-of-war (POW), with two never to return. *America* and her air wing, CVW-6, would be awarded the Navy Unit Commendation for their efforts. The ship completed the deployment and returned home to Hampton Roads on 16 December 1968.[12]

Rumble was next appointed as Assistant Chief of Staff to Commander Naval Air Force, U.S. Atlantic Fleet at NAS Norfolk until April 1970 when he became Chief of Staff to Commander Second Fleet, serving under four different flag officers. His selection for rank of Rear Admiral was approved by the President on 26 April 1972.

In November 1972 he reported as Commandant of the First Naval District, with headquarters at the Boston Naval Shipyard, Boston, Massachusetts, with the additional duty as Commander of the Naval Base, Newport, Rhode Island.

Rumble later stated that it was an unusual choice of assignment given that most of his experience had been at sea, rather than shore duty. Additionally, as a newly minted admiral, it was unusual that he would be posted to commands usually reserved for about-to-retire senior officers. Nonetheless, it was this posting that allowed him to preserve an icon of American history.

"The DOD Base Realignment ordained during my tour presented me with the opportunity to establish the USS *Constitution* Museum Foundation and concurrently to convince the National Park Service of the wisdom of establishing a National Naval Park in partnership with the Navy and the Museum Foundation. The initiative insured a permanent home for the USS *Constitution* with the infrastructure to support the upkeep of the ship as well as support facilities for the crew."[13]

The result is the USS *Constitution* Museum, located in the Charlestown Navy Yard, Boston, which serves to preserve the heritage of a national treasure, "Old Ironsides." The tour of the ship, still a commissioned U.S. Navy warship, includes the ship's spar deck (top deck), gun deck and berth deck and explains the history of the ship. There is also a learning center and museum.

Rumble was relieved of the additional duty of commanding the Naval

Captain Rumble (left) during a celebration aboard the USS *America* October 20, 1969 (official U.S. Navy photograph).

Base at Newport when it was disestablished, on 1 July 1974. Later that month he was ordered to duty as Commander Naval Safety Center, Naval Air Station, Norfolk, Virginia.

"I believed my new orders belied the end of my Navy career, however before I actually took command, I was asked to take command of the Fifth

Naval District and the Norfolk Naval Base. My predecessor had been fired and my mandate was to restore "good order and discipline" and clean up the base. I was also ordered to present a plan for combining the Naval Station and the Air Station, and present it (the plan) in thirty days."[14]

His tour at Norfolk was interrupted when he was ordered to London as Deputy Commander in Chief, U.S. Navy—Europe (CINCUSNAVEUR), to report immediately. His relationship with his boss was, as he later described it, "difficult," perhaps because of the officer's disinclination towards aviators. When CINCUSNAVEUR was downgraded, and the incumbent replaced by an aviator, it was decided to reassign him, possibly to avoid having both top spots filled by aviators.

An interview with the Chief of Naval Personnel created an awareness as to the unlikeliness of a three-star assignment when he was advised that you had to be "next to the bull" to get promoted to Vice Admiral. He accepted a position based at Norfolk, Virginia, as Chief of Staff to Adm. Harry D. Train, the SACLANT (Supreme Allied Commander—Atlantic), one of two NATO Supreme Commanders, the other being SACEUR (Supreme Allied Commander—Europe). The mission of SACLANT was to safeguard NATO's Sea-lines of Communication (SLOC) and protect NATO's Sea-based Nuclear Deterrence.

On 30 August 1981, after forty-one years of Naval service, Rear Admiral Rumble retired from the Navy. He passed on opportunities in defense related businesses, opting instead to help establish, and then serve as director of a Maritime Museum housed in an abandoned, now refurbished, Coast Guard Lifesaving Station. After seven years, he retired again and was presented with a putter as a going away gift. Having decided to purchase the rest of the clubs, he now spends his time playing golf when he can with a group of retirees of all ranks called the "swindlers."[15]

Rear Admiral Rumble's awards include two awards of the Legion of Merit, Meritorious Service Medal; Navy Expeditionary Medal (Cuba) and the Vietnam Service Medal with bronze star. He has also been awarded the Philippine Liberation Ribbon and the Republic of Vietnam Gallantry Cross.

Notes

1. USS *Salt Lake City* website http://ussslcca25.com/slc-history.htm
2. Ibid.
3. Interview with Richard Rumble, January 2013.
4. Ibid.

    5. Ibid.
    6. History of the USS *Salt Lake City*—December 11, 1929–27 September 1945, U.S. Navy Dept. Office of Public Information http://ussslcca25.com/1929-45.htm#top.
    7. St. John, Philip. USS *Boxer.* Turner Publishing Company, Nashville, Tennessee (2000) ISBN 978-1-56311-610-0.
    8. Interview with Richard Rumble, January 2013.
    9. Ibid.
    10. Ibid.
    11. Ibid.
    12. The USS *America* Virtual Museum—http://ussamerica-museumfoundation.org/history.html
    13. Interview with Richard Rumble, January 2013.
    14. Interview with Richard Rumble, January 2013.
    15. Interview with Richard Rumble, January 2013.

Capt. Thomas B. Hayward
(December 1969–November 1970)

Aboard the Seventh Fleet Carrier USS *Intrepid* (CVS-11) the tall, slender Navy commander used no notes as he spoke. Holding onto the microphone with one hand, he began his remarks more as a personal conversation than as a formal speech. The occasion, on 23 June 1966, marked his departure from the ship on which he had served seven months and from the air wing which he commanded almost a year.

Cdr. Thomas B. Hayward of Jacksonville, Florida, was being relieved of his command of Carrier Attack Air Wing Ten, which had deployed with the *Intrepid* for duty in the Western Pacific. His air wing began training aboard the "Fighting I" the previous November in preparation for assignment to the South China Sea and support of the allied commitment to South Vietnam.

In the first month of aerial operations against enemy concentrations in that country, Commander Hayward himself flew more than thirty strike sorties earning him three Air Medals in addition to the eight he already wore.

His tour as Commander, Air Group (CAG) at an end, the affable commander presented his thoughts on CVW-10 and *Intrepid.*

"The word is SQUARE—S-Q-U-A-R-E.

"Back not too many years ago this word, square, was one of the finest words in our language. You gave your fellow officer or shipmate a square deal if you treated him fairly and justly.

"You stood foursquare for what was right—and square against everything else. At inspection you stood with your shoulders square—proud to be known as one who was squared away. And there was something special about looking another square in the eye. It was a mark of integrity, courage and honor.

"Then somehow, as the years passed, this grand old word lost this meaning and took on a new connotation. Square became the parent who could not do the frug. The odd ball. He's the Aviation Technician who gets a special kick out of doing his job just a little bit better than anyone else. The Ordnanceman who volunteers to sweat it out in the hot sun at Dixie Station when he could easily avoid the extra effort and sit it out in the shade. He's the boob who gets so engrossed in his work that he has to be told when to quit and 'go home.' He's the guy who feels a chill run down his spine when a parade goes by...

"The opposite of square is round. And being round is so much simpler. Responsibilities and problems are easily shrugged off. And it's so easy to roll down the middle-of-the-road—not having to take a position—just following along in a comfortable rut.

Adm. Thomas B. Hayward during his tenure as Chief of Naval Operations, 1977 (U.S. Navy).

"Well, I stand here this morning, after twelve months as Commander, Attack Carrier Air Wing Ten, proud to proclaim that it has been great serving with the finest group of SQUARES ever assembled. In particular during these past forty days I have seen literally hundreds of squares hard at work. There are no round shoulders in this outfit!

"I have watched ordnancemen hauling, loading and reloading bombs, never giving up until the job is completely done—mechanics, plane captains, hydraulicsmen, painters, storekeepers, personnelmen—literally all hands volunteering for work they could easily avoid ... unfortunately, my day-to-day work does not bring me into contact with every man in Air Wing Ten. However, I have my own barometers with which to measure the merit of this great Air Wing—daily aircraft availability, readiness, morale, ability to meet every commitment...

"Of course, seated behind me is the boss man of all squares—Captain Macri. Captain Macri has given this Air Wing as square a deal as any air wing has ever been given. He has been quick to recognize and applaud us in our successes, patient and enduring when we have stumbled and shown something less than our best.

"Captain Macri, the Champagne Air Wing is going to sorely miss your firm and steady guidance when you depart in a few weeks.

"I would like to believe that I could be counted among the squares of Air Wing Ten—fighter pilot though I am." (Ed. Note: Commander Hayward had been kidded about his years as a fighter pilot prior to leading this all attack Air Wing).

"Before I read my orders I would like to relate a brief story about the squarest American I know. This story has special meaning to me because the individual concerned is a close personal friend, but I am certain there are hundreds more like him serving in South Vietnam, on Dixie Station, on Yankee Station and many like him standing and sitting in Hangar Bay One of USS *Intrepid* this morning.

"This officer's name is Cdr. Jerry Denton. At this moment he can be found in a damp, darkened cell in solitary confinement where he has been for the past twelve months. Nearly one year ago, Commander Denton was shot down and captured on a mission over North Vietnam. Since that time he has seen no other American and has heard only what the North Vietnamese want him to hear concerning the progress of the war. He has been interrogated day after day by some of the most expert interrogators known to military history, men trained in the art of breaking a man's will, of realigning his thinking, of indoctrinating him into the communist way of life.

"Two months ago, Commander Denton was interviewed in Hanoi by a member of the Japanese press, an interview that was filmed in part and shown on television in the United States. Among the millions of TV viewers were Commander Denton's wife and seven children. They saw a haggard, drawn, exhausted shell of a man who was once a great athlete.

"He spoke with great difficulty, as though drugged or deprived of sleep for several days in preparation for the interview. But when he spoke, he spoke clearly and squarely! After one year of constant effort by skilled interrogators to drive a wedge in this man's loyalty to the United States, to cast doubts about the U.S. policy in Vietnam, to encourage criticism of American statesmen and Department of Defense civilians, to deride the judgment of our admirals and generals over their handling of the war in Vietnam, he had this to say:

'I don't know what is happening in Vietnam, but whatever my government's policy is, I support it.

'I believe in my government, yes sir, I am a member of that government and will support it as long as I live.'

"These are humbling and inspiring words. They make us realize what a privilege and honor it is to be in Vietnam, to serve with the Seventh Fleet, to serve our country in the execution of its policies. As your departing Air Wing Commander, I want you to know it has been a privilege and honor for me to have served for Commander, Task Group 77.5 (Captain Macri), and with Attack Carrier Air Wing Ten—the best there is!"

Commander Hayward then read his orders, and following brief remarks by his relief, Commander Burrows, was officially relieved of his intrepid and square command.[1]

Commander Hayward would go on to reach the rank of full Admiral and become the twenty-first Chief of Naval Operations (CNO). As CNO he brought to his position an extensive background in Navy program planning and management, and a long and distinguished career in Naval Aviation, including fighter pilot experience in Korean and Vietnam combat operations and duty as a Navy test pilot. He has commanded aviation squadrons and a carrier air wing, a stores ship and an aircraft carrier, served as Commander, U.S. Seventh Fleet, and was Commander-in-Chief, U.S. Pacific Fleet, prior to taking over as Chief of Naval Operations in 1978.[2]

A year before his retirement on 1 July 1982, he was awarded the Society of Experimental Test Pilots James H. Doolittle Award. After retirement Admiral Hayward became chairman of the Ethics Resource Center of America and worked to promote ethics curriculum and programs. He actively participated in the establishment of several Navy related museums, including the USS *Missouri* Foundation and the Military Aviation Museum. He worked tirelessly for literacy reform in public schools through Voyager Expanded Learning, a company he co-founded in 1994, which served over a million at risk public youngsters.

In 2007 Admiral Hayward received the U.S. Naval Academy's Distinguished Graduate Award.

On 8 December 2009, Voyager Learning Company was acquired by Cambium Learning Group, Inc., headquartered in Dallas, Texas. The company employs over four hundred employees and continues to provide "at risk" student education. The Cambium Learning Group is the largest U.S. company focused primarily on serving the needs of at risk and special student population.[3]

Thomas B. Hayward was born in Glendale, California, in 1924, during the "Roaring Twenties." He attended Glendale Junior College and Occidental College at Los Angeles, and in 1943 was appointed a Naval Aviation Cadet in the V-5 Program of the U.S. Naval Reserve. He entered the U.S. Naval Academy in 1944 on appointment from the state of California and upon graduation was commissioned Ensign in the U.S. Navy on 6 June 1947.[4] At the Academy Hayward impressed everyone he met. A fellow midshipman would recall years later that "even then he possessed the marks of an exceptional individual." The Lucky Bag (Academy yearbook) noted that "anything tickling the funny bone would be sure to bring out the abundant sense of humor possessed by this genial ambassador from the West Coast."[5]

Following graduation from the Academy, Hayward served aboard the aircraft carrier USS *Antietam* (CV-36) as a "black shoe" engineer until he entered flight training at Pensacola, Florida, in 1948. He earned his gold wings in July 1950 and was assigned to Fighter Squadron Fifty-One. During his tour with VF-51 and Air Wing Five he spent sixteen months in the Korean theater which included two combat cruises. He flew 146 combat missions in F9F Panther fighter jets embarked in the carrier USS *Essex* (CV-9), and later in the *Valley Forge* (CV-45) earning the Distinguished Flying Cross, ten Air Medals and three Navy Commendation Medals with Combat "V." In 1951 he made a wheels-up forced landing on an outlying field due to flak damage and in late November 1953 he ditched his aircraft after a catapult launch.[6]

In January 1954, he reported for test pilot training at the Naval Air Test Center, Patuxent River, Maryland, and upon completion of training remained there as a test pilot and project coordinator. While at Patuxent he flew a dozen different types of jet and prop aircraft during his thirty-one month tour. Next, he attended the Aviation Safety Officers School at the University of Southern California at Los Angeles, after which he served with All Weather Fighter Squadron Three from December 1956 to July 1958 flying F8U Crusader jets. In August of 1958 he reported for instruction at the Naval War College, Newport, Rhode Island, and in December 1959 joined Crusader Fighter Squadron Two Hundred Eleven as Executive Officer on USS *Lexington*. He continued duty with that squadron making a nine month WestPac cruise until July 1961, when he became Administrative Aide to the Secretary of the Navy.[7]

In December 1963 he served as Executive Officer, later Commanding Officer, of Fighter Squadron One Hundred Three and made a Mediterranean cruise on board the USS *Shangri-La*. It was during this deployment that Hayward assumed command of Attack Carrier Air Wing Ten. After return of the Wing to the U.S., Hayward commenced reorganization of the Air Wing in preparation for combat duty with the USS *Intrepid* off Vietnam. Air Wing Ten became the only all-attack wing to serve with the Seventh Fleet. "For meritorious service ... from September 1965 to June 1966" he was awarded a Gold Star in lieu of the Second Navy Commendation Medal. The citation further states in part:

> ...Commander Hayward was able to reorganize, reassign and subsequently deploy Attack Carrier Air Wing Ten against enemy forces in Southeast Asia. In the remarkable short period of six months, he effected the integration of Attack Squadrons Fifteen, Ninety Five, One Six Five, and One Seven Six, transitioning from propeller to jet aircraft and fusing the Wing into a fully trained, combatant organization mated with an antisubmarine support aircraft carrier. Successfully completing an Operational Readiness Inspection, the Wing arrived off Vietnam and began delivering maximum quantities of aviation ordnance as a part of Task Force 77.5 against communist guerrilla forces....

Philippine President Ferdinand Marcos (left front) and his wife visit the *America*, flagship of Vice Adm. Frederic A. Bardshaw, under the command of Captain Hayward (behind Marcos) (official U.S. Navy photograph).

In 1967 Hayward completed a year of instruction at the National War College, after which he served as Commanding officer, USS *Graffias* (AF-29) serving again with the Seventh Fleet. In December 1969 he assumed command of the USS *America* (CVA-66), deploying to the Seventh Fleet as Flagship to Commander Task Force Seventy Seven. With Air Wing Nine embarked, *America* supported combat operations from May to November 1970 earning the Meritorious Unit Commendation. Captain Hayward received the Gold Star in lieu of a Second Legion of Merit as Commanding Officer. He was promoted to Rear Admiral in November 1970 and reported as Commander Hawaiian Sea Frontier and Commandant of the Fourteenth Naval District with headquarters at Pearl Harbor, Hawaii, with additional duty as Commander Fleet Air, Hawaii and Commander Manned Spacecraft Recovery Forces Pacific.[8]

In 1975, Vice Admiral Hayward assumed command of the Seventh

Fleet. A year later, Admiral Hayward served a Commander-in-Chief, U.S. Pacific Fleet. In 1978, he became Chief of Naval Operations and a member of the Joint Chiefs. His four year tenure was marked by a surge in pride and professionalism within the ranks, an increase in fleet readiness and a bold zero tolerance drug policy that stopped a growing problem in its tracks.[9]

Admiral Hayward retired from the Navy on 1 July 1982. During his career he had logged a total of 4,600 flight hours, made 450 fixed wing carrier landings, flew 146 mission in the Korean War and thirty-six during the Vietnam conflict.[10]

Military Awards: Two Distinguished Service Medals, Three Legion of Merit Medals, the Distinguished Flying Cross, Thirteen Air Medals, three Navy Commendation Medals, Korean/United Nations/Vietnamese/China/Japanese Service Medals and numerous campaign ribbons with devices, and unit/personal citations.[11]

Notes

1. Official *U.S. Navy News* Release: "'SQUARE' SPEECH MARKS DEPARTURE OF *INTREPID* WING COMMANDER," 27 June 1966.

2. Official Biography of Admiral Thomas B. Hayward, USN, Naval History and Heritage Command, Washington, D.C.

3. Admiral Thomas B. Hayward, USN (Ret.), Distinguished Graduate Award–2007 (www.usna.com/document.doc?id=277)

4. Official Biography of Admiral Thomas B. Hayward, USN, Naval History and Heritage Command, Washington, D.C.

5. www.usna.com/document.doc?id=277

6. Official Biography of Admiral Thomas B. Hayward, USN, Naval History and Heritage Command, Washington, D.C.

7. Ibid.

8. Ibid.

9. www.usna.com/document.doc?id=277

10. Official Biography of Adm. Thomas B. Hayward, USN, Naval History and Heritage Command, Washington, D.C.

11. Ibid.

Capt. Thomas B. Russell, Jr.
(November 1970–April 1972)

In August 1950 Russell was assigned as Flight Officer of Composite Squadron Eleven (VC-11), which deployed with Carrier Air Group Two as a unit of Task Force Seventy-Seven. Engaged in combat operations against North Korea the squadron was split, flying from two decks, the USS *Valley Forge* (CV-45) and USS *Philippine Sea* (CV-47). Russell flew a variant of the Douglas Skyraider, the AD-3W. The single engine aircraft provided anti-submarine and airborne early warning protection for the Task Force. Because they were configured with a big belly radome which housed a search radar, the aircraft were called "Guppies."

Although American naval jet aircraft such as the Banshee and Panther eventually entered the fray, the real work horse of naval aviation during the Korean War was the Douglas AD Skyraider.

Capt. Thomas B. Russell, Jr. (official U.S. Navy photograph).

Important among its qualities was the ability of the "Able Dog" to absorb flak damage and return its pilot to a heaving carrier deck. The "Sandy" as it was later called during the Vietnam War would continue to play a major role in that war.

Russell was awarded his first combat medals when as commander of Carrier Air Wing Fourteen deployed aboard the USS *Ranger* (CVA-61) he engaged enemy forces in Southeast Asia. "For heroic and meritorious achievement in the planning and execution of aerial strikes against the Viet Cong ... on 31 January 1966..." he was awarded the Distinguished Flying Cross. He also received the Air Medal with Gold Stars in lieu of the Second and Third awards, "For meritorious achievement in aerial flight ... during missions in support of combat operations in Southeast Asia against the Viet Cong" during the period 15 January to 8 March 1966.

Born in Charleston, Missouri, on 18 December 1923, Russell worked as a bank teller for two years after graduating from high school. He entered the Naval Aviation Cadet Program in August 1943 and was designated a Naval Aviator and commissioned an Ensign nineteen months later. He subsequently advanced in rank to that of Rear Admiral in September 1973, having transferred from the Naval Reserve to the Regular U.S. Navy in 1946.

After receiving his commission, he underwent four months' operational training at the Naval Air Station, Deland, Florida, and later was transferred to a series of squadrons, Bombing Fighting Squadron Ninety-Seven, Bombing Fighting Squadron Eighteen (F-6F Hellcat), Fighting Squadron Eight-A (F-6F Hellcat) and in July 1948 to Fighting Squadron Seventy-Two (F-6F Hellcat). In 1949 he attended Iowa State College at Ames under a Five Term Program.

In 1950 Russell was next assigned as flight Officer of Composite Squadron Eleven (as mentioned above) flying combat missions during the Korean War. As a result of his participation in that war he was entitled to wear the ribbon for, and facsimile of, the Navy Unit Commendation awarded the *Valley Forge*. Following the end of the Korean War he attended the Naval Postgraduate School in Monterey, California, then served as a flight instructor at the Naval Air Basic Training Command in Pensacola, Florida. In 1955 he joined the ships' company aboard the USS *Siboney* (CVE-112) as First Lieutenant (ship's company officers were assigned various duties in administration, maintenance, operations, navigation, etc. departments). The First Lieutenant was in charge of unrated seamen who worked in the mess kitchens, cleaned up living spaces, etc. Once rated, they were moved into various departments. After attending Safety Officer School at the University of Southern California, he was attached to the Jet Transitional Training Unit at NAS Olathe, Kansas, after which he served as Instrument Flight Instructor with the Fleet All Weather Training Unit, U.S. Atlantic Fleet. In 1958/59 he had similar duty with Fighter Squadron Twenty-One (F9F Panther jets/F3H-2 Demon jets).

After attending the Armed Forces Staff College in Norfolk, Virginia, he headed the Navy's Airborne Requirements, Electronic Countermeasures and Communications Section in the Pentagon in Washington and in November 1959 he joined the fleet again as Executive Officer of Attack Squadron One Hundred Fifty-Five where he flew A-1 Skyraiders and A-4D Skyhawk jets. He assumed command of the squadron in 1964. A year later he served as Commander Carrier Air Wing Fourteen. In August of that year the Air Wing consisting of F-4B Phantom IIs/A-3B Skywarriors/F-8E Crusaders/A-4C Skyhawks/A-1 Skyraider prop aircraft and E-1B Tracer prop aircraft deployed aboard the USS *Constellation* (CV-64) participated in the first retaliatory strike against North Vietnam. He planned and executed Air Wing strikes and subsequently was awarded the Distinguished Flying Cross and the Air Medal with two Gold Stars for meritorious achievement in aerial flight.

It was back to a desk job in Washington in late 1966 for JCS duty, then the National War College, and George Washington University from which he received the Bachelor of Science degree in Political Science in 1968. He then assumed command of the USS *Tulare* (AKA-112) and was awarded the Bronze Star Medal for meritorious service during combat operations against the enemy off the coast of the Republic of Vietnam while sustaining Marines ashore during two critical combat operations. His citation reads in part, "...Captain Russell displayed exceptional qualities of leadership while his unit was assigned to Amphibious Ready Group BRAVO of the U.S. Seventh Fleet. During the period 24 February to 3 June 1969, the Amphibious Ships remained at sea off the coast of the Republic of Vietnam in direct support of combat operations. His personal example of initiative and devotion to duty inspired his crew to maintain a high degree of combat readiness while sustaining Marines ashore during Operations Defiant Measure II and Defiant Measure III. Through his ability, *Tulare* significantly contributed to combat support operations...." Following his relief of command of the *Tulare* Captain Russell returned to Washington and served as Assistant Director for Captain Detail (Aviation) for which he was awarded the Meritorious Service Medal.

In November 1970 he assumed command of the USS *America* relieving Capt. Thomas B. Hayward in the Gulf of Tonkin, off Vietnam. The ship completed her fifth line period and then made port at Subic Bay, Philippines, for one last rowdy liberty in Olongapo, a city adjacent to the Naval base. The *America* had completed five line periods off Vietnam and had flown approximately 10,000 sorties, expended over a thousand tons of ordnance while suffering few combat losses.

Captain Russell took the *America* back to its home port arriving at Pier 12, Naval Operating Base (NOB) Norfolk, Virginia, on 21 December 1970. Port calls along the way included Sidney, Australia, and Rio de Janeiro, Brazil. The ship entered the Norfolk Naval Shipyard in January 1971 for three months to undergo some much needed repairs. Departing the yard on schedule in March, *America* operated in the Virginia Capes area and exercised in Puerto Rican waters with U.S. Naval forces and Royal Navy combatants, HMS *Ark Royal, Cleopatra*, and *Bacchante*. Her third Mediterranean deployment began when she departed Norfolk on 6 July 1971.

During her deployment Captain Russell was relieved in April 1972 by Capt. Burton H. Shepherd, the seventh commanding officer of *America*. Before the ship returned from deployment in December of that year she had participated in eight exercises with foreign navies and made ten port calls.

Captain Russell stayed in the Norfolk area next serving on the Joint Staff of the Commander in Chief, Atlantic, with additional duties on the

It was traditional for the *America* to invite each newly crowned Miss America on board to have lunch with the ship's crew in the enlisted mess. The Carrier Onboard Delivery (COD) aircraft was used to fly passengers and mail to and from the ship. The C-2A Greyhound was named Miss America as can be seen in the above photograph of Captain Russell and the 1971 Miss America, Phyllis George, who eventually married Kentucky Governor John Y. Brown and later became the first NFL female sportscaster (official U.S. Navy photograph).

Staff of the Commander in Chief, U.S. Atlantic Fleet and the Commander in Chief, Western Atlantic from May 1972 until July 1973. He then reported as Commander Naval Air Reserve with Headquarters at the Naval Air Station, Glenview, Illinois. He also served as Commander Naval Air Reserve Force, Deputy Chief of Naval Reserve (Air). Added to these duties he was assigned as Commandant of the Ninth Naval District and Commander Naval Base, Great Lakes. He was promoted to Rear Admiral in September 1973 and became Deputy Chief of Naval Reserve, headquartered at New Orleans, Louisiana, in 1974 with additional duty as Commander Naval Air Reserve Force. Before retiring in September 1978, he was Commander, Naval Forces Japan, and Naval Component U.S. Forces, Japan.

Military Awards: Distinguished Flying Cross, Bronze Star Medal, the Meritorious Service Medal, three Air Medals, China/Korean/United Nations and Vietnamese Service Medals, numerous campaign stars/personal/unit citations.[1]

Notes

1. Official Biography of Captain B. Russell, Jr., USN (Ret.). Navy History and Heritage Command, Washington, D.C.

Capt. Burton H. Shepherd
(April 1972–April 1973)

"I am not worried about the capability and spirit of those who will be manning the cockpits and aircrew stations of Navy Aircraft in the years ahead. They are eager and well trained to meet the challenges of the future."—Rear Admiral Shepherd commenting as Head of Naval Air Training Command—*Naval Aviation News*, March 1977

Burton Hale Shepherd was the seventh commanding officer of the *America*. As Commander of Air Wing Sixteen (July 1967–January 1968) aboard the USS *Oriskany* he led numerous air strikes over North Vietnam during Operation Rolling Thunder, a massive bombing campaign to break the will of the North Vietnamese and end the Vietnam War. As commander of the air wing he was awarded numerous medals including the Navy Cross (the Navy's highest award), several Distinguished Flying Crosses and many Air Medals.

Shepherd was born in Kansas City,

Rear Adm. Burton H. Shepherd (official U.S. Navy photograph).

Kansas, on 11 November 1927, son of Orin A. and Mary Ellen (Smith) Shepherd. He attended Wyandotte High School in Kansas City, Kansas, prior to enlisting on 17 December 1945, in the U.S. Naval Reserve at Kansas City, Missouri. As a V-5 student (Reserve Naval Aviation Cadet) he attended Southwestern University, Georgetown, Texas, and Omaha University, Omaha, Nebraska. On 13 June 1947, he was appointed Midshipman and had training at the Naval Pre-Flight School, Ottumwa, Iowa. He reported in July 1947 for flight training at the Naval Air Station, Pensacola, Florida, and on 24 November 1949, was designated a Naval Aviator. He was commissioned an Ensign on 9 September 1949, and subsequently advanced in rank to that of Rear Admiral to date from 1 July 1973, having transferred to the U.S. Navy on 20 January 1954.

After receiving his commission in 1949, he joined Composite Squadron Thirty-One in December of that year and in June 1950 was released from active duty. During the period July 1950 to July 1952 he maintained his status in the Naval Reserve serving as a pilot with Organized Reserve fighter squadrons at the Naval Air Stations in Denver, Colorado, and Glenview, Illinois. In the spring of 1952 he received the degree of Bachelor of Arts from Western State College of Colorado at Gunnison and was a graduate student at the University of Chicago that same year when he was ordered to return to active naval service.

From August 1952 to January 1954 he served with Fighter Squadron One Hundred Fifty-One, which operated off the USS *Boxer* (CV-21) in the Korean area of hostilities. "For meritorious achievement ... as a pilot of a jet fighter plane attached to fighter Squadron One Hundred Fifty-One ... on 11 July 1953..." he was awarded the Navy Commendation Medal with Combat "V." The citation continues in part:

> (He) led a section of jet planes through adverse weather conditions and over mountainous terrain to attack a large concentration of enemy trucks north of Sep'o-ri in Communist North Korea. Despite intense and accurate enemy anti-aircraft fire, he pressed home repeated attacks, personally destroying five trucks and damaging seven others with two direct bomb hits. His accurate strafing caused two large secondary explosions resulting in fires which were still burning when the flight left the area....

He was also awarded the Air medal and Gold Stars in lieu of the Second and Third Air Medals for meritorious service in aerial flight in Korea from 13 May to 14 July 1953.

In February 1954 he reported as a Project Pilot with Project Cutless (Chance-Vought F7U fighter for the Navy which was the first Navy Production aircraft to fly at supersonic speed), at the Naval Air Station, Miramar, California. He remained there until October 1954, after which he was a Transitional Training instructor with Composite Squadron Three. From April 1955 to August 1956, he served in the Office of Naval Officer Procurement, Kansas City, Missouri, then was assigned as Instructor-Pilot and Maintenance Officer with Jet Transitional Training Unit, Naval Air Station, Olathe, Kansas.

In December 1958 he joined Attack Squadron One Hundred Twenty-Five as Weapons Training Officer and in September 1960 transferred to Attack Squadron Twenty-Two to serve as Operations Officer and Executive Officer. He reported in January 1963 as Special Projects Assistant Officer in the Bureau of Naval Personnel, Navy Department, Washington, D.C., where he remained until June 1964.

Following an assignment, which extended to October 1964, as a Fleet Replacement Pilot with Attack Squadron Forty-Three, he became Executive Officer of Attack Squadron Eighty-One. He assumed command of that squadron, which was attached to the USS *Forrestal* (CVA-59), in October 1965. Between October and December 1966 he had duty on the Staff of Commander Readiness Attack Carrier Air Wing Four, after which he was Commander Attack Carrier Air Wing Sixteen, which operated off the USS *Oriskany* in waters off Vietnam. Samples of citations for medals he was awarded are included below which tell of the intensity of the air battles encountered during Rolling Thunder.

Navy Cross: "For extraordinary heroism on 26 October 1967.... As the strike leader of an eighteen-plane strike group launched against the strategically located and heavily defended Hanoi thermal power plant in North Vietnam, Commander Shepherd, although hampered by adverse weather conditions en route, maintained the precise timing necessary to properly execute an intricate strike plan. Skillfully maneuvering to avoid the numerous tracking missiles and intense and accurate barrage of 57 mm and 85 mm flak, he led the strike group to the optimum roll-in point and then aggressively pressed home his attack, releasing all bombs on target. Egressing from the target area in a hail of enemy fire, he retired to the relative safety of the Karst hills and checked in his strike group. After proceeding expeditiously to the coast to refuel, Commander Shepherd returned to an area south of the target to search for one of his missing strike pilots. Continuing the search for more than an hour over enemy terrain in the face of the most concentrated enemy fire in North Vietnam, he finally returned to the coast after reaching a low fuel state...."

USS *America* being refueled by USS *Ponchtoula* at Yankee Station in the Gulf of Tonkin, circa 1970 (official U.S. Navy photograph).

Distinguished Flying Cross: "For extraordinary achievement ... on 29 July 1967. Commander Shepherd led an Air Wing strike against the Loi Dong Barracks complex and located concentrations of anti-aircraft guns and surface-to-air missiles in North Vietnam. Though opposed by intense anti-aircraft fire and within the surface-to-air missile envelope, (he) led his group of twenty-two aircraft in a manner which completely deceived as to his intended area of attack. Attaining ascendancy during the enemy's dilemma, Commander Shepherd then led his strike force in a perfectly executed bombing attack, inflicting heavy damage to the target and completely silencing two heavy caliber flak sites...."

Silver Star Medal: "...As strike leader of a twenty plane major air wing strike on 4 September 1967, Commander Shepherd conceived and executed a brilliant plan of attack against the Haiphong Highway Bridge South-Southeast, North Vietnam, a vital link in the enemy's lines of communications to the South. Exploiting known enemy weaknesses, he effectively deployed his support forces in a feint, which initially split and deceived the enemy's defenses. In spite of diluting the enemy defenses, it was necessary for Commander Shepherd to maneuver the strike group through repeated surface-to-air missile attacks. Encountering intense anti-aircraft fire as he approached, he directed the flak suppression elements into coordinated attacks against those sites posing the major threat, then positioned the strike group for optimum attack. Disregarding the enemy's lethal barrage of anti-aircraft fire, Commander Shepherd placed his bombs directly on target. Following his example, the strike force bombed with equal precision, destroying four of the five bridge spans while minimizing collateral damage to the surrounding civilian area. Completing his attack, (he) remained over the target to ensure that all aircraft cleared the high threat area safely. As a direct result of (his) faultless execution of his strike plan, this vital and heavily defended link in the enemy's logistic network was destroyed without loss to the strike force...."

Legion of Merit: "For exceptionally meritorious conduct ... from 14 July 1967, to 12 January 1968, during combat operations against the enemy. Commander Shepherd displayed exceptional leadership, superb professionalism and devoted concern to his pilots in personally directing daily combat operations in a hostile environment of surface-to-air missiles, anti-aircraft artillery fire, constant small arms fire as well as unpredictable fighter aircraft activity...."

In addition he was entitled to wear the Strike/Flight Numeral "3" on his Air Medal and the Ribbon for, and a facsimile of, the Navy Unit Commendation awarded to USS *Oriskany*.

In March 1968 Shepherd was assigned to the Office of the Chief of Naval Operations in Washington, D.C., where he was Head of the Tactical Air Team in the Systems Analysis Division. In September 1969 he reported as Senior Aide and Executive Assistant to the Vice Chief of Naval Operations and between 1970 and 1972 he held the same assignments for the Chief of Naval Operations. He commanded the USS *America* (CVA-66) and then held various Pentagon positions until he was promoted to Rear Admiral and designated Naval Inspector General. Shepherd was Chief of Naval Air Training from 1975 to August 1978 when he retired from the Navy.[1]

From 1978 to 1981 he attended the Episcopal Seminary in Austin, Texas. He became a Deacon in June 1981 and an Episcopal priest in January 1982. Subsequently he served the church in southern Texas as Curate, Vicar and finally as Rector, Epiphany, Kingsville, Texas, from 1983 to 1990 when he retired from full-time church ministry. He moved to Florida in 2008 and continues to serve the Episcopal Church and participate in various volunteer endeavors.[2]

Military Awards: Navy Cross, two Silver Stars, six Distinguished Flying Crosses, Four Legion of Merits, Bronze Star, eight Air Medals, Several campaign medals.[3]

Notes

1. Official Biography of Rear Adm. Burton Hale Shepherd, USN (Ret.), Navy History and Heritage Command, Washington, D.C.
2. Correspondence with Rear Admiral Shepherd, January 2013.
3. Official Biography of Rear Adm. Burton Hale Shepherd, USN (Ret.), Navy History and Heritage Command, Washington, D.C.

Capt. Thomas H. Replogle
(April 1973–September 1974)

Everything worked like clockwork. This is just the first exercise, and I'm sure we'll have quite a few to follow.—Admiral Thomas Replogle commenting on the amphibious landing at Guantanamo Bay, 17 October 1979

On Wednesday, 17 October 1979, most Americans were anxiously awaiting the seventh game of the World Series, with the Pittsburgh Pirates and Baltimore Orioles tied 3–3, or perhaps they were focused on Mother Theresa being awarded the Nobel Peace Prize. As a result, the amphibious landing by Marines onto the beaches of Cuba might have gone unnoticed.

But on that day, in torrential rains, an assault force of 2,200 Marines of the 38th Marine Amphibious Unit (MAU)

Capt. Thomas H. Replogle (courtesy Thomas H. Replogle).

were carried through fierce winds by helicopter and over churning waves by landing craft to safely deploy at the Guantanamo Bay Naval Base on Cuba's southern coast to reinforce the force of 420 Marines stationed there.

A television address to the American people by President Jimmy Carter on 1 October 1979, revealed the presence of a Soviet combat brigade in Cuba, and outlined the measures he planned to take to counteract their presence. The United States had demanded their withdrawal on 22 September, but the Soviets had taken no action.

The U.S. was in the midst of negotiations with the Soviet Union to adopt the provisions of the second Strategic Arms Limitation Treaty (SALT II) and Carter defined the challenge as, "to act in a firm, decisive way without destroying the basis for cooperation which helps to maintain world peace and control nuclear weapons."[1]

Carter went on to state, "I am establishing a permanent, full-time Caribbean Joint Task Force Headquarters at Key West, Florida. I will assign to this headquarters forces from all the military services responsible for expanded planning and for conducting exercises. This headquarters unit will employ designated forces for action if required. This will substantially improve our capability to monitor and respond rapidly to any attempted military encroachment in the region." He further added, "We will expand military maneuvers in the region, and we will conduct these regularly from now on. In accordance with existing treaty rights, the United States will, of course, keep our forces in Guantanamo."[2]

The next day, 2 October, Rear Admiral Thomas E. Replogle was named to command the new Caribbean Joint Task Force; Replogle was already the commander of the Tactical Air Wing—Atlantic, and he would carry out his new duties concurrently.

Later, Admiral Replogle would recall the circumstances of the notification of his appointment: "I was aboard a helicopter flying north for a meeting with the Air Force when I was contacted on the radio by Vice Adm. Don Engen, the 7th Fleet Chief of Staff, who told me I had to return immediately, as I was scheduled to brief the Commander in Chief, U.S. Atlantic Fleet (CINCLANTFLT), Admiral Kidd. I said, 'I don't have a briefing for the CINC' and he said 'Yes you do. You're staging an amphibious landing in 15 days.'"[3]

The training exercise, codenamed Reinforcex '79, was meant to demonstrate American power and resolve in the Caribbean by landing troops at the only military base on Communist soil. Col. Mark Fennessy, the commander of the Marines at Guantanamo, praised the move to beef up his four hundred permanent troops for a month. "It went like a ballet," he said.[4]

The Marines were delivered to the island by a three warship flotilla, consisting of the USS *Nassau* (LHA-4), a Tarawa-class amphibious assault ship, the USS *Plymouth Rock* (LSD-29) a *Thomaston*-class dock landing ship, and the USS *Spartanburg County* (LST-1192), *Newport* class tank landing ship. They were trailed by a suspected Cuban intelligence ship, sporting an antenna and the number H-102, which monitored the landing.

The USS *Nassau* was a brand new, and thus untested, class of ship, undergoing its first full-scale operation. It was designed to carry a complete Marine Battalion Landing Team, and all supplies, equipment and vehicles needed, and to land the team ashore either by helicopter and/or small amphibious craft. In this operation, twelve CH-46 Sea Knight and CH-53 Sea Stallion helicopters delivered their Marines, while the *Spartanburg County* and *Plymouth Rock* launched seven waves of amphibious landing craft, including two carrying 50-ton M-60 tanks. The operation was covered by ten Marine A-4's, flying cover from Cherry Hill, North Carolina.

The landing, extensively covered by eighty photographers and reporters, put 2,200 Marines ashore, under adverse conditions, in under four hours. There were no confrontations, despite the call up of 3,000 Cuban reservists. The landing demonstrated American resolve to remain active and vigilant in the Caribbean.[5]

It would not be the last time that Admiral Replogle would have to deal with Castro's Cuba.

Thomas E. Replogle was born in Pittsburgh, Pennsylvania, on 4 June 1929, and, after graduating Bethel Township High School, studied science and physics at Westminister College in Western Pennsylvania. He learned to fly at age fourteen, taking off from an airstrip his father had built in an apple orchard he owned. By September 1949, when he accepted an appointment as a Naval Aviation Cadet, he had over four hundred hours of flight time.

Following flight training at Pensacola Florida and Corpus Christi, Texas, in the Grumman F6F Hellcat, a World War II era carrier based fighter, Replogle was commissioned an ensign and awarded his gold Navy Aviator wings in April 1951.

On 24 May, he reported to the Navy's first transitional jet training squadron at NAS Whiting Field, Milton, Florida. From there, he was sent to U.S. Naval School All Weather Flight, at Corpus Christi, Texas, from 25 June until 5 July 1951, where he flew SNB-5 aircraft, after which he was

Left to right: **Ens. Tom Replogle, Lt. Jim Lee, Lt.(jg) Bob Dresen, Lt. George Tally aboard the USS *Kearsage* with VF-11 off the coast of Korea, 1953 (courtesy Thomas H. Replogle).**

assigned to Fighter Squadron Eleven (VF-11) the World Famous Red Rippers flying the McDonnell F2H-2 Banshee. "We spent most of our time in the Jacksonville area aboard the USS *Wasp* (CV-18) doing night carrier landings and group air wing tactics, mostly bombing and strafing on towed targets behind the carrier."

The country was entering its third year of involvement in the "police action" in Korea when VF-11 deployed to the Far East, departing San Diego aboard the aircraft carrier USS *Kearsarge* (CV-33), as part of Carrier Air Group Fourteen (CAG-14) on 11 August 1952. After intensive flight training in the Hawaiian Islands, the carrier arrived at Yokosuka, Japan, on 8 September, and joining the fast carrier Task Force Seventy-Seven (TF-77) off the east coast of Korea six days later, joining the USS *Oriskany* (CVA-34) and the USS *Valley Forge* (CVA-45) under command of Rear Adm. A. Soucek and later Rear Adm. R.F. Hickey. Three days after that, on 17 September, Lieutenant (Junior Grade) Replogle flew his first combat mission.

"Korea, like Vietnam later, saw very little air-to-air combat. I saw only one MiG (Russian jet fighter) the entire time I was there. It was high up at 40,000 feet going back into China. I did a lot of orbiting waiting for them to come up but none did on my watch. Most of my effort as a fighter pilot was dropping bombs on bridges, tunnels, and enemy lines of communication in order to keep the bad guys' supplies from coming south. I flew the F2H Banshee, a single seat carrier-based jet fighter."[6]

The Banshees were initially utilized as an escort for long-range USAF bombers, but as the war progressed USN fighters were primarily assigned to ground attack missions, including close air support of ground troops and destruction of the North Korean army's supply lines. But as air defense tactics still depended on being able to see the enemy, it was soon discovered that an F2H-2P flying alone at high altitude was almost impossible to spot from the ground, and Banshees were soon in high demand for battlefield photography missions.[7]

Despite little air-to-air combat, and the F2H's ability to fly at high altitudes, the squadron was not without losses. "My section leader, Lt. Jim Lee, went down on 30 Dec 1952. I was just behind him dive bombing a bridge fifteen miles west of Wonson, over North Korea."[8] Three weeks later, on 23 January 1953, the squadron lost its skipper when Cdr. Denny Powell Phillips failed to eject after being hit by AAA fire in the same area. "The skipper, Commander Phillips, was shot down 23 Jan 1953, off my right wing by a 57mm. He never got out of the aircraft."[9]

Nearly 6,000 sorties were flown from the *Kearsarge's* deck, before she completed her tour in late February and she departed for San Diego, arriving on 17 March as the newly designated CVA-33. She later appeared as Admiral Halsey's flagship in the 1954 movie *The Caine Mutiny*.

Replogle left VF-11 on 7 January 1954, and spent most of 1954 as an Instructor Pilot at NAS Pensacola, before being assigned to the Navy's Jet Transition Training Unit (JTTU) at NAS Olathe, Gardner, Kansas, on 16 December. After taking leave, Replogle reported in and flew his first flight at Olathe on 11 February 1955. He remained, "primarily teaching old navy pilots how to fly jets," usually in F9F-8s until 19 July 1957.

On 28 August 1957, Replogle reported to the Naval Postgraduate School in Monterey, California, but departed on 6 June 1958, after which he was assigned to the VX-3 Fighter Development Squadron at NAS Oceana, Virginia Beach, Virginia. VX-3 was one of four air development squadrons (VX) that the Navy formed, testing newly developed jet aircraft to develop and evaluate jet fighter tactics, among other tasks. "We did the pressure suit testing for the astronauts," Replogle recalled. "I would take an F4D Delta wing up as high as I could get it, 59–60,000 feet and flame out the engine so the pressure suit would blow up, record what was happening and relight it, and go up again about three times. I did this for about three weeks. No problems except the first light off on the first flight. I tried to light it off to high at 25,000 feet and I was about to dead stick it into Cherry Point Marine Air Base when it finally relit at about 2,000 feet."

Replogle next spent a year of exchange duty, 15 January 1960, through 14 June 1961, with the USAF at Otis AFB on the western edge of Cape Cod, Massachusetts, where he flew the McDonnell F-101 Voodoo, a nuclear-capable supersonic jet fighter, and then he returned to the Naval Postgraduate School to complete his B.S. degree, graduating in 1962.

Replogle, now a lieutenant commander, was assigned to Fighter Squadron One Hundred Twenty-One (VF-121) "Pacemakers," a Fleet Replacement squadron stationed at NAS Miramar, near San Diego, California, where he remained until 6 November 1964. Replogle recalled:

> I was stationed at NAS Miramar, training pilots to fly the F4 Phantom, when the operations officer of VF-151 Vigilantes turned his wings in, and I was sent in to replace him. The squadron departed on the USS *Coral Sea* (CVA-43) bound for Vietnam, on 9 November 1964. The *Coral Sea* had already left San Francisco when I received my orders, so I flew a replacement F4 and landed aboard her on 11 December 1964, while she was on her way to Hawaii. We spent some time in Hawaii while the ship had some extensive repair work done prior to its departure for Vietnam, and we had a great time under the Banyan trees on Waikiki Beach.
>
> We headed west for Vietnam on 6 January 1965, and arrived in the Philippines for a short stop. I flew my first combat flight in Vietnam on 15 February 1965. It was similar to air combat during the Korean War, with lots of orbiting, waiting for MiGs and lots of bombing lines of communication to stop supplies from going south. We were not very effective, as the North Vietnamese were extremely good at supplying their troops. My last combat mission was on 13 October 1965.[10]

Like Replogle, it was VF-151's first deployment to Vietnam, as part of Carrier Wing Fifteen (CVW-15), and in its eleven months deployed, the squadron would fly nearly 1,500 combat sorties, participating in Operation Rolling Thunder, the aerial bombardment of North Vietnam, beginning in March 1965. The squadron's deployment ended 1 November 1965.

"Transferred to VF-121, January 1966. Last flight VF-121, 30 November 1966. Transferred to VF-161, December 1966. Transferred to VF-143, 12 July 1967, when their skipper got shot down. Flew first combat flight on 13 July 1967 with Jim Capps the senior squadron RIO. Got my permanent RIO

(Malchiodi) in August 1967 who flew with me for the rest of the cruise, a great performer until we got back to the states and I was transferred back to VF 121 in December 1967."

Replogle was ordered back to VF-121 in January 1966, training F4 pilots, but then was transferred to VF-161 as executive officer on 22 December 1966. He flew with them until 6 July 1967.

On 28 June 1967, Cdr. William P. "Bill" Lawrence was the commanding officer of Fighter Squadron One Hundred Forty-Three (VF-143) part of CVW-14 onboard the USS *Constellation* (CV-64), when Lawrence and his co-pilot, Lt.(jg) James W. Bailey, flew a mission over Nam Dinh, North Vietnam, in their F4B Phantom. The aircraft was hit by enemy fire and the crew was forced to eject. Both Lawrence and Bailey were captured by the North Vietnamese and interned in the infamous Hanoi Hilton until 1973. Replogle was selected to take over command of the squadron.

"When Bill Lawrence got shot down and taken prisoner in Vietnam, I was again selected as the duty replacement pilot, and I was flown out to Saigon, South, Vietnam, and then out to the *Constellation* to take command of VF-143 'The Pukin' Dogs.' I arrived aboard on 12 July 1967. As I got out of the COD (Twin engine turbo aircraft used to deliver people and supplies aboard the carriers). I heard over the One MC 'Commanding Officer of VF 143 report to the Chief of Staff of the Admiral immediately.' I wondered what that was all about. The Chief of Staff held up the morning carrier newspaper. On the front page was a big picture of a humped up dog barfing, (the squadron seal for all their displays including the painting on the aircraft.). He said 'Commander, I don't want to see any more of this, particularly when I'm eating my breakfast and you can change the name of that squadron as one of your first duties.' I went down to the ready room and met the pilots, some of whom I knew, and told them what the Chief of Staff had ordered. They replied, 'Ah come on boss, you have got to be kidding. This squadron has had that name forever.' I held my composure for a moment and then said, 'Yes, I'm kidding and so was the Chief of Staff.' He'd been my skipper in VX-3 and we were just having some fun.

"My first combat mission on my second deployment was on 13 July 1967, and I flew my last combat mission on 9 November 1967. As indicated earlier, combat on the second cruise was much the same as the first with the exception of the Surface to Air Missiles (SAMs)."

It was not an easy deployment, as the then CAG of CVW-14, Rear Adm. Ernest "Gene" Tissot recalled: "The carrier operated first on Dixie Station, a patrol area about sixty miles (100 km) off South Vietnam with strikes in the Iron Triangle region, and then moved north to Yankee Station, a patrol area about fifty miles (80 km) off North Vietnam for a total of 121 days on the line.… The eight-month deployment ended in December, having totaled losses of sixteen aircraft and twenty personnel, including seven KIAs and eight POWs.[11]

It was during this second tour that it became apparent to Replogle that there needed to be a change in tactics. "The SAMs by far accounted for most of our losses. They had just started coming into use as I was leaving Vietnam after my first cruise. When I was called again to replace the skipper of VF-143, and I joined the squadron, I found only three operable F-4 Phantom aircraft in the squadron because of losses or damage caused by the SAMS. They had also lost fourteen or fifteen A-4C Skyhawk aircraft. I asked the air wing commander what his tactics were.

"The CAG was an A-4 pilot who had never been in combat. He told me that he had the A-4's down low flying at 10,000 feet and the F-4's flying at 20,000 feet trying to stay behind them. A fully loaded A-4 might fly at three hundred knots, but if you want to come back home, you don't ever let an F4 fly under four hundred knots. As a result, the SAMs were knocking both aircraft down like clay pigeons. So I told the CAG, 'With all due respect sir, your tactics are dead wrong!' I told him to reverse it, and put the F4's at 10,000 feet flying a minimum 400kts, where they could dodge and outmaneuver the SAMs and the A4's at 20 to 25,000 feet. The SAM's wouldn't see the A-4's and the F4's could outmaneuver them. It worked, and we lost no more aircraft in the air wing.

"Robert McNamara, the Secretary of Defense (SECDEF) invited the CAG back to Washington, and he took me with him to explain to them how we were able to do it. They were about to award a contract to re-engine all the A-4 aircraft because the engine smoked and they thought that was the reason for all the losses. We showed it was tactics, and saved the Navy a lot of money."[12]

With over four hundred combat missions in two wars, Replogle was assigned "Combat Limited" status in 1968 and he left the squadron to assume the duties of Fighter Training Officer at COMNAVAIRPAC where he initiated the Top Gun Program under the auspices of the Ault Committee. The purpose of the committee was to investigate why U.S. air-to-air missiles were not performing to expectations. The Navy formed a blue-ribbon review board, later to become known as the Ault Committee, named for its leader Capt. Frank Ault, to determine the causes and to recommend corrective action. Replogle provided the insight of an experienced combat pilot.

"We were used to shooting bullets at targets between 300 to 500 feet away, but now we were shooting missiles at targets one-two miles distant, and there was an uncertainty as to at what point a target would be in range with a particular missile. The sidewinder was an infrared missile, and presented no problem because they would emit a tone when they were in range. But as for radar missiles, we really didn't know what to do with them.

"I recommended that they needed an instrumented range. Something where you could put a 'bug' on an airplane and let it fly, go into a simulated dogfight, and when the pilot felt he was in position to fire a missile, he would sound-off and say 'Fox-1 simulating a firing' and the computer would send a signal down to the big screen below being monitored by engineers.

"They finally decided we needed such a range to teach and train pilots and also as a platform to test and develop tactics we could use against enemy aircraft we would be fighting. From that idea of a combat range emerged the Top Gun Program."

What followed was an eighteen-month tour as Commanding Officer of Air Wing Seventeen (CVW-17) including time in the Mediterranean aboard the USS *Forrestal* (CVA-59) but Replogle characterized the deployment as "uneventful."

In April 1971 Replogle was ordered to Washington, D.C., for his first, and only, Pentagon assignment in charge of aircraft funding, responsible for the funding of any new Navy aircraft, including the F-14 Tomcat.

After only eight months in the Pentagon, Replogle was ordered back to sea, taking command of the USS *Nashville* (LPD-13), an *Austin*-class amphibious transport dock, at Norfolk, Virginia, on 9 June 1972. "I got promoted to captain early, primarily because I spent only eight months at the Pentagon instead of two years. They gave me the *Nashville* as something I could 'bump the fenders' on before they gave me the *America*."

Three days after taking command, on 12 June, the *Nashville* departed Norfolk for Western Europe on NATRONLANT-72, a Naval Academy midshipmen training cruise, with stops in England, France, and Germany. After a brief return to Norfolk, she departed again on 23 August on Operation Pegasus, the transportation of 151 dependent women and children, their pets, automobiles, and household goods to Athens, Greece, where Destroyer Squadron Twelve would now be homeported under a pilot program of the CNO. The operation necessitated the creation of an onboard nursery, playground and kennel, as well as the laying in of products (diapers, bottles, etc.) not usually carried in the Ship's Store. Despite the challenge, all were delivered safely.

After one last cruise to Puerto Rico, Martinique, Barbados, and St. Croix in January, Replogle transferred command of the *Nashville* to Capt. George A. Church in a shipboard ceremony on 21 February 1973. In April, he took command of the USS *America*, relieving Capt. Burton H. Shepherd.

"I took over command of the *America* shortly after it came back from Vietnam, on 11 April 1973. It was in the Portsmouth Naval Shipyard. We got underway and brought her out of the shipyard on 10 August 1973, but she was only running on three screws, as one of the four engines wasn't ready to go yet. COMNAVAIRLANT, Admiral Michaelis, said that if I could handle that, he would let me proceed, which I did.

"I was operating up off Atlantic City because of a hurricane that was coming north. We were qualifying young pilots to land upon the carrier when the Lebanon Crisis emerged. Since we were the duty carrier, I was required to come back into Hampton Roads and load on ordnance; ammunition and so forth.

"The duty officer called me and said, 'You'll have to return immediately,' and I said, 'Have you guys taken a look out your window lately, we've got a hurricane coming up the coast. That's why were up here in Atlantic City. The best I can do is be down at the entrance of the channel at about seven o'clock in the morning.'

However, with the flood tides associated with the hurricane, the tugs wouldn't be able to dock me, particularly since there was a new tunnel being put in and I only had about a two-hundred yard turning radius. But the senior pilot said, 'That's not a problem, you can go ahead and come on up.' I was there at 7:00 a.m. and started up the channel, and about halfway up I got a call that said, 'Hey, you're right. We won't be able to hold you. Turn around and go back.'

"Well, you can't turn a thousand foot carrier around in a five hundred foot channel. So I had to keep coming and backing down because of the flood tide was pushing me at about seven knots and we got to the point where I had to make my turn into the anchorage area.

"Normally, you have about two thousand yards to turn, but since they were making that new tunnel, I only had about two hundred yards and there was a Swedish tanker at short stay and with his anchor with smoke coming out and it looked like he was getting ready to get underway.

"I told him I'd pass him port to port because I couldn't stop. There was no report from him so I kept going, and finally I got to the point where I had to cross his bow. Just in case he did come out, I put on a full bell, just to kick the carrier forward.

"I got a tap on my shoulder, and it was the Senior Pilot for the area who had flown aboard on the helicopter, and I looked up at him. He was a big, tall guy, about 6'5" and I asked him, 'Do you think you can handle this better than I can?' and he said. 'Yes Sir, I do!'

"I ordered, 'Pilot has the conn,' and he immediately reversed my engine calls and ordered all back full on the engines, and things started to happen. Very shortly, the number one generator went out, the number two generator went out, the number one engine went out, and the number two engine went out. Within a period of four minutes, we were stuck dead in the water, with no engines and no generators.

"What had happened, of course, is that when he put a 'full-back' bell on, we pulled all the tires and all the other garbage off the bottom of the channel and it completely clogged all our condensers, engines and generator.

"So I ended up with one engine, and I told the Chief Engineer, 'This is a flood tide. It's going to stop in about thirty-two minutes, then we're going to get an ebb tide, and if you can't get me some engine power by then, this carrier is going to be sitting on its side in Hampton Roads aground.'

"As it was, I wasn't moving, but I was pretty certain I wasn't aground; I thought I was probably just up against the channel bank. In any case, I put my Chief Quartermaster over the side to watch the tide. He kept dropping wood chips over. In about thirty-three minutes, the chips went dead in the water, and then they started moving back, meaning we were getting an ebb tide which would lower the carrier about 6–8 inches and that would probably put me aground.

"I took the conn away from the pilot and told the Chief Engineer I needed two engines. I told him to do his best, and to do whatever was necessary, but that I needed at least two engines in the next thirty-two minutes, otherwise our great carrier would be aground.

"So he took all the crew out of the other two engine rooms and they did everything they could. They were able to get two engines online in about twenty-nine minutes, and he gave me a full bell. I took over the conn, and told the pilot I would take it from here.

I had the quartermaster pulling a bearing, and nothing happened. We were stuck, but then we were moving just a little bit, and all of a sudden, he advised we were slowly getting underway. I had a full bell on, and as soon as we broke the suction, I came back to standard throttle and I proceeded to take the ship on into port and dock it.

I went back to my cabin and wrote everything down. They flew an Admiral on board to hold a Board of Inquiry and find out what happened.

Because I was the duty carrier, I'd had to send a message to the Joint Chiefs telling them I was aground in Hampton Road.

"Anyway, I went back to my cabin and wrote down exactly what happened. The Admiral looked over my report and said, 'Tom, you did exactly the right thing. But, a captain who puts his ship aground at any point loses his command. I'm afraid your career and your command are gone.'

"So I went home that night feeling pretty gloomy and I remembered something the previous commanding officer had told me about taking some photos of the hull and the propellers when he was down in Subic Bay before he came back from Vietnam.

"I said, 'How about we go down and look at that,' and he said, 'Tomorrow,' and I said, 'No, let's go look at that right now.' So at 2:00 a.m. we went down and we laid out the pictures they'd taken that showed the damage to the hull, the bottom of the ship, and the props.

"Sure enough, there wasn't a mark of difference. So the next morning, I took the photos in to the admiral, laid the photos out and showed him. He turned, gave me a big grin and said, 'Captain, here's your ship and your career back.'

"Fortunately, I wasn't aground. I had only come alongside the channel bank, and fortunately they didn't take pictures of the side. They only took pictures of the bottom, to see if you'd gone aground. So, we got away with it. I was once told, 'If you're ever going to get promoted to flag rank, you've got to get some notoriety.' That got me some notoriety.

"After that, as we were still the duty carrier, we loaded up and went out to sea. We carrier qualified a few more pilots, and then set off for the Mediterranean to relieve the carrier on station."[13]

The *America* relieved the USS *Independence* (CV-62) at Rota, Spain, on 11 January 1974, and became the flagship for Rear Adm. Frederick C. Turner, Commander of Task Force Sixty (TF-60), and commenced operations in the western Pacific for the next several weeks.

"When the *Kennedy* and the *America* were initially built they installed anti-submarine sonar on the bow and placed a five-inch gun behind the LSO platform.

"They were going to remove them, but I told them to leave them on, because our sonar was at the very bottom of our keel, probably thirty feet below where the destroyers had theirs. When you get to the Mediterranean, there's a thermal level which the sonar bounces off of, and this means they don't always pick up the submarines, but our sonar, being lower, could see beneath the thermal layer.

"It caused some amusement when we misread a whale as a submarine during the crossing, but it proved its worth in the Straits of Gibraltar. We had four or five destroyers with us, and our sonar picked up a submarine trailing us. We contacted the senior destroyer captain and said, 'We've got a bad guy under you at six o'clock, and it looks like he's going to simulate firing a torpedo at you.' And he came back saying, 'No. We're clear.' And at about that time a star shell came out, and I said, 'Sorry about that captain, but you just lost your ship.'

"It was a U.S. submarine, of course, playing the game they do when we are there. Every U.S. Navy ship that comes through, they simulate torpedoing them. The whole time they're in the Med, they continue to simulate attacks. Because I was able to keep the ship moving at thirty knots and with the sonar, I could see the submarines out there, and I could turn away from them, so they were never able to get a fire control solution on me. This continued the entire time I was in the Mediterranean, until finally, just before I departed, they snuck in and got a torpedo in me, when I was anchored in port.

"The Navy awarded the ship as the most effective anti-submarine ship that had ever been in the Mediterranean, obviously because our sonar was on the bow, down under the thermal layer, so we could see the submarines, even when the destroyers had a tough time seeing them."[14]

Turning over command of the *America* to Capt. Daniel G. McCormick on 29 September, Replogle was ordered to Japan aboard the light cruiser USS *Oklahoma City* (CL-91) in October 1974 to be Chief of Staff, Seventh Fleet, during which he was selected for Rear Admiral.

"After the *America*, I was sent to the Seventh Fleet as Chief of Staff, and I spent nine to ten months out there before I was ordered back to CIN-CLANT as Inspector General for CINCLANT and SACLANT, a NATO command. I didn't turn up anything much.

"My boss at the time was Adm. Issac C. Kidd, Jr. His father, Rear Adm. Issac C. Kidd, was killed on the bridge of the battleship USS *Arizona* during the attack on Pearl Harbor, the only U.S. Admiral killed in World War II, and was posthumously awarded the Medal of Honor. His son was one of the finest officers I worked for. Anyway, in August 1978, he says, 'Tom, you haven't been getting enough airborne time, so I'm sending you to take over as Commander, Tactical Wings, Atlantic Fleet (COMTACWINGSLANT).' It was an admiral's job, supervising the training of all fighter pilots on the East Coast. I divided my time between NAS Oceana in Virginia and NAS Cecil Field in Florida, and included responsibility for all carrier training. This gave me the opportunity to get in a lot of flying."[15]

On 2 October 1979, Replogle was handed the additional assignment as commander of the newly created Caribbean Joint Task Force. The amphibious landing at Guantanamo was only the first of numerous military exercises that would be carried out to demonstrate America's resolve to prevent and counter Communist influence in the region. During one of these exercises, Solid Shield 80, Castro allowed approximately 100,000 Cubans to depart Cuba by boat, concurrently emptying his prisons and mental institutions into the refugee population. CINCLANT gave Replogle the responsibility to coordinate the Naval and Coast Guard operations to recover and process the fleeing refugees of what would later be called the 1980 Mariel Boatlift.

"CINCLANT said to me, 'Replogle, you're in charge. A lot of criminals are coming out. You have the Coast Guard and five amphibious ships. Pick them up, bring them in, and create a processing center to separate the criminals from the good guys.' And that's what we did." He, and others, were awarded the Humanitarian Service Medal for their efforts by the Secretary of Defense.[16]

Rear Adm. Thomas Replogle retired from the Navy on 31 August 1980, after thirty-one years of service, including 9,200 flight hours in 74 different aircraft, and 675 carrier landings, the last of which, as an admiral, was in an A-6 aboard the USS *John F. Kennedy* on 8 May 1979. "I was up for my third star. I'd always been an operator and if I took the third star, it looked like I'd be down in the tank in the Joint Chiefs for three or four years, and I decided I didn't want to do that, so I retired. I've never regretted my decision. For peace of mind, I know I retired at the right time."[17]

His awards include the Legion of Merit, Bronze Star, Distinguished Flying Cross, Air Medal with thirteen Gold Stars, and two Navy Commendation Medals with combat "V."

Notes

1. Transcript of U.S. President Carter's TV Address on Measures to Counteract the Presence of a Soviet Combat Brigade in Cuba, from Washington, D.C., Monday, 1 October 1979. http://www.thegrenadarevolutiononline.com/carterspeech.html

2. Ibid.

3. Interview with Thomas Replogle, 19 February 2013.

4. Daniloff, Nicholas. "2,200-Man U.S. Force Lands at Guantanamo." *Sarasota Herald Tribune,* Thursday, 18 October 1979.

5. Ibid.

6. Interview with Thomas Replogle, 19 February 2013.

7. McDonnell F2H Banshee http://americanmilitaryhistory.devhub.com/blog/871301-mcdonnell-f2h-banshee/

8. Interview with Thomas Replogle, February 2013.

9. McDonnell F2H Banshee losses http://www.ejection-history.org.uk/Aircraft_by_Type/Banshee.htm

10. Ibid.

11. Tissot, Rear Adm. Ernest. *CAG—The Ultimate Experience.* The Brown Shoe Project http://www.thebrownshoes.org/

12. Ibid.

13. Ibid.

14. Ibid.

15. Ibid.

16. Ibid.

17. Ibid.

Capt. Daniel G. McCormick III
(September 1974–April 1976)

He had all the "right stuff" even then, and was obviously destined for great things. If there is a heaven, Dan is probably in command of a good portion of it already.—Joe Haggard, a former shipmate in VA-104 remembering his friend

Daniel Gilbert McCormick III was born in Key West, Florida, on 8 May 1930, the son of Mr. and Mrs. D.G. McCormick of Miami, Florida. He graduated from the Georgia Institute of Technology with a Bachelor's Degree in Mechanical Engineering prior to entering the Navy as an Aviation Cadet in March 1952.[1] He was commissioned as an Ensign and designated a Naval Aviator on 2 September 1953, upon completion of flight training. McCormick's first fleet

Capt. Daniel G. McCormick III (official U.S. Navy photograph).

assignment was with Attack Squadron One Hundred Four (an AD Skyraider squadron) at the Naval Air Station, Cecil Field, Florida. Two deployments to the Mediterranean aboard the USS *Coral Sea* (CVA-43) were completed during this tour of duty. In 1956 during the Suez War, the squadron operated off the coast of Egypt providing air support for the evacuation of Americans and foreign nationals from that country.[2]

His next assignment was to the Naval Air Test Center (NATC), Patuxent River, Maryland, as a student in the Test Pilot School. Upon graduation in June 1957, he was assigned to the Board of Inspection Branch of the Electronics Test Division. Projects included BIS trials of the A-4D (Skyhawk), F-8U (Crusader), A-3D (Skywarrior), F-3H (Banshee), F-9F (Panther), AD-5 (Skyraider), A-3J (Vigilante), and UF-1 (Albatross) series aircraft.

Assignment as Flag Lieutenant and Aide to Commander, Carrier Division Five deployed in the Western Pacific followed duties at NATC, Patuxent River.

His next assignment in June 1962 was with Fighter Squadron One Hundred Fourteen, the first West Coast Fleet Squadron to receive the F-4 Phantom aircraft. During this tour, two deployments to the Western Pacific were made on board the USS *Kitty Hawk* (CVA-63).

In 1964 McCormick attended the Armed Forces Staff College, Norfolk, Virginia. This was followed by a tour in the Office of Chief of Naval Operations (OP-90) Program planning and budgeting. In November 1965 he was assigned to Fighter Squadron One Hundred One, Key West, and in May the following year he became the First Assistant Officer in Charge of VF-101 Detachment Oceana. Next came a tour of duty as Executive Officer of Fighter Squadron Forty One deployed aboard the USS *Independence* (CVA-62). He later assumed duties as Commanding Officer of VF-41 in February 1967. VF-41 became the first Navy Squadron to receive the newest F-4 series aircraft, the F-4J, the same month.

In March 1968 he was assigned duties as Air Operations Officer of the USS *Ranger* (CVA-61) then deployed to Southeast Asia. The next twenty-six months aboard *Ranger* included two combat cruises on Yankee Station and assumption of duties as the Operations Officer.

In July 1970, McCormick served as Commanding Officer of VF-101, NAS Key West, Florida. VF-101 with its detachment at NAS Oceana, Virginia, was the Navy's largest fleet replacement training squadron, responsible for training all east coast F-4 aircrews and enlisted personnel.

Detached from FITRON 101 in July 1971, he became Head, Fighter Design Branch, Naval Air Systems Command in Washington, D.C. In this capacity, he was responsible for coordinating the technical aspects of the F-4 and F-14 programs. During his tour he became the eighth Naval Aviator to fly the F-14 Tomcat.[3]

In December 1972, he joined the Amphibious Forces Atlantic Fleet, as Commanding Officer, USS *Trenton* (LPH-14). He served in this capacity until 1974.

Prior to assuming command of USS *America* (CVA-66) on 29 September 1974, he served as Safety Officer on the Staff of Commander Naval Air Force, U.S. Atlantic Fleet, from May to September 1974. During his tour, *America* supported the evacuation of Americans from Lebanon in May 1976.[4]

Following his command of *America* McCormick returned to the Pentagon and was selected for Rear Admiral on 1 March 1978. He was then assigned to a NATO post in Naples, Italy. During his "twilight" tour he was designated the twenty-fourth Navy Inspector General (August 1980–October 1981) before retiring.

Rear Admiral McCormick logged approximately 4,500 hours of flight time and over 600 day and night carrier landings during his Navy career. His awards included the Navy Meritorious Unit Commendation, the Navy Commendation Medal and the Bronze star.

Upon his retirement Admiral McCormick worked for the McDonnell Douglas Training Systems, then spent his later years sailing the Caribbean in his sail boats before settling in North Carolina.

Rear Adm. Daniel Gilbert McCormick, USN, passed away on 10 March 2011 in Longmont, Colorado.

Notes

1. Official Biography of Rear Adm. Daniel Gilbert McCormick III, USN, Navy History and Heritage Command, Washington, D.C.

2. Gossnick, Roy A. *Dictionary of American Naval Aviation Squadrons, Volume 1.* Washington, D.C., Naval Historical Center, Department of the Navy, 1995.

3. Official Biography of Rear Adm. Daniel Gilbert McCormick III, USN, Navy History and Heritage Command, Washington, D.C.

4. *Dictionary of American Naval Fighting Ships*, 9 vols. Department of the Navy, Naval Historical Center, Washington Navy Yard, Washington, D.C., 1959–1991.

Capt. Robert B. Fuller
(April 1976–April 1978)

America! My America! How beautiful you are! I stand here tonight as a free man thanks to the American people, the love and devotion of my darling wife and mother, and to our great Commander-in-Chief.—Speech delivered by Captain Fuller upon arrival at Naval Air Station, Jacksonville on the night of 8 March 1973, following his release by the North Vietnamese four days earlier after almost six years as a POW

On 7 September 1976, in a change of command ceremony on the hangar deck of the USS *America*, Captain Robert Byron Fuller accepted command of the carrier from Captain Daniel G. McCormick III, becoming the *America's* tenth commanding officer. In so doing, he won a challenge made at Hoa Lo Prison in Hanoi years earlier.

Robert Byron Fuller was born 23 November 1927, in Quitman, Mississippi, but the family moved first to Atlanta, Georgia, and then to Jacksonville, Florida, when he was in the third grade. He attended Landon Junior-Senior High School in Jacksonville, then Emory at Oxford. He enlisted in the U.S. Navy toward the end of World War II on 14 July 1945, at age seventeen.

Following boot camp at San Diego, Fuller was assigned to the USS *Waldron* (DD-699), a 2200-ton *Allen M. Sumner* class destroyer newly commissioned in June 1944 and named for Lt. Cdr. John C. Waldron, a naval aviator killed in action on 4 June 1942 while leading Torpedo Squadron Eight (VT-8) during the Battle of Midway.[1]

Fuller reported aboard the *Waldron* at Pier 31, San Francisco harbor, upon her return from the Far East on 20 January 1946, and was assigned to the forward fire room working the boilers. The *Waldron* sailed first to San Diego, and then transited the Panama Canal on 14 February to arrive at Nor-

Capt. Robert Byron Fuller (official U.S. Navy photograph).

folk, Virginia, on the 19th. After operations along the east coast, *Waldron*
put in at the Boston Naval Shipyard in May for extensive repairs. During
the yard period, Fuller took and passed the Naval Academy entrance exam.
Fuller left the ship and was honorably discharged with the rank of Fireman
First Class on 6 August 1946.[2]

Upon his release from active duty, Fuller remained in the naval reserve
while attending Emory College, Oxford, Georgia, for a year of study until
being admitted to the U.S. Naval Academy in July 1947, a member of the
Class of 1951. One classmate, future astronaut James Irwin, would walk on
the moon as part of the Apollo 15 mission. Another classmate, William P.
Lawrence, future Vice Admiral and Superintendent at Annapolis would be
shot down and captured sixteen days (28 June) before Fuller was downed
and the two would be confined together for almost six years. Three other
classmates would also be shot down and confined at Hoa Lo Prison: Capt.
(then Commander) Allen C. Brady (19 January 1967) and Capt. (then Commander) Charles R. Gillespie, Jr. (24 October 1967) were also interned in
Room Seven. Capt. (then Commander) James Mehl (30 May 1967) was also
confined at Hoa Lo, but in a separate room.[3]

Following his graduation in June 1951, Ensign Fuller remained at
Annapolis for an additional three months as an instructor of new incoming
plebes. In October, he was accepted for flight training and reported to NAS
Pensacola for basic flight training, then to Kingsville and Corpus Christi,
Texas, for advanced training, qualifying as a naval aviator and earning his
"wings of gold" on 7 November 1952. The following five weeks of all-weather
flight training were interrupted by Christmas leave, during which Fuller
married Mary Anne McGinley on 27 December, a Jacksonville girl whom
he describes as "the love of my life."

In March 1953, Fuller was assigned to Fighter Squadron 192 (VF-192),
the "Golden Dragons" at Moffet Field, California. The squadron, newly
returned from combat operations in Korea was in the process of transitioning from propeller-driven F4U-4 Corsairs to the jet-driven F9F-5 Panthers. Fuller deployed to the Pacific twice with the squadron aboard the
Essex-class carrier USS *Oriskany* (CVA-34).

On the first Western Pacific (WestPac) deployment in September 1953,
the *Oriskany* sailed from San Francisco to join the Seventh Fleet engaged
in monitoring the truce in Korea, arriving at Yokosuka, Japan, on 15 October. Following operations in the Sea of Japan and the East China Sea, the
Oriskany supported Marine amphibious assault exercises at Iwo Jima before
returning to San Diego on 22 April 1954.

Between deployments, Fuller attended the USAF Fighter Weapons School at Nellis AFB, Nevada, for twelve weeks' training with the F-86 Sabrejet. In the interim, the *Oriskany* was overhauled at the San Francisco Naval Shipyard which was completed on 22 October 1954 when she again put out to sea. During this second deployment, the ship participated in the production of the film *The Bridges at Toko-Ri*. Because Fuller's aircraft was "the shiniest in the squadron," it was used in the movie. A film segment of Fuller flying the Panther was used to depict the fictional "Lieutenant Brubaker," the character played by William Holden. "I had two plane captains who kept her in tip top condition," Fuller recalled.[4]

In November 1955, Fuller left the *Oriskany* to attend Combat Information Center (CIC) School at NAS Glynco, Georgia, the site of the present Federal Law Enforcement Training Center, which trained Navy personnel to receive, evaluate, and transmit intelligence information throughout a ship or task force. While there, Fuller flew four different types of jets, and four different prop-aircraft.

In November 1958, Fuller began a tour of duty as Flag Lieutenant to Rear Admiral William E. Gentner, Jr., Commander Carrier Division Seven (ComCarDiv–7) and from April to December 1959 deployed to the Far East aboard the *Essex*-class carrier USS *Lexington* (CVG-21), the "Blue Ghost." Ports of call included Pearl Harbor, Yokosuka, Hong Kong, Iwakuni, Beppu, Subic Bay and Sasebo, before returning to California.[5]

From May through September 1960, Fuller was assigned to VA-126 "Bandits" at NAS Miramar. VA-126 was an A-4 Replacement Air Group (RAG) whose mission was to provide training prior to deployment with the fleet air wing, and Fuller trained flying Douglas A-4 Skyhawks.[6]

In September, he joined Fighter Squadron Fifty-Five (VA-55) "Warhorses" at NAS Lemoore as Operations Officer. During his twenty-six months with the squadron, he deployed twice aboard the USS *Ticonderoga* (CVA-14) for operations in the Western Pacific.

In November of 1963, Fuller was rotated to shore duty in Washington D.C., assigned to the Navy Bureau of Personnel (BUPERS) followed by attendance at Armed Forces Staff College at Norfolk, Virginia, from August 1965 until January 1966. In Southeast Asia, the war in Vietnam was escalating, and the need for aviators was increasing proportionally.

In February 1966, Fuller reported to Cecil Field, Florida, near Jacksonville, and was unexpectedly appointed Executive Officer of Attack Squadron Forty-Four (VA-44) "Hornets" an A-4 RAG. He divided his time between administrative duties and training for his next assignment and then in September, he transferred to the west coast, assigned as Executive Officer of Attack Squadron Seventy-Six (VA-76) "Spirits" flying the A-4 out of NAS Lemoore in California.

The commanding officer of VA-76, Cdr. Albert D. McFall, had only been in command a little more than two months when, on 6 December 1966, he died in a training accident. The squadron was operating about forty-five miles off the coast of San Diego aboard the USS *Bon Homme Richard* (CVA-31) when, during night launching operations, McFall's A4-C Skyhawk (BU149549) crashed into the ocean shortly after take-off . Fuller took over as the squadron's twelfth commanding officer.[7]

On 26 January 1967, the squadron embarked as part of Air Wing Twenty-One (CVW-21) aboard the *Bon Homme Richard* en route to its second Vietnam deployment. The *Bon Homme Richard* had seen combat in Vietnam as early as August 1964.

Commander Fuller flew his first combat mission over North Vietnam on 26 February 1967. Over the next five months, Fuller and squadron pilots flew almost continuously, so that by the afternoon of 14 July, Fuller was preparing to fly his 110th combat mission.

At 4:40 p.m. Fuller took off in the lead of an Alpha Strike, a large air attack by a carrier air wing. He was followed by flight of thirty-five aircraft, including A4 Skyhawks from VA-76 and VA-212 and six F-8 Crusaders flying fighter cover. The A4s carried a payload of one 2,000 lb. bomb and two 1,000 lb. bombs on its wings. It was the end of the monsoon season and command was opening up targets further north. The target that day was the Cao Tri railroad bridge near the city of Hun Yen, in the Hai Hung Province south of Hanoi. As Fuller later recalled, "the Surface to Air Missiles (SAMs) were up and ready for us that day."[8]

Fuller had scouted the area by accompanying the morning Alpha raid and had decided on flying west into the target area. "We saw three SAMs coming at us out of the southeast, and there was heavy radio traffic, but I radioed that they were going to go high. Then three more came at us from the west, but again, they went high. But the three SAMs that came from the Hanoi area left no time for evasive measures. Later I would be told that my wingman, Lt. John Waples, had thirty-six holes in his aircraft. I must have gotten a fair share in my own.... It was a direct hit!"

Fuller's aircraft was hit as he was beginning his delivery run northwest of the city and after dropping his payload he ejected. "I dropped my load on target, but was still about seventy miles from the Gulf of Tonkin. I felt that if I could make it to the Gulf, I had a good chance, but if I ejected over the target area, I'd have no chance. I could hear voices on the radio calling out 'Bail out! Fire! Eject! Eject!' I pulled up but had lost A-1 control. I still had rudder control but I was losing altitude. I ejected, but was hit in the shoulder and head by my canopy.[9]

Fuller was knocked semi-unconscious. Lt.(jg) Steven R. Grey, one of VA-212's "Rampant Raiders" would later recall the shoot-down in his book by the same name: "We were attacking the Cao Tri bridge about ten miles south of Hanoi when a bunch of SAMs from Hanoi streaked toward us. VA-76's skipper, Commander 'By' Fuller was hit right over the target area and immediately ejected. As his parachute floated down almost directly over the target, we saw to our horror a 37mm gun firing at him. The parachute canopy was riddled with holes and some of it was smoldering when he hit the ground hard just yards from the revetment of the flak site that had been shooting at him. Commander Fuller lay motionless at the edge of the ground and enemy gunners swarmed out of the revetment to take him captive."[10]

Fuller's was not the only plane of VA-76 shot down that day. A second pilot, Lt. J. N. Donis was hit by flak on an armed reconnaissance mission and ejected, but was rescued by a helicopter and returned to the carrier.[11]

The errant canopy had shattered Fuller's left shoulder and given him a concussion. His accelerated descent and subsequent hard landing also resulted in two broken bones in his left hand and a dislocated left knee, an injury from which he still suffers to this day. His captors fashioned a net of vines, suspended from bamboo poles and carried him into a village where he was abused by villagers who pelted him with rocks. He was transported to Hoa Lo Prison in Hanoi, arriving about midnight. Most Americans are more familiar with the name American POWs gave the facility, "Hanoi Hilton."[12]

Hoa Lo was a prison built by the French between 1886 and 1889 and was constructed primarily of bricks covered by stucco. The name translates to "fiery furnace" or "stove," perhaps from the wood stoves that used to be sold along the street. It was damp and unventilated and was by all accounts thick with the odor of sweat, urine, feces and fear. Hot in the summer and freezing in the winter, it was infested with all manner of vermin from rats to cockroaches. Worst of all was the isolation and the brutality of the interrogations, aimed less at obtaining military information than in breaking the spirit of the prisoners. POWs were routinely kept separate and isolated, confined in leg irons and tortured.

Fuller was brutally interrogated for seven days, the Vietnamese being interested in information on the AGM-62 "Walleye," an early prototype of "precision guided munitions" or smart bombs, information which Fuller did not possess. On 21 July, Fuller was relocated to "Golden Nugget Cell #1" and was given a cellmate, USAF pilot Maj. Wayne Waddell, who remained with him for the next ninety-one days. Fuller credits Waddell for his survival: "He saved my life. He set my bones. Wiped my ass. Fed me. Bathed me. He'd use his water ration to daub my heat rash."

On 19 October, Fuller and Waddell were moved to "Thunderbird Cell #1," but Waddell was removed from the cell on 25 October, which began twenty-five straight months of solitary confinement for Fuller, that lasted until 25 November 1969, when Commander Ken Coskey was placed in his cell.[13]

Meals were served twice a day, at 10:30 a.m. and 2:30 p.m. and consisted of bland pumpkin or cabbage soup and a bowl of rice. Despite prohibitions against it, prisoners developed ways to communicate and organize, even at the risk of severe consequences. Metal drinking cups, one of the prisoners' few possessions, would be placed against the wall to amplify the tapping in code that facilitated communications. The "tap code" could also be coughed or sneezed out, letter by letter and on occasions when they were in view of each other, hand signals could be used to pass on rumors, news and orders from the senior POWs. Being caught communicating resulted in harsh torture, yet although prisoners of war, they continued to resist and refused to accept defeat.[14]

On 27 November 27 1969, Fuller and Coskey were joined by USAF Lt. Col. Carl Crumpler, who also grew up in Jacksonville and things began to improve marginally. On 5 October 1970, Fuller and Coskey were moved into "Desert Inn Cell #3," where they remained for the next eighty-one days. It was the Son Tay Raid, however, on 20 November 1970, that significantly altered how the POWs were confined.

The target of the raid was Son Tay Prison, a POW camp 23 miles west of Hanoi, where intelligence analysts believed as many as 55 Americans were confined. The plan was for a joint operation where USAF resources would insert 56 Army Special Forces soldiers (Green Berets) into Son Tay during hours of darkness to rescue the POWS while the Navy conducted a diversionary simulated attack on Haiphong Harbor northeast of Hanoi.[15]

On the evening of 20 November, six helicopters, two large support aircraft and five attack aircraft flew from Thailand to Son Tay. Although the mission was not a success in the sense that no POWs were rescued, as they had been evacuated earlier, the only casualty of the 27 minute raid was a single broken ankle and the (intentional) loss of one helicopter. The mission was also a success in that it resulted in a substantial change by North Vietnam in the treatment of American POWs.

Fears of subsequent raids caused the North Vietnamese to consolidate their prisoners into fewer camps, which facilitated communication and organization among the POWs. Additionally, morale soared as the raids put to rest the lie their captors had asserted; that they were forgotten by their government. At the Hanoi Hilton, the prisoners were consolidated into seven large rooms.[16]

On 26 December 1970, Fuller was placed in "Room 7" with 46 others including Cdr. (later Vice Admiral and Vice-Presidential candidate) James Stockdale, the ranking Navy POW, and Maj. (later Colonel) Everett "Bud" Day, both of whom would be awarded the Medal of Honor for their actions while prisoners. Also interned in "Room 7" were future presidential candidate Lt. Cdr. (later Captain and Senator) John McCain, Cdr. (later Rear Admiral and Senator) Jeremiah Denton, Lt. Col. (Later Brigadier General) Robbie Risner, the ranking USAF POW, and Lt. Col. Hervey Stockman, a former U-2 pilot. Overall, they were an extraordinary group of individuals. Not surprisingly, "Room 7" was a center of resistance to their captors. They remained together 82 days.

On 18 March 1971, Fuller was moved to Building Zero, into a small two-man cell with Cdr. Al Brady, USAF Lt. Col. Fred Crow, and Cdr. Mel Moore, but on 29 June, Brady and Crow were moved to a separate cell. On 21 September 1972, Fuller and 18 other senior officers were moved to "Room #9" at the "Mayo Clinic." (The POWs gave names to all camp buildings, e.g., Las Vegas, Alcatraz, etc.)

Fuller's most memorable Christmas as a POW was the Christmas of 1972. Peace talks between North Vietnam and the United States had stalled and the talks collapsed on 13 December. Five days later, on 18 December 1972, President Richard Nixon ordered Operation Linebacker II in which American B-52s and fighter-bombers dropped over 20,000 tons of bombs on the cities of Hanoi and Haiphong. The United States lost 27 aircraft during the attacks in which North Vietnam claimed over 1,600 civilians killed. The bombings were successful in that North Vietnam resumed negotiations on 29 December. The Paris Peace Accords were signed at the Majestic Hotel in Paris on 27 January 1973.

Fuller recalled, "They told us we'd been forgotten by our country. The sound of the explosions and the flashes disproved their lies." "We cheered and we cried," recalled Crumpler. "When we heard the B-52s we knew the war was over because America was committed. It was the greatest day of our lives because we knew it was just a matter of time before we'd be going home."[17]

Fuller was still confined at the "Mayo Clinic" cell when on 31 January 1973, the POWs were informed of the Peace Agreement that had been signed on 27 January. Fuller was moved twice more before finally boarding a C-141 bound for Clark AFB in the Philippines on 4 March 1973, ending 2,060 days as a POW. The released Americans remained impassive and unemotional in front of their captors, but gave out a loud cheer once the plane lifted off.[18]

During his captivity, Fuller had frequently communicated with Stockdale over their futures once they were released and returned to the Navy. They disagreed as to which of them would be the first to command a carrier, and it was only Stockdale's promotion to flag rank that allowed Fuller to win the "bet." As returning POWs, they wanted nothing special, only the opportunity to compete fairly with their peers for command positions.

Fuller had been promoted to captain while a prisoner and, after debriefing, took several months of accumulated leave. There were plenty of available billets at the war colleges and the Naval Postgraduate School as well as positions in administration, recruiting and shore commands, but Fuller wanted to rejoin the fleet with a command at sea. After some successful campaigning with the Chief of Naval Operations (CNO) and old colleagues, he was screened by a convening board and selected for a deep draft command. This was followed by almost non-stop training with a temporary assignment (TAD) to the Fleet Training Center at Virginia Beach, Virginia.

After courses in Combat Information Center (CIC), Damage Control, Intelligence and Communications, Fuller departed for the Mediterranean, arriving to take command of the USS *Detroit* (AOE-4), a *Sacramento*-class fast combat support ship, on 6 August 1974. *Detroit* was the last of four in that class to be commissioned. Essentially an oiler and supply ship, she carried ammunition and supplies, but had sufficient speed to keep up with carrier battle groups.

While commanding officer of the *Detroit*, the ship made two deployments to the Mediterranean, the first beginning on 14 July 1974, when she departed Norfolk to support Sixth Fleet operations, and participated in contingency operations when trouble broke out in Cyprus. On 20 July 1974, Turkey staged a military invasion of Cyprus in response to a Greek military junta-backed coup in Cyprus. In August, shortly after Fuller arrived to

Captain Fuller greets his family and well-wishers upon his release, March 1973 (courtesy Robert B. Fuller).

assume command, an agreement to divide the island, with terms favoring Turkey, was signed by Greece. The *Detroit* remained in the area until returning to Norfolk in December.

On 19 August 1975, the *Detroit* returned to the Mediterranean, completing two hundred replenishments before returning home on 28 January

1976. While deployed, Fuller had been screened for command of an aircraft carrier, and he relinquished command of the *Detroit* on 19 November 1975.

To prepare for taking command of the *America*, Fuller attended the new Senior Engineering Course at Arco, Idaho, for seventeen weeks, taught by Adm. Hyman Rickover. Fuller also attended the Naval Tactical Command course, and took some accrued leave. Finally, Fuller departed for the Mediterranean to join his ship, flying in a Boeing 747 for the first time. He subsequently spent several days aboard *America* meeting with department heads, squadron commanders and crew members before formally taking command on 7 September 1976.[19]

As Fuller assumed command, he became the first released POW to command an aircraft carrier, which fulfilled the promise he'd made to himself years earlier in that Hanoi cell. However, Fuller will tell you that this was only possible because his friend Stockdale had the "bad fortune" to be promoted to Rear Admiral, over-qualifying him for carrier command.

Prior to Fuller's arrival, the *America* had been involved in support of Operation Fluid Drive, the evacuation of Americans and other foreign nationals from war-torn Beirut, Lebanon, after the American Ambassador Francis E. Meloy and Economic Counselor Robert O. Waring were kidnapped and murdered while en route to a meeting with Lebanese President Elias Sarkis on 16 June 1976.

President Gerald Ford, upon consulting with Secretary of Defense Donald Rumsfeld, CIA Director George H.W. Bush and White House chief of staff Dick Cheney, as well as Secretary of State, Henry Kissinger, and national security adviser, Brent Scowcroft, ordered Operation Fluid Drive to commence on 20 June.

While 263 Americans and other foreign nationals were evacuated from a beach by unarmed sailors aboard a landing craft from the USS *Spiegel Grove* (LSD-32), the *America* lay one hundred miles offshore with her fighters on short alert, capable of responding to the area within minutes. She also maintained surveillance of the Soviet Mediterranean Fleet during this time and provided support for a second evacuation on 27 July.[20]

Shortly after taking command, Fuller and the *America* were underway, involved in several international maritime exercises in the Mediterranean, most notably Display Determination, a NATO exercise involving forty-five Allied warships, including vessels from Italy, Greece, Portugal, Turkey and Great Britain, in October 1976. The exercise involved convoy operations simulating wartime reinforcement and resupply of NATO's southern region by sea. Upon conclusion of the exercise, *America* sailed to Rota, Spain, where she was relieved by the USS *Franklin D. Roosevelt* (CV-42), and she returned to Norfolk on 28 October.

America's second Mediterranean deployment under Fuller's command got underway on 29 September 1977, with Air Wing Six (CVW-6) and Rear Admiral C.C. Smith aboard, reaching Rota on 9 October and operating in the Mediterranean until 25 April 1978, when she returned home. In the interim, Fuller was advised of his selection for flag rank in February 1978.

On 17 April 1978, while still at sea, Fuller turned over command of the *America* to Capt. William F. Meyer and Adm. C. C. Smith "frocked" Fuller to the rank of Rear Admiral and presented him with the shoulder boards worn by former CNO Adm. James L. Holloway, III, when he was first promoted to flag rank. After the change of command ceremony, Fuller took off from the deck of the *America* and flew to the Azores, where a waiting P-3 *Orion* was to transport him to Norfolk.[21]

Captain Fuller departs the USS *America* after passing command to Capt. William F. Meyer, 17 April 1978 (courtesy Robert B. Fuller).

When asked what he remembered most about his time aboard the *America*, he unhesitatingly replied, "the crew." "They were an outstanding group of young men. Their average age was twenty-one, and they worked at the toughest job 18–20 hours a day. They were magnificent, and came through in every way."[22]

Almost immediately after reaching the states, in May 1978, he assumed the position of Director of the Joint Reconnaissance Center (JRC), assigned to the Joint Chiefs of Staff at the Pentagon in Washington, D.C.

Established in 1960 following the shoot-down of a CIA U-2 spy plane, piloted by Gary Francis Powers, while flying a reconnaissance mission over the Soviet Union, the JRC was created to coordinate all military reconnaissance flights. Its mission was "Global Force Management of all conventional Intelligence, Surveillance and Reconnaissance (ISR) and Maritime Patrol and Reconnaissance Aircraft (MPRA) for the Department of Defense." Fuller coordinated approval from all parties regarding reconnaissance overflights, became familiar with both the SR-71 and U-2 aircraft and gained a first-hand education in the workings of the government. For his service as Director, he was presented with the Defense Superior Service Medal citing his leadership, dedication to duty, and far-reaching imagination and foresight as "directly responsible for the successful completion of vital worldwide military operations of great sensitivity and utmost concern to the National Command Authorities."[23]

After twenty-three months at the "Puzzle Palace," in April 1980, Fuller was once again ordered to sea, this time to the Indian Ocean as Commander—Carrier Group Four (CCG-4) normally tasked with training and preparing Atlantic Fleet Carrier battle groups and additional assigned ships to conduct joint and combined maritime operations. Upon his arrival aboard the USS *Dwight D. Eisenhower* (CVN-69) on 20 June 1980, he took command of the carrier group which included the carrier USS *Midway* (CV-41) and the nuclear-power guided missile cruisers USS *California* (CGN-36) and USS *South Carolina* (CGN-37).

What came to be known as the Iranian Hostage Crisis was in full swing following the taking hostage of fifty-two Americans by Islamist students at the American Embassy in Tehran on 4 November 1979. An attempt to rescue the hostages, Operation Eagle Claw, on 24 April resulted in eight American servicemen killed and the loss of two aircraft before the mission was aborted. The *Eisenhower* arrived in the area three days later and relieved the USS *Nimitz* (CVN-68).

The carrier group remained on station off the coast of Iran for an unprecedented 254 days at sea, taking only a short liberty in Singapore from 17 through 22 July, before being relieved by the USS *Independence* (CV-62) and returning to Norfolk on 22 December.

Back on shore, Fuller learned that he was being considered for another carrier group assignment, this one with a home port of Naples, Italy. Reluctant to be away from family for another two years, and not interested in a shore command, Fuller informed the CNO of his desire to retire at the convenience of the Navy, and awaited his relief.

In the interim, Fuller again went to sea, embarked on the USS *Nimitz*, and was aboard on 26 May 1981, when an EA-6B Prowler crashed on the flight deck, killing fourteen crewmen and injuring forty-five others. Low on fuel after a missed approach, its crash and the subsequent fire and explosions destroyed or damaged eleven other aircraft. After hard work, the *Nimitz* deployed on schedule. Fuller then switched his flag to the USS *John F. Kennedy* (CV-67) to oversee her preparations for deployment to the Mediterranean.

From 30 April through 3 August, the *Kennedy* was at the Norfolk Naval Shipyard undergoing upkeep and overhaul maintenance, then departed Norfolk for three weeks of ship/air wing refresher operations in the Jacksonville/Guantanamo area, returning to Pier 12 on 14 September. Training continued through October including four days of "carquals" (carrier qualifications) and fly-on operations for Air Wing Three (CVW-3) which resulted in three fatalities on 29 October, when an EA-6B Prowler of VAQ-138 crashed killing the crew and serving as a reminder of the seriousness of their mission.

From 30 October to 4 December the *Kennedy* sailed to Puerto Rico to take part in ReadiEx 1-82, an exercise involving the Atlantic fleet and the Royal Navy. Thirty ships participated, which included the *Eisenhower,* and two hundred aircraft in a coordinated dual carrier battle group operation.

After a month back at Norfolk, the *Kennedy* departed on her tenth deployment to the Mediterranean on 4 January 1982, with CVW-3 embarked and arrived in the Mediterranean on the 17th. On 21 January, she participated in National Week XXXI, a multinational exercise, then transited the Suez Canal on 3 February and sailed into the Indian Ocean, where in February, Fuller relinquished command to his relief, Rear Adm. Edward H. Martin who like Fuller was an Academy graduate (Class of 1954) and former POW.[24]

Fuller flew from Diego Garcia to Hawaii, San Diego, and Jacksonville, Florida, where he was assigned to the staff of Commander Fleet Air at Jacksonville while he processed out of active service. He spent several months doing research, assisting on projects, completing paperwork and taking his exit physical.

Fuller retired with the rank of Rear Admiral on 1 December 1982. His decorations include the Navy Cross, two Silver Stars, the Defense Superior Service Medal, two Legions of Merit with Combat "V," four Distinguished Flying Crosses, two Bronze Star Medals with Combat "V," two Purple Hearts, the Vietnamese Air Gallantry Cross with Silver Wings, and the POW Medal.

Upon retirement, Fuller took a position the following day as Vice President of Sun State Marine, Inc., a tug and barge towing company. He retired as President of the company in December 1994. He resides in Jacksonville, Florida.

Surprisingly, Fuller bears no ill will toward the North Vietnamese. "They were doing their job, and I was doing mine."[25]

Rear Adm. Jerry C. Breast, on Captains McCormick and Fuller

Rear Admiral Jerry C. Breast served aboard the *America*, first as Operations Officer, then as Executive Officer, for fourteen months; he served under two captains. A native of Shelbyville, Tennessee, he graduated from Vanderbilt University and entered active duty on 4 June 1958, with an NROTC commission and a degree in physics. He was designated a naval aviator in September 1959.

Between 1967 and 1973 he deployed three times on combat tours to Vietnam and flew 336 missions over North Vietnam flying light attack aircraft. This included one tour aboard the *America* (June 72–May 73) flying A-7C Corsairs as commander of Attack Squadron 82 (VA-82) Marauders. He left the *America* in July 1974 to attend the U.S. Naval War College.

"After being ordered to the U.S. Naval War College in Newport, Rhode Island, twelve months prior to the end of my command of Attack Squadron 82 (VA-82) aboard the *America*, I failed to screen for air wing commander. I was very disappointed but that was somewhat short-lived when I was picked up two years early for promotion to captain (O-6). Coming out of the War College, I was ordered back to USS *America* as the Operations Officer and arrived there in July of 1975.

"The Commanding Officer of CV-66 at that time was Dan McCormick and, because of my new rank, he appointed me the Executive Officer (XO) shortly after I was frocked. Captain McCormick was a fighter pilot, a test pilot and a superb ship handler. He was extremely comfortable on the bridge and knowledgeable about all aspects of flight operations. It was a pleasure to watch the ease and confidence with which he maneuvered the ship relative to the rest of the formation or coming alongside. Although I had qualified as OOD Underway in the early 60's, Captain McCormick shared his knowledge and confidence with those of us who as department heads wished to gather greater ship-handling experience.

"During that first cruise to the Mediterranean, the change of command ceremony, during which Captain McCormick was relieved by Capt. Byron Fuller, was planned and executed while in Palma, Mallorca. It was a fun time and I remember that both commanding officers and the embarked flag (admiral) enjoyed the celebration. Naturally, as the executive officer, I was very much involved and responsible for the ceremony. I was sad to say goodbye to Dan McCormick but happy to welcome our new skipper. In those days we lustily sang 'America, the Beautiful' at every ceremony and ship's party.

"An unusual event had happened while we were in port at Naples, when a senior member of the embarked flag staff had ordered the ship to take aboard some 'personal articles' of a foreign national which needed transport back to the states. A number of boxes were moved aboard and placed in a locked stateroom and a Marine guard was posted outside for security. Soon after the change of command, it became apparent that Captain Fuller had not been briefed on this cargo and the flag's intentions for it. When he found the nature of the arrangements he became concerned that we perhaps should not be transporting it under the existing rules for U.S. Naval warships carrying civilian cargo. Captain Fuller had the legal officer check out the regulations thereto and the flag and legal authorities in Naples decided that it likely was not in accordance with regulations.

"The final result of this incident took place when the *America* returned to the states. U.S. Customs authorities came aboard and confiscated what turned out to be treasures brought from China after the Communist victory in about 1947. They were claimed to be the property of a Chinese tailor who had been a very close friend of several senior U.S. Naval officers. The interesting factor of this case was that Captain Fuller had the insight and care to ensure that this incident did not develop into one which reflected badly on the ship or our Navy. As the XO, I was very impressed with his integrity and the balanced way that he went about handling what could have been a significant problem.

"Because of injuries he had sustained from his ejection and imprisonment of several years by the North Vietnamese, Captain Fuller's bridge presence was a thing of wonderment to me. He was almost always on the bridge of the *America* and always in a very pleasant mood. He would sit for hours, being unable to raise his arms much above his shoulder level. His physical discipline far outperformed those of us who were younger but had never experienced the rigors of torture. Department heads would come to the bridge to deliver reports and it was always so pleasant there that they were never in a hurry to leave. Adding to the merriment was the navigator, Cdr. Dick Vosseler, who was very capable and therefore helped to create a comfortable environment. Suffice it to say, every carrier bridge is not filled with such congeniality!

"Part of the necessary relationship between the captain and the XO of a carrier is that the CO depends greatly on the XO to keep him advised of the daily functioning of the ship below the flight deck. On the *America*, just like every carrier I ever sailed on, we had lots of fires break out. For the most part they were insignificant in magnitude and damage and were usually put out within minutes. But obviously the skipper is going to be very alarmed at what is going on that he cannot see and could hazard his vessel. Therefore, part of my job as the XO was to go immediately to the fire and, as quickly as possible, report back to the CO himself. This was not an unusual task since that is exactly where I needed and wanted to be ... but it made Captain Fuller very happy to hear from me that the fires were under control. To some degree, I was his 'wet security blanket' that was thrown on the fires.

"We did have one particular situation which could have been deadly. One of the damage control survey teams making their regular inspection of the voids, deep in the bowels of the ship, tapped a valve which ruptured. This valve was part of the Chemical Holding Tank (CHT) which processes the human waste aboard ship. When it ruptured, a great flow of hydrogen sulfide escaped and the men were quickly overcome. Fortunately a chief petty officer realized that he had lost communications with them and sent an investigative team to rescue them. The rescue was successful and both men lived, but one of them was comatose for over a year. I mention this only to point out the hundreds of hazards to men and machinery that exist and fail every day aboard a ship of the complexity and size of one of our super-carriers.

"Let me emphasize the importance of quality department heads to the success of a naval vessel. On aircraft carriers, at least in the last few decades since World War II, the Navy has gone to every extreme to ensure experienced and capable middle-grade officers (O-4 and O-5) are slotted into those positions. From the Chief Engineer, the Navigator, the Weapons Officer, the Operations Officer to the men in the tower who control the flight and hangar decks ... there was not a weak performer in the group. USS *America* was a taut ship and a happy ship.

"I cannot tell you what an honor it was to work for and with Capt. Byron Fuller. I will never forget his physical and emotional discipline, moral courage, and deep integrity. We often use the phrase: 'In the finest traditions of the United States Navy.' Byron Fuller is the personification of that terminology."

Following his time aboard the *America*, Breast went on to command the replenishment oiler USS *Savannah* (AOR-4), and the carrier USS *Independence* (CV-62), before being promoted to flag rank on 7 June 1983. Later, while assigned Commander Carrier Group Two onboard USS *Coral Sea* (CVA-43), he took the first F/A-18 squadrons to the Mediterranean and demonstrated their capability in combat during operational strikes against Libya in 1986. He finished his career as Director of Operations (J-3) U.S. Space Command and retired as a Rear Admiral (Upper Half) on 30 March 1990. His awards include the Distinguished Service Medal for operations in Libya, a Silver Star earned in Vietnam, three Distinguished Flying Crosses and six Air Medals.

Notes

1. Mooney, James L. *Dictionary of American Naval Fighting Ships*, U.S. Navy History Division—Volume VIII, 1981.

2. Baron, Scott. Telephone interview with Robert B. Fuller, 16 July 2012.

3. Ibid.

4. Ibid.

5. Andrew, R.D.M. (Ed.). *1959 USS* Lexington *CVG-21 Far East Cruise Book*. Daito Art Printing Company: Tokyo, Japan, 1959.

6. A-4 Skyhawks Association—VA-126/VF-126 Bandits—http://a4skyhawk.org/3e/va126/va126.htm

7. "Carrier Pilot Lost at Sea." (UP) *Long Beach (Ca.) Press Telegram*, 8 December 1966.

8. Marbutt, Max. "Checking Into and Checking Out of the Hanoi Hilton." *Jacksonville (FL) Daily Record*, Friday, 13 July 2012.

9. Baron, Scott. Telephone interview with Robert B. Fuller, 24 July 2012.

10. Gray, Stephen R. *Rampant Raider—An A4 Skyhawk pilot in Vietnam*. Annapolis MD: Naval Institute Press, 2007.

11. Mersky, Peter. *U.S. Navy and Marine Corps A-4 Skyhawk Units of the Vietnam War*. Oxford: Osprey Books, 2007.

12. Soergel, Matt. "Out of a Tortured Past." *Florida Times-Union*, Sunday, 23 March 2008.

13. Ibid.

14. Interview with Robert Byron Fuller. http://link.brightcove.com/services/player/bcpid1460849479?bctid=1467273699.

15. Son Tay Raid Fact Sheet—National Museum of the Air Force—posted 24 March 2011. www.nationalmuseumaf.mil

16. Ibid.

17. Marbutt, Max. "Checking Into and Checking Out of the Hanoi Hilton." *Jacksonville (FL) Daily Record*, Friday, 13 July 2012.

18. Baron, Scott. Telephone interview with Robert B. Fuller, 27 July 2012.

19. Fuller, R. Byron. "Life After the Hanoi Hilton." *National Museum of Aviation Foundation Magazine*, Spring 1996.

20. Hoffman, Fred S. "Operation Fluid Drive." *St. Petersburg (FL) Times*, Monday, 21 June 1976.

21. Fuller, R. Byron. "Life After the Hanoi Hilton." *National Museum of Aviation Foundation Magazine*, Spring, 1996.

22. Baron, Scott. Telephone interview with Robert B. Fuller, 1 August 2012.

23. Defense Superior Service Medal citation.

24. Mooney, James L. *Dictionary of American Naval Fighting Ships*, vol. VIII. U.S. Navy History Division, 1981.

25. Fuller-Kalb, Peggy. "More Memories From the Home Front." *Florida Times Union*, 9 November 2003.

Capt. William F. Meyer
(April 1978–August 1979)

William F. Meyer was born in Hamler, Ohio, on 21 June 1932. He graduated from Ohio Northern University with a Bachelor of Science Degree in Civil Engineering and commenced Officers Candidate School on 19 January 1955. Commissioned on 6 May 1955, he completed flight training and was assigned to VA-96.[1] Nicknamed the "Eagles" the squadron of AD-6/7 Skyraiders was based at NAS Miramar and later at NAS Moffett Field. While Meyer was aboard, the squadron made a WestPac deployment on the USS *Keasarge* (CVA 33) operating in the vicinity of Taiwan following the build up of Chinese communist forces opposite the offshore islands to Taiwan.[2]

In April 1958, he was assigned as flight instructor with VA-125 (In June 1958 the squadron's mission was changed from "Air to Ground/Surface Attack" to "Indoctrination and Training of Pilots and Enlisted Personnel in Attack Aircraft for Assignment to Combat Carrier Squadrons." Based at

Moffett Field, squadron aircraft consisted of AD Skyraiders and A-4 Skyhawks (Rough Riders). After a tour as special projects pilot for the Bureau of Naval Weapons at North American Aviation, he received refresher training prior to becoming Operations Officer of Reconnaissance Attack Squadron Five. During this tour, Meyer deployed to Southeast Asia aboard the USS *Ranger* and participated in the first deployment of the RA-5C aircraft.[3]He received a Secretary of the Navy Letter of Commendation for his efforts as Special Projects Officer evaluating the RA-5C reconnaissance systems and the Integrated Operational Intelligence Systems during the deployment for the period of November 1964 to March

Capt. William F. Meyer (official U.S. Navy photograph).

1965. Commander Reconnaissance Attack Wing One, Capt. R.E. Fowler, Jr., made the presentation on 28 October 1966. The Secretary of the Navy described the work of Lieutenant Commander Meyer as resulting in "substantial savings for the Navy in terms of future improvements to RA-5C reconnaissance systems.[4]

Meyer was the only former commanding officer of the *America* to fly the RA-5C Vigilante aircraft. The RA-5C evolved from the Navy's heavy attack aircraft program. To carry an atom bomb a large, powerful aircraft was needed. A land based patrol aircraft, the P2V Neptune, was considered but it was too slow and too large to be safely recovered aboard a carrier. North American Aviation designed and built the AJ Savage and it was tested. With two reciprocating engines and a supplemental jet engine encased in the fuselage, the first carrier based multi-engined carrier aircraft was still too slow. It eventually became a tanker and saw service for only a few years. Douglas Aircraft finally introduced a suitable aircraft to meet both a conventional and nuclear mission requirement. However, the A3D Skywarrior was subsonic and supersonic became the key requirement of the time. Thus, the Navy replaced it with the Mach 2 Vigilante. When the Polaris submarines entered the fleet, the Navy discontinued the aircraft's strategic nuclear mission.[5]

After attending the Armed Forces Staff College in Norfolk, Virginia, Captain Meyer became Readiness Officer on the staff of Reconnaissance Attack Wing One. In September 1969, he joined RVAH-9 as Executive Officer and subsequently assumed command of the Squadron. Meyer then attended the Naval War College in Newport, Rhode Island, before assuming command of Carrier Air Wing Seven.[6]

After assignment as Staff Operations Officer on Carrier Division Four, he assumed command of USS *Concord* (AFS 5). Upon completion of the Senior Officer Ship Materiel Course in Idaho Falls, Idaho, Meyer served as Chief of Staff for Service Group Two on 17 April 1978. He then took command of the USS *America* (CV 66).[7]

In addition to various campaign and service awards, he wore the Meritorious Service Medal, Air Medal, Navy Commendation Medal and Navy Achievement Medal.[8]

Captain Meyer passed away on 27 March 2009.

Rear Admiral Smith (center) returns Captain Fuller's salute as Capt. William F. Meyer takes command of the *America* in April 1978 (official U.S. Navy photograph).

Capt. William F. Meyer, Bomb Damage Assessment Run

The following is a reprint of an article written by Robert R. "Boom" Powell, former Vigilante pilot, Virginia Beach, Virginia, July 2004. It appeared in the Osprey Combat Aircraft publication #51, *RA-5C Vigilante Units in Combat*. Permission has been granted by Robert Powell and Osprey editor Tony Holmes for the authors to reprint this article. The said publication #51 was initially published in Great Britain in 2004 by Osprey Publishing 1st Floor Elms Court, Chapel Way, Botley, Oxford, OX29LP

BDA Run

"The dust, dirt and debris from 100 Mk 82 500-lb bombs was still settling back to the ground as the Vigilante began its photo run. The pilot had both afterburners blazing, and he lowered the nose of his aircraft to pick up more speed. In the back cockpit, the Reconnaissance Attack Navigator (RAN) checked that the film counters were running down, the image-motion bars were tracking and the inertial navigation readouts were correct, all the while watching the ALQ scope for any signs of SAM radar lock-ons and missile launches. The Vigilante was doing 650 mph as the wings snapped level over the primary target. Inside the planned turn, the Phantom II escort was in full afterburner trying to keep up.

"The Vietnamese gunners who had not been injured in the attack had reloaded their weapons as fast as they could, and they began to shoot as the RA-5C came over the target. The smaller guns tracked the fast moving aircraft while an 87 mm site put up a barrage of exploding shells where they hoped the Vigilante would be.

"The pilot jinked left to throw off the track of the gunners, avoid the shell bursts and get closer to one of the SAM sites which had been attacked. Tracers streaked the air, the ALQ screen was a mass of golden strobes and missile lock warnings warbled in the crew's earphones. The RAN continued to monitor the reconnaissance and navigation systems as the aircraft swerved and bounced. The Radar Intercept Officer (RIO) in the escorting Phantom II called out gunfire when he saw it.

"After long, breathless minutes, the two airplanes clear the target area. The RAN moved a cursor handle, punched a button and told his pilot to 'Follow steering.' On the pilot's instrument panel a needle swung towards the southeast, and the distance to their carrier spun up. They were still forty miles from the safety of the Tonkin Gulf, and remained in afterburner until they were off the coast, and having reported 'Feet Wet' to the carrier.

"Such was a typical Bomb Damage Assessment (BDA) mission flown by RAVH squadrons during the whole of air war in Vietnam.

"The vast majority of RA-5C flights were either BDA or route reconnaissance. The Vigilante had the most sophisticated suite of reconnaissance systems of any aircraft flying at the time. It also had the highest loss rate of any carrier-based aircraft during the war in South-East Asia.

"The Vigilante crews used to taunt the attack and fighter pilots: 'We have to get back from our missions to be successful. Once you hot-shots have dropped your bombs, you're done. Furthermore, it is our photos that are firm evidence that a target has been destroyed so you don't have to go back. Our cameras don't lie.'

"'Unarmed and Unafraid' was the cynical motto of the Vigilante photoreconnaissance crews who flew into the world's most heavily defended airspace."

Notes

1. Official Biography of Captain William F. Meyer USN (Ret.), Navy History and Heritage Command, Washington, D.C.
2. *Dictionary of America Naval Aviation Squadrons-Volume 1*, p. 164.
3. Official Biography of Captain William F. Meyer USN (Ret.), Navy History and Heritage Command, Washington, D.C.
4. Command History, Reconnaissance Attack Squadron Five, dated 20 June 1967.
5. Powell, Robert R. "Boom." *RA5-C Vigilante Units in Combat*. Oxford, Great Britain: Osprey Publishing Limited, 2004.
6. Official Biography of Captain William F. Meyer USN (Ret.), Navy History and Heritage Command, Washington, D.C.
7. Ibid.
8. Ibid.

Capt. Rene L. "Sam" Leeds (August 1979–February 1981)

> In general we got solid interest and support of our maritime strategy ideas—Captain Rene Leeds commenting on the Strategic Studies Group's reception by Senior Navy and USMC officers[1]

Rene "Sam" Leeds was born in 1934, one of two sons born to Mr. and Mrs. William E. Leeds of Overland Park, Kansas. He graduated Shawnee Mission High School near Kansas City, followed by an Engineering degree from General Motors Institute of Technology (GMI) at Flint, Michigan, in September 1956.

Leeds enlisted in the U.S. Navy as an Aviation Officer Candidate in November 1956, and after four months of pre-flight training at NAS Pensacola in Florida, he received his commission as an ensign and was awarded his naval aviator wings of gold on 29 March 1957.[2]

His first fleet assignment was to the Fighter Squadron Hundred Ninty One (VF-191) "Satan's Kittens" flying the Grumman F-11F Tiger. The F-11F, Tiger, later designated the F-11 in 1962, was the first

Capt. Rene "Sam" Leeds (official U.S. Navy photograph).

supersonic single-seat carrier based fighter in the fleet and they were used by the Blue Angels flight team from 1957 to 1969.

The squadron deployed from NAS Miramar, California, on a Western Pacific (WESTPAC) cruise as part of Air Wing Nineteen (CVG-19) aboard the USS *Bon Homme Richard* (CVA-31) on 1 November 1958, and made port calls at Bombay, India; Subic Bay, Hong Kong, and Japan before returning home on 16 June 1959.[3]

From 1960 through 1961, Leeds was assigned to the Naval Missile Center at Point Mugu, California, involved in Aerospace Flight Operations.

For the next three years (September 1961–September 1964), Lieutenant Leeds attended the Naval Postgraduate School in Monterey, California, studying nuclear physics. While a student, on 21 November 1961, Leeds and another student, Marine Capt. Robert E. Solliday, were flying into Monterey Regional Airport in a North American T-2 Buckeye when engine failure forced them to eject from their aircraft at three hundred feet. The jet crashed into the side of a hill. Both Leeds and Solliday were recovered uninjured.[4]

His thesis, "Computer Simulation Studies of Copper Atoms in 110 Channels of Copper Crystals," earned him a Master's Degree in Physics. He graduated in 1964 and then returned to the fleet.

In September 1964, Leeds reported to NAS Miramar, near San Diego, California, assigned to Fighter Squadron One Hundred Twenty One (VF-121) "Pacemakers," a Replacement Air Group (RAG) for fleet replacement training, in order to transition to the McDonnell Douglas F-4 Phantom II, a tandem, two-seat, twin-engine, all-weather, long-range supersonic jet interceptor fighter/fighter-bomber which became the Navy's principal air superiority fighter during the Vietnam War. He completed his transition in November. "They rushed my transition into the -F4 to make VF-21's deployment to Vietnam. As a result I did my Carrier Qualifications in VF 21 during her workup on the Midway headed for Vietnam."[5]

Following the completion of his training in November, Leeds reported to Fighter Squadron Twenty One (VF-21) "Freelancers" as Maintenance Officer. While assigned to the squadron, Leeds made two combat cruises to Vietnam.

On 17 June 1965, during his first deployment, from 6 March through 23 November 1965, as part of Air Wing Two (CVW-2) embarked in the USS *Midway* (CVA-41), pilots of VF-21 downed two MiG-17s over the Gulf of Tonkin. The first MiG-17 was downed by Cdr. Louis C. Page and Lt. John C. Smith, and the second by their wingman, Lt. David Batson and Lt. Cdr. Robert Doremus. Thus, VF-21 earned the distinction of the first Navy air-to-air combat kills of the Vietnam War.[6]

Leeds recalled: "It was early in the Vietnam War. It was a sunny day over the beach in North Vietnam with a few scattered clouds. A division of MiG-17s made two mistakes that day. First, they picked on VF-21s Cdr. Lou Page (XO of VF 21) and his Radar Intercept Officer (RIO) Lt. Cdr. J.C. Smith and their wingman Lt. Dave Batson and Lt. Cdr. Bob Doremus. Page had run this type of dogfight in his mind and with his section many times. J.C. (Smith) was a leading RIO in his community and very good at adapting the Phantom, which was designed for all weather intercepts against bombers, to the dogfight. Our Phantoms had missiles but no guns for the close-in fight. So head-on they had to shoot no later than three miles separation or the Sparrow would fail and go stupid.

"The day would be J.C.'s day. J.C. held the four tracks on his radar as did Bob Doremus. J.C. locked up the lead target and Bob picked another. One critical problem remained. Were these radar tracks good guys or bad guys? They had to be visually identified before shooting.

"The four MiGs made their second mistake. They saw the smoking engine trails that our Phantoms always made and turned toward the VF-21 section, now fully armed with the sections crewmen staring for a visual sighting and Talley Ho (I see you), all except J.C. who was fixed to his radar—realizing it would be a minimum range shot at best and that the missiles had to come off the rail at the right angle. The dot on his radar screen showed they were not getting the best angle. Page, seeing the MiGs, was starting a right turn more toward them. J.C. screamed, 'Come left to get the DOT' just as they identified the flight of four as enemy MiGs.

"Lou (Page) responded with a hard pull left and the section launched two Sparrows at minimum range. At a speed of 600–700 knots closure, the engagement was over in a few seconds. Both Sparrows hit their targets. A third MiG pilot ejected leaving a lone MiG to escape.

"This was the first MiG shoot-down of the war and the first by missiles, not to mention head-on at minimum range. Everything had to go perfectly and it did! We didn't see MiGs after that for some time, I suppose because of the lone pilot's report of how they were shot down before they could start an attack. But that's not the only significant thing that happened that day.

"Those of us in Phantoms who heard this shoot down explained understood it marked a different chapter in fighter aviation. Air-to-air missile dogfights would be challenging and very much a crew effort. Pilots, or rather front seat observers, as J.C. loved to call them in the ready room, did not control the radar or the set-up of a radar intercept.

"It was a team effort all the way to the award ceremony. The shootdown was a major news event, but not without J.C. At the planned awards ceremony in Saigon, the Navy proposed to give the two pilots Silver Stars and the two RIOs Distinguished Flying Crosses (a lower award). J.C. responded simply, 'We all get Silver Stars or you can forget us.' They all proudly wear Silver Stars today and appropriately so. Aircrews are families."

(Aircraft from the *Midway* would also score the last air combat victory of the Vietnam War when Phantoms of VF-161 downed a North Vietnamese MiG-17 on 12 January 1973.)

Leeds, and the squadron, deployed again to Vietnam on 29 July 1966, again as part of CVW-2, but this time aboard the USS *Coral Sea* (CV-43). Proceeding via Pearl Harbor, the ship reached Yokosuka, Japan, on 14 August and relieved the USS *Ranger*, then departed on 20 August, bound for the Philippines. Despite severe weather conditions generated by Typhoon Winnie on the 21st and 22nd, the *Coral Sea* arrived at Subic Bay on 25 August, and departed the following day for Yankee Station, but damage to two propellers made operational speed impossible and required her return to the Subic Bay drydocks for repairs.

Coral Sea arrived at Yankee Station on 13 September, and began launching strikes against enemy lines of communication and supply facilities.[7] *Coral Sea* departed Yankee Station on 20 October and returned to Subic for further repairs, then departed on 30 October to return to Yankee Station until 4 December.

Following upkeep at Subic (6–17 December), the ship visited Hong Kong from 20–26 December before returning to the line, where she ushered in 1967 with round-the-clock combat operations against Communist supply lines in North Vietnam. Their efforts were not without cost. CVW-2 lost sixteen more aircraft, six aircrew killed, three missing and six more prisoners or war. Relieved by the *Bon Homme Richard*, the *Coral Sea* sailed for home 9 February, reaching Alameda on the 23rd.[8]

In September 1966, Leeds returned to VF-121, assigned as a Tactics Phase Leader, teaching combat tactics to new and transitioning pilots. "I was getting F 4 aircrews ready to go into Vietnam combat. I also helped set up Top Gun, taught ACM and bombing and flew in some great projects."

By the mid–60s, the Navy had come to the conclusion that there was a need to revise fighter tactics, based in part on the high losses they were suffering in Vietnam, approximately one loss for every two enemies killed. This was significantly higher than the 10–1 ratio during World War II.

Following the Korean War and the dawn of the Cold War, fighters were trained in tactics to intercept Soviet nuclear bombers, and little training was provided in Air Combat Maneuvering (ACM) or "dogfighting." The F-4 Phantom, developed in 1960, was tailored to fit the role of interceptor, so much so that guns were deemed unnecessary.[9]

The initiation of air combat in Vietnam coincided with the advent of Beyond Visual Range Air to Air Missiles (BVRAAM), air-to-air missiles capable of engaging at ranges up to twenty nautical miles. American fighters were facing an opponent flying the smaller, more maneuverable MiG-17, 19 and 21.

Additionally, Rules of Engagement (ROE) called for a visual identification, and by the time that was achieved, they were within minimum range. Frustrated, in 1968, Capt. Frank Ault, skipper of the *Coral Sea*, wrote a letter to the Pentagon outlining the problem. Tasked with defining the problem, the resulting "Ault Report" concluded, in part, that the problem stemmed from inadequate air-crew training in air combat maneuvering and recommended establishment of an "Advanced Fighter Weapons School."[10]

The solution was the creation of the Naval Fighter Weapons School (NFWS) at NAS Miramar, initially as a department within VF-121. As head of tactics, Leeds was first in being considered to head the school and "ride herd on the best of the best." But Leeds' RAG tour was about finished, and he was scheduled for a new post on the east coast. "I could have been selfish and taken it (the job) and left in the middle," Leeds later recalled "but this was going to be a long term program. It wouldn't have been right to whoever followed."[11]

The squadron Operations Officer, Lt. Cdr. Dan Pedersen, originally scheduled to take over Tactics, was next in line. "At first, he didn't want to do it," Leeds said of Pedersen. "I don't remember the details other than the school was an unknown entity and we don't know how it would turn out." Pedersen also admitted he was suspicious why Leeds wasn't taking the command. Ultimately persuaded, Pedersen took command of the Naval Fighter Weapons School, also known as Top Gun, on 3 March 1969. Despite its humble beginning in a single portable metal trailer in which offices, classes and research were all conducted, it accomplished its purpose, with a 13–1 kill ratio by the end of the Vietnam War. In 1996, the School was merged into the Naval Strike and Air Warfare Center at NAS Fallon, Nevada.

In April 1969, Lieutenant Commander Leeds moved east and reported to Norfolk, Virginia, assigned to Fighter Squadron Eleven (VF-11) "Sundowners" as the Operations Officer. The squadron, part of Air Wing Seventeen (CVW-17), embarked aboard the USS *Forrestal* (CVA-59) on a Mediterranean cruise from 2 December 1969 until 8 July 1970 with port calls in Italy, France, Spain, Greece and Malta. Leeds recalled, "I ejected from a Phantom into the Mediterranean on 20 January 1970, my birthday. There were no serious injuries to my RIO, Lt. Cdr. Al Johnson or me, but the water was cold."

By June 1971, Leeds was back at NAS Miramar, assigned as Fleet Introduction Coordinator for the Grumman F-14 Tomcat, in charge of the training and logistics program for the F-14 build-up and integration into the squadrons.

With the failure of the General Dynamics-Grumman F-111B interceptor to meet the needs of both the Navy and Air Force, and its unambiguous rejection by Vice Adm. Tom Connolly, Deputy Chief of Naval Operations for Air Warfare, who felt that the F-111B was totally unsuitable as a carrier based aircraft, the aircraft was never put into production. Admiral Connolly told Congress "There isn't enough thrust in Christendom to get the F-111 airborne."

In 1968, U.S. Secretary of Defense Robert McNamara formally directed that the services study the development of a single aircraft that would satisfy the needs of both the Navy and Air Force. General Dynamics, McDonnell Douglas, North American Rockwell and Ling-Temco-Vought (LTV) all put in proposals. Grumman's Design 303E, that would evolve into the F-14 Tomcat, was announced as the winner on 14 January 1969. It was named "Tomcat" to honor Admiral Connolly.

Air Test and Evaluation Squadron Four (VX-4) "Evaluators" received its first Tomcats in the fall of 1972 and began working on operational tactics. Meanwhile, the first two fleet squadrons, VF-1 and VF-2, were established at NAS Miramar, and the aircrews trained by VF-124 "Gunfighters," the first Tomcat Fleet Readiness Squadron (FRS). Cdrs. Dick Martin and Sam Leeds were selected as the first squadron commanders.

On 14 October 1972, Commander Leeds took command of VF-1 "The Wolfpack" at NAS Miramar, even as Commander Martin took command of VF-2 "The Bounty Hunters," however the first Tomcats didn't arrive until 1 July 1973.

VF-1 and the F-14A made their first operational deployment aboard the USS *Enterprise* (CVN-65) in September 1974 and Tomcats flew air cover during Operation Frequent Wind, the evacuation of Saigon, in April 1975.

By that time, Leeds was gone, having been ordered to Washington, D.C., in April 1974, assigned to the Staff of the Deputy Chief of Naval Operations for Air Warfare as the F-14 coordinator.

On 23 December 1976, Leeds relieved Cdr. W.H. Byng and assumed command of Carrier Air Wing Eleven (CVW-11) embarked in the USS *Kitty Hawk* (CV-63) at NAS North Island, outside San Diego, California.[12]

Leeds took command of his first naval vessel, when on 25 August 1978, he relieved Capt. (later Rear Adm.) John R. Batzler as commanding officer of the USS *Ashtabula* (AO-51), a Cimarron-class fleet oiler, home ported at Pearl Harbor, Hawaii. Leeds recalls, "*Ashtabula* was built and sailed during World War II and had a downed Japanese fighter to her credit. Her engineering plant was of that vintage. As I viewed the water in her bilges and many other challenges, I asked our engineer what speeds she could reliably do? He responded, '12 Knots, Sir.' I never ordered more than twelve knots. We transited independently at twelve knots and brought ships alongside at twelve knots and *Ashtabula* made all her commitments though we left early for almost all events."

Ashtabula having already deployed on a WESTPAC cruise on 30 June, Leeds joined the ship at Pattaya Beach, Thailand, and sailed her to Australia, Singapore, and Hong Kong, with a stop for upkeep at Guam before returning to Pearl Harbor on 18 January 1979.

"Steaming independently, *Ashtabula* was headed for the Pearl Harbor. At 2:00 a.m. Lieutenant Hillary, the OOD, woke me from a deep sleep to brief me that he had spotted a flare-up light on the horizon for a short time. I moved to the bridge. Lieutenant Hillary believed that it was a possible distress signal but he no longer saw any lights. He had marked the bearing to the light. We turned the ship to that bearing for thirty minutes to see if the signal reappeared. It did. We found a large raft adrift with eight Vietnamese down to water rations. Their engine had failed days ago and they were unable to repair it. The map they had hoped to navigate by was a world hemisphere map, measuring 3 inches × 3 inches. Having drifted far off any shipping lanes they fortunately saw *Ashtabula*'s running lights on a quiet sea state. With them safely aboard and generally healthy we resumed course for the Philippines. Lieutenant Hillary had undoubtedly saved their lives."[13]

The rest of his command was spent in the usual activities of training, inspections, and local operations. On 14 July 1979, Leeds turned over command to Capt. Brian D. Woods.[14]

On 23 August 1979, Leeds relieved Capt. Frederick Meyer as commanding officer of the USS *America* during her Mediterranean deployment, while in port at Augusta Bay, Sicily. Vice Adm. George Kinnear was the guest speaker. Following the turnover of duty to the USS *Nimitz* (CVN-68) *America* sailed for home, arriving at Norfolk on 22 September.

October was spent operating off Mayport, Florida, and in the Gulf of Mexico conducting carrier qualifications, highlighted by the first arrested carrier landing of the new McDonnell-Douglas F/A-18 Hornet, and several days of rigorous testing of its capabilities. Leeds credits any success he had as skipper of the *America* to the professionalism of the crew, from teenaged deck hands to seasoned senior petty officers and first rate officers.

"One night an A-7 hit the ramp, the back of the landing area, and burst into flames as it careened up the deck. It caught an arresting wire and slowly slid, or so it seemed, across the deck and into a catwalk hitting and destroying our landing mirror, which on a carrier is the number one aid to final landing. The A-7 has some magnesium parts that when ignited will not go out and so the fire continued around the A-7. My deck crew immediately responded and fought and contained the fire. They approached within a few feet of that plane as they fought it. Heroes all! On the bridge, I had my finger on the fog foam system that could flood the deck, in case the fire spread. The Air Boss called and asked for some time, and proposed pushing what was left of the plane over the side. I was glad to see that bird depart

America. No one was injured and amazingly the pilot had climbed out safely and joined the deck crew to help fight the fire. God bless the fight deck crew and those professionals. I didn't have to push the button to avoid a *Forrestal* size fire."

Three days after returning to Norfolk, on 6 November, *America* entered the Norfolk Naval Shipyard for overhaul and alterations including the installation of NATO Sea Sparrow missiles and the multi-barreled Phalanx machine-gun for close-in defense. "The CNO, Admiral Hayward, visited *America* while she was in overhaul. Overhaul lasts many months and for a carrier is much like open-heart surgery. Gear is everywhere and the ship is pretty messy and busy. Admiral Hayward had been CO of *America* ten years earlier and his visit was special. During our rounds he asked about the drug problem, which in 1980 had reached a major crisis. I told him I estimated almost half of the crew was using or had used drugs. He soon announced to the Navy 'Not in My Navy.' Within a year the drug problem had almost disappeared. We started several programs that showed our crew that we cared about their careers and future. It paid off! They are professionals and should be treated that way."[15]

Following her post-repair sea trials 27–29 October 1980, she spent the remainder of the year operating in the Virginia Capes, and performing upkeep in port at Norfolk. "My chief engineer, Cdr. Arny Ristad, was one of the best, and a professional. After a full overhaul, under his leadership, he and I opened her up one night, operating all eight boilers, and we got her to over thirty knots."

On 14 January 1981, *America* earned a footnote in U.S. naval history when Ens. Brenda Robinson, USNR, became the first black female naval aviator to be carrier qualified when she landed a Grumman C-1A Trader COD aircraft onto *America*'s deck.[16]

While returning to Norfolk, on 29 January, after conducting carrier qualifications for Air Wing Eleven (CVW-11), *America* received a call of distress from the Greek vessel *Aikaterina,* and responded to the scene. Helicopters of Helicopter Anti-Submarine Squadron Twelve (HS-12) transported damage control equipment and repair parties over to the ship and assisted until the arrival of the Coast Guard.

"Air Wing Eleven was a west coast wing and placing them on an east coast carrier was a challenge. I welcomed it. I had commanded Air Wing Eleven Commander some two years before. I knew many of the wing personnel and traveled to the west coast to welcome them and make our support clear. More professionals! For example, Air Wing Eleven was the first air wing to go to the USAF Red Flag Exercise at Nellis AFB. F-14 Tomcats and A-7s, E-2 vectored to the target and engagement with F 15s. Great dogfight too and CVW-11 looked combat ready throughout. Mission accomplished."

Shortly after returning to Norfolk, on 11 February 1981, Leeds turned over command of *America* to Capt. James Francis "Yank" Dorsey, Jr., in a ceremony aboard the *America* while docked at Pier 12, with Rear Adm. Gordon R. Nagler, Commander Cruiser/Destroyer Group Two (COM-CRUDESGRUTWO) as the guest speaker.

In April 1981, at a strategy forum, Adm. Thomas Hayward, former C.O. of the *America* and current Chief of Naval Operations, announced the creation of the Naval Warfare Studies Center, to be located at the Naval War College, Newport, Rhode Island.

At the same time, citing "a lack of strategic thinking, even at the fleet commander level" Hayward ordered the formation of a Strategic Studies Group to "fill the void." He hoped this group of "the best and brighter of our military officers" would provide a variety of viewpoints, and as CNO, Hayward personally reviewed the service records of the first group, and made the selections. Among those selected for the first group was Captain Leeds.[17]

The first Strategic Studies Group, under the direction of former Undersecretary of the Navy Robert J. Murray, and comprised of six Navy and two Marine field-grade officers, supported by a staff of three, met on 31 August 1981.

As defined, their two key tasks would be to develop a near-term offensive strategy and an offensive strategy of the future with regards to any future war with the Soviet Union. The maritime strategy they proposed took full advantage of the situation and the introduction of new capabilities across the fleet including the F-14. It placed a great deal of pressure on the Soviet Fleet and their flanks. Their discussions with leaders in Washington, D.C., and with senior naval commanders opened much needed debate in the Navy.

"The group reported directly to the CNO. What Hayward wanted was not an instantly created strategy, but a well-framed understanding of the issues with possible resolutions."[18]

The first Strategic Studies Group completed its work in June 1982, and Leeds was sent to Gaeta, Italy, in the Mediterranean, assigned as the Sixth Fleet Chief of Staff, about the time when armed conflict broke out in Lebanon.

In 1984, Leeds returned to the Naval War College, assigned the number two position at the Center for Naval Warfare under Director Robert Wood. Leeds spent his final years on active duty and several more later, as a civil servant, implementing ideas from the maritime strategy. He retired from active duty in September 1986 after nearly thirty years.

Following his retirement, Leeds went to work at the Navy Doctrine Center in a career civil service position (GS-15), and then he went to work as part of the USMC team assigned to the Joint Forces Command. He continues to work in the field of Joint and Combined Operations, concerned with how to best integrate the individual armed services to be best prepared to prevent, and if necessary fight the war of the future.

Notes

1. Interview with Sam Leeds, 26 June 2013
2. Ibid.
3. *U.S. Navy Naval Aviation News*, May 1959.
4. *Pacific Stars and Stripes*, Friday, 24 November 1961.
5. Interview with Sam Leeds, 7 July 2013.
6. The Midway Phantom website—http://www.midwayphantom.com/index1a.htm.
7. USS *Coral Sea* Tribute site—http://www.usscoralsea.net/pages/mtjas.php.
8. Ibid.
9. Elder, Adam. "Top Gun—40 Years of Higher Learning." *San Diego Magazine*, October, 2009.
10. Michel III, Marshall L. *Clashes; Air Combat Over North Vietnam 1965–1972*. Annapolis, MD: Naval Institute Press, 1997, 2007.
11. Wilcox, Robert K. *Scream of Eagles: The Dramatic Account of the U.S. Navy's Top Gun Fighter and How They Took Back the Skies Over Vietnam*. London: Simon & Schuster, 2005.
12. *Kitty Hawk* Command History 30 April 1977. http://www.history.navy.mil/ship hist/k/cv-63/1976.pdf
13. Interview with Sam Leeds, 10 July 2013.
14. USS *Ashtabula* http://www.navsource.org/archives/09/19/19051a.htm
15. Interview with Sam Leeds, 7 July 2013.
16. *Dictionary of American Naval Fighting Ships*, Naval History and Heritage Command http://www.history.navy.mil/danfs/a8/america-iii.htm.
17. Hattendorf, John B. "The Evolution of the U.S. Navy's Maritime Strategy, 1977–1986." *Naval War College Newport Papers*, 2003. http://www.dtic.mil/cgi-bin/GetTRDoc? AD=ADA422147.
18. Ibid.

Capt. James F. Dorsey, Jr.
(February 1981–July 1982)

"While at the helm of the *America* Captain James 'Yank' Dorsey, Jr., transited the Suez Canal in April 1981 on her way to the Indian Ocean, the first super carrier to make the crossing. In October of that year she once again passed through the Suez Canal, with escort from the Egyptian Army, Navy and Air Force due to the recent assassination of Egyptian President Anwar Sadat."[1]

James F. Dorsey, Jr., was born in Baltimore and reared in Washington, D.C. Entering the Navy in 1955 through the Naval Aviation Cadet Program, he earned his commission and designation as a Naval Aviator in 1956 after completing advanced fighter training in the F-9F Panther at Corpus Christi, Texas.

Dorsey reported to the first of his nine squadron assignments in October 1956, with Fighter Squadron Sixty-One at Naval Air Station Oceana, Virginia. He subsequently served tours homeported at Oceana with Fighter Squadron Forty-One, One Hundred Two, and One Hundred-One Detachment Alpha, where in 1962 he participated in the program that introduced the F-4B Phantom II aircraft into Atlantic Fleet Service.

After serving a year as an instructor pilot with VF-101 in Key West, Florida, he left the east coast in December 1965 and began studies at the Naval Postgraduate School, Monterey, California, earning a degree in Political Science. Ordered to NAS Miramar, he served as Operations Officer for Attack Carrier Air Wing Two and flew with Fighter Squadron Twenty-One until March 1971, when he became the Executive Officer of Fighter Squadron One Hundred Twenty-One and then he became the squadron's Commanding Officer from December 1971 until May 1972.

Capt. James F. Dorsey, Jr. (official U.S. Navy photograph).

Dorsey was then assigned to VF-21 as Executive Officer and then Commanding Officer until July 1974. Following a tour as a member of the Staff of Commander, Fighter Airborne Early Warning Wing, Pacific, he reported for his third command assignment with VF-121 in December 1974, homeported at NAS Miramar, California.

In May 1976, he reported to Yokosuka, Japan, to serve as Executive Officer of the Navy's only overseas homeported aircraft carrier, USS *Midway* (CV-41). During his tour *Midway* was twice recognized for her combat readiness by award of the Battle Efficiency Pennant. In addition, *Midway* received the Ney, Flatley and Golden Anchor Awards.

In July 1978, Captain Dorsey took command of the USS *Calooshatchee* (AO-98), a multi-product underway replenishment ship, homeported at Norfolk, Virginia. As a result of this tour, Captain Dorsey was awarded the Meritorious Service Medal. In June 1980, he reported for duty as Assistant Chief of Staff for Readiness and Deputy Chief of Staff, on the Staff, Commander Naval Air Force, U.S. Atlantic Fleet.

On 12 February 1981, Captain Dorsey assumed command of the aircraft carrier USS *America* (CV-66) homeported in Norfolk with the U.S. Atlantic Fleet. He next served as Deputy Director Joint Program Office of the Defense Communications Agency, then as Commander Carrier Group Four.

Dorsey was promoted to Rear Admiral in September 1986 and advanced to the rank of Vice Admiral on 1 February 1989. At the time of his retirement in July 1991 he was Commander, Third Fleet.

During his naval career, Vice Admiral Dorsey had flown more than 4,700 hours in sixteen types of aircraft, ranging from the SNJ basic trainer to the latest and most advanced carrier aircraft. He had flown from eleven different carriers and completed 226 Vietnam combat missions flying F-4J fighter jet aircraft. His medals and awards include the Defense Superior Service, Defense Distinguished Service Medal, Legion of Merit with one Gold Star in lieu of second award, Meritorious Service Medal, Air Medal (individual), twelve Air Medals (Strike/Flight), Armed Forces Expeditionary Medal (Cuba) with one Bronze Star in lieu of second award (Sea of Japan), Vietnam Service Medal with three Bronze Stars.[2]

Since departing active Naval service, Vice Admiral Dorsey has been self-employed and has consulted for the Center for Naval Analysis, Raytheon Corporation, TRW Corporation, BETAC Corporation, Grumman Aircraft Corporation, Norden Systems, and is an Associate of Burdeshaw Associates, LTD.

He served for over three years as the co-chairman of the Secretary of the Navy's Retiree Council. In this capacity he was recalled to active duty each year for several weeks and worked to maintain and enhance the rights and benefits of both active duty personnel and retirees.[3]

Fighter Squadron One Twenty-One Command History

1 January to December 1971 (Excerpts)

On 1 January 1971, Fighter Squadron One Twenty-One (VF-121) began its eleventh year of training naval aviators, radar intercept officers (RIOs) and maintenance personnel to operate the supersonic F4 Phantom II fighter from the decks of west coast attack carriers. VF-121 is an all weather fighter squadron under the command of Commander Fleet Air Miramar. It is the largest naval fighter squadron in the world. Graduates of this command report directly to carrier-based fighter squadrons which are currently active in Southeast Asia operations.

Permanently based aboard U.S. Naval Air Station, *Miramar, California,* the Pacemakers's mission is to support fleet Phantom squadrons with combat-ready flight crews, train maintenance personnel, review and develop combat tactics, monitor a constantly updated standardization program (NATOPS) for F4 aircraft, and provide general support and guidance to fleet and shore activities concerned with F4 operations.

From 15 July 1970 until 28 May 1971, VF-121 was commanded by Capt. Billy D. Franklin, USN. He was relieved on 28 May by Cdr. Donald B. Pringle. Commander Pringle received orders in December 1971, and on 21 December Cdr. James F. Dorsey, Jr., USN, assumed command of Fighter Squadron One Twenty-One.

Flight crew training is the priority mission of VF-121. During 1971, 105 fleet replacement pilots and eighty fleet radar intercept officers completed the VF-121 syllabus. Among these were fifteen F8 pilots from VF-51 and VF-111 who were transitioned to the F4 Phantom II. Familiarization training and standardization check were provided to the Blue Angels. For both pilots and radar intercept officers the course averages thirty weeks and includes seven weeks of ground training before the new air crewmen actually fly the Phantom.

- The prior-to-flight phase includes fire fighting training, deep water environmental survival training; Survival Evasion, Resistance, and Escape School, Air Intelligence and Officer

Orientation Course; Instrument Refresher Ground School and aircraft systems schools.

- Supported by an extensive lecture series, the VF-121 flight crew syllabus is divided into six major phases: transition, weapons (radar, intercept, missile), electronic warfare, carrier qualification, tactics, and conventional weapons.

- During the transition phase the ready replacement pilot (RRP) ready replacement radar intercept officer (RRRIO) is indoctrinated during a one week course offered by NAS Miramar's Naval Aviation Maintenance Training Detachment and a one week prior-to-flight course.

- The task of the weapons systems phase is to instruct fleet replacement aircrews in the operation of the AN/AWG-10 weapons system and associated electronic countermeasures equipment.

- VF-121's Electronic Warfare phase is designed to acquaint replacement aircrews with current state-of-the-art information on electronic countermeasures, Southeast Asia electronic threats to fighter aircraft and utilization of electronic countermeasures aboard F4B/F4J aircraft.

- During the carrier qualification phase in 1971, seven detachments were sent to attack aircraft carriers to make carrier qualification landings. A total of 1,126 carrier landings were logged.

- The purpose of the tactics ground and flight phase is twofold: to spark the enthusiasm, aggressiveness, and spirit of attack of the novice F4 fighter crew, and to establish and develop the tactical principles and methods of attack which are the stock and trade of the F4 fighter pilot and RIO.

- The conventional weapons training phase is conducted from NAS Miramar to targets located in the Imperial Valley. Primary consideration is placed on forty degree dive bombing with practical ordnance.

- During 1971, the VF-121 Navy Fighter Weapons School ("Top Gun") continued to train fighter crews.

As of 1 December 1971, there were 1,132 officers and men assigned to VF-121. This number consisted of:

78 Permanent Officers
39 Replacement Pilots

33 Replacement RIOs
02 Royal Navy Exchange Officer
979 Enlisted Personnel[4]

Notes

1. Official Biography of Vice Adm. James F. Dorsey, USN (Ret.), Navy History and Heritage Command, Washington, D.C.
2. Ibid.
3. Ibid.
4. Fighter Squadron One Twenty-One Command History, 1 January to December 1971 (Excerpts), Navy History and Heritage Command, Washington, D.C.

Capt. Denis T. Schwaab
(July 1982–February 1984)

It is always hard to say the losses are acceptable, because they aren't acceptable.—Rear Admiral Schwaab commenting on air show accidents in a 4 September 1988 article for the *Los Angeles Times*

Denis T. Schwaab, born in Gloucester, New Jersey, was commissioned an Ensign in 1957 through the Officer Candidate Program at Newport, Rhode Island. Upon commissioning and after a short tour aboard the USS *Talbot County* (LST-1153), he proceeded to flight training where he was designated as a Naval Aviator in July 1958.

Following an initial tour with Guided Missile Group Two at NAS, Chincoteague, Virginia, and VC-8 at Naval Station, Roosevelt Roads, Puerto Rico, Schwaab received assignments to

Capt. Denis T. Schwaab (official U.S. Navy photograph).

various fighter squadrons and the Research, Development, Test and Evaluation Community. He joined VF-33 in April 1962. The squadron was flying F8U-2NE Crusaders from the world's first nuclear powered aircraft carrier, the USS *Enterprise* (CVN-65) and took part in the blockade of Cuba.

In February 1968 he was ordered to Fighter Squadron One Hundred Sixty One which had transitioned from F-3B Demons to F-4B Phantom II's. Between June 1967 and April 1969 during the squadron's second and third Vietnam combat tours aboard the USS *Coral Sea* (CVA-43) VF-161 flew a total of 3,209 combat sorties. He was Executive Officer of VF-151 from December 1972 until he took command of the Phantom squadron in August 1973 while home ported in Japan aboard USS *Midway* (CVA-41). After turning over command to Cdr. E.D. Conner in December 1974, shore assignments consisted of a tour as a Project Officer at the Naval Missile Center, Point Mugu, California; Head of the Ordnance Branch at Naval Air Test Center, Patuxent River, Maryland; and once again back to Point Mugu as Head of Flight Test at the Pacific Missile Test Center.

After completing a tour as Executive Officer of the USS *Independence* (CVA-62), Captain Schwaab commanded the USS *Coronado* (AGF-11) which functioned as the flag ship for the Commander, Middle East Forces. He also served as Assistant Chief of Staff for Readiness/Training and Deputy Chief of Staff for Commander, Naval Air Force, U.S. Atlantic Fleet. His next assignment was as Commanding Officer of the USS *America* (CVA-66), where deployments ranged from the North Atlantic through the Mediterranean to the Indian Ocean. Following his command tour he served as Deputy Director, Defense Mobilization Systems Planning Activity, in the Office of the Secretary of Defense. He then served as Director, Carrier, and Air Station Programs Division (OP-55). Captain Schwaab was designated Rear Admiral (lower half) while serving in billets commensurate with that grade. He was promoted to Rear Admiral (lower half) on 1 August 1985. He next served as Commander, Naval Safety Center, Norfolk, Virginia.

Rear Admiral Schwaab received his bachelor's degree from Muhlenberg College in Allentown, Pennsylvania, in 1956. In 1965 he attended the Naval War College where he graduated with distinction. While at the War College he took advantage of a cooperative program with George Washington University where he received a master's degree in Internal Affairs.

Rear Admiral Schwaab retired from the Navy in 1988 following the end of his tour as Commander of the Naval Safety Center in Norfolk. He passed away on 18 September 2010 in Jupiter, Florida, and is buried in Arlington National Cemetery.

During his career, Rear Admiral Schwaab flew more than 5,000 hours in twenty-four types of aircraft and logged 750 carrier arrested landings. He had over 250 combat missions to his credit.

Military Awards: Defense Distinguished Service Medal, Legion of Merit, Meritorious Service Medal with one Gold Star, Air Medal with Silver Star, Navy Commendation Medal with Combat "V" and one Gold Star in lieu of second award, Navy Expeditionary Medal (Cuba), Armed Forces Honor Medal First Class by the Republic of Vietnam and various unit citations and campaign ribbons.

Capt. Leighton W. "Snuffy" Smith, Jr.
(February 1984–July 1985)

"With Leighton Smith in charge, we've got a Navy admiral running a predominantly land campaign.... As the U.S. continues to withdraw from overseas bases, Naval Forces will become even more relevant in meeting American forward presence requirements."—U.S. Secretary of the Navy John Howard Dalton in an address in Newport, Rhode Island (11 June 1996)

On 6 October 1972, as the end of the war in Vietnam was being negotiated in Paris, four navy pilots of Attack Squadron Eighty-Two (VA-82) Marauders aboard the USS *America* (CV-66) were preparing their Vought A-7C Corsairs for a mission. Their target was the infamous Thanh Hoa Bridge, located just north of the city of Thanh Hoa, capital of the Thanh Hoa Province, approximately seventy miles south of Hanoi.

Adm. Leighton W. "Snuffy" Smith, Jr. (official U.S. Navy photograph).

Known as the Ham Rong Bridge (Dragon's Jaw) by the Vietnamese, it was a 540 foot long rail and highway bridge that spanned the Song Ma River and was a major throughway for men and materiel from North Vietnam into the south. As such, it was a major target for American air power. But seven years, 873 sorties, and countless tons of ordnance had failed to bring the bridge down.[1]

The bridge, one of the few routes from the north, was an early target of Operation Rolling Thunder, a campaign of aerial bombardment of North Vietnam carried out between 2 March 1965 and 2 November 1968 by U.S. Air Force, U.S. Navy, and Republic of Vietnam air assets.

The original bridge, destroyed by the Viet Minh in 1945, had been replaced in 1964 and had a width of thirty-eight feet, with highways running both sides of a center railroad. It was protected by an extensive air defense system, including Surface to Air Missiles (SAMs), Anti-aircraft artillery (AAA) and MiG fighter aircraft. Its proximity to the coast, with the resulting bad weather, provided an additional measure of protection, as did its reinforcement by eight massive concrete piers.

Between the first attack on 3 April 1965 in which forty-six Republic F-105 Thunderchiefs of the 67th Tactical Fighter Squadron "Fighting Cocks," flying out of Korat RTAB, Thailand, supported by twenty-one North American F-100s, two McDonnell RF-101s, and ten tankers attacked the bridge, until the end of Rolling Thunder in November 1968, nearly seven hundred air sorties had only been able to damage but not destroy the bridge.[2]

By 1972, the bridge was a symbol of resistance to the North Vietnamese even as its destruction became an obsession with the American high command. On 27 April, 12 F-4 Phantoms of the Eighth Tactical Fighter Wing, based at Ubon, Thailand, attacked the bridge with laser-guided bombs (LGB). The raid was successful; the bridge had been dislodged from its western abutment, with one half falling into the river. To complete the destruction, a second attack was ordered for 13 May. Fourteen F-4 fighters attacked the bridge's central supporting pillar with 2,000 lb. LGB. Once again the attack was successful and the bridge was rendered completely unusable.[3]

In order to hinder repair efforts, the Air Force flew two more missions against the target and the Navy flew eleven additional missions between May and October. There was an expectation that the raid on 6 October would completely demolish the remainder of the structure.

The four Navy pilots, Lt. (jg) Jim Brister, Lt. (jg) Marv Baldwin, Lt. Cdr. Leighton Smith and Cdr. Don Sumner, recently promoted to squadron commander of VA-82, were advised at briefing that elements of Carrier Air Wing Eight (CVW-8) would carry out diversionary raids on near-by rail-yards. For one of the Corsair pilots, it would be his third bite at the apple.

Lt. Leighton "Snuffy" Smith had flown a mission against the bridge on 23 September 1966, while assigned to Fighter Squadron Twenty-Two (VA-22) "Redcocks" aboard the USS *Coral Sea* (CV-43) which resulted in damage that was rapidly repaired. Two days earlier, on 4 October, Smith had flown another mission and he recalled:

"When we rolled in, my weapon came off but it got hit by a 30 mm shell. It disintegrated as soon as it left my aeroplane, or at least became stupid." Now, he was preparing to make his third attempt.[4]

Leighton Warren Smith, Jr., was born in Mobile, Alabama, on 20 August 1939, the second of four children. His father, forced to leave college during the Great Depression, raised his children with a strong work ethic. When Smith was about thirteen, his father moved the family back to the family farm outside Union Church, Alabama. "I learned a hell of a lot about life while living on that farm … I watched my father work his butt off and basically lose everything he had because we had three years of horrible 'farming weather.' I learned that the absolute last thing I wanted to do was be a farmer!"[5]

At fifteen, Smith moved back to Mobile to live with his grandmother and aunt. Difficult behavior had resulted in his being expelled from one of his classes, and he was saved only by the intervention of his father. "Dad asked that I be reinstated, and said that I would apologize to the teacher, that I would make up all assignments that I had missed and that I would be the best damn student that teacher had! He then looked at me and said, 'I have your word on that, do I not?' To Dad, one's 'word' was a trust con-tract!! You never, ever, went back on your word! In looking back, that one thing may have been one of the most important things Dad ever did for me because, in those days, if you had ever been expelled from class, for any reason, you were not even considered for the Naval Academy. Of course that wasn't even on my radar in those days." Smith was reinstated and, true to his word, made up the work he had missed and toed the mark. Once he had passed that semester, he left that school for Murphy High School where he graduated in 1957.

After graduating from high school in June 1957 with barely passing grades, he attended business classes at the University of Alabama, but finances were a concern, and his father suggested the possibility of attending the Naval Academy. His uncle, Page Smith, had attended Annapolis, Class of 1924, and later retired as a full admiral, which certainly played a part in his deliberations. "I wasn't sure what I wanted to do, but I was certain what I didn't want to do, and I didn't want to be a farmer." He collected sixty-three letters of recommendation which persuaded Congressman Frank W. Boykin to appoint Smith to the Class of 1962 and he entered Annapolis in July 1958.

Smith soon discovered that recommendations and good intentions would not be sufficient to overcome the academic rigors presented at the Naval Academy and by November of his first semester, of his five classes, he was failing three classes, and had Ds in two others. He would later joke, "My real claim to fame is (that) I made the upper 95 percent of my class look good." But failure was a real possibility. Smith credits what happened next as a defining moment in his life.

He was ordered to report to the Office of the Commandant of Midshipmen who at the time was Capt. William F. "Bush" Bringle, Naval Academy Class of 1937, whom Smith would later describe as "looking every bit the warrior, except for his eyes. There was a gentleness in his eyes."

"I walked in, and I shall never, ever forget that session," Smith recalled. "He asked me why I was failing? I answered with the standard 'No excuse, Sir,' but Bringle persisted. "I want to know why. Are you having a problem around here that I don't understand and I need to know about? What is causing you to be unsat in three subjects, and having a D in the other two? Do you need some special help? Are the midshipmen of the upper-class giving you a hard time? Are the instructors not giving you the amount of time you need?"

Then, as Smith would frequently recall, Bringle said four words, not encouragement but an assessment of him that forever changed him: "Midshipman Smith, you can do this," and he gave Smith ten days to improve his grades or face another visit to the Commandant's office.

"I realized that it wasn't anybody else's fault ... I realized it was me. And I figured, if I really wanted to do anything with my life, that he was giving me a chance. So I went and saw every one of my instructors. I talked to my classmates. I said, 'I need help. I don't want to go home.' And they all turned to and helped me."[6]

He also learned a lesson in leadership. "He (Bringle) went way, way down to one of the plebes at the Naval Academy who was having trouble to say, 'I'm going to give you a second chance.' And he did. And I worked real hard. And I made it." Bringle would later retire from the Navy with four stars.

Upon graduating from the Naval Academy in the lower third of his class, in June 1962, Ensign Smith was assigned temporary duty aboard the USS *Krishna* (ARL-38) one of thirty-nine *Achelous*-class landing craft repair ships built for the United States Navy during World War II.

"I was aboard that ship for only about six weeks," Smith recounted. "I was a brand-new Ensign that didn't know anything, and I had the great fortune to eat breakfast each morning with three warrant officers, all of whom had been at Pearl Harbor on 7 December 1941. They were experienced sailors who literally took me under their wings and mentored me in how to be an effective leader and Naval Officer. The officer who supervised me was critical in my fitness report, stating that I was too friendly with these three 'junior officers.' I ran into that guy later when I was a commander. He was still a lieutenant-commander and I often wondered what he might have been able to do if he had also listened to those three gentlemen."

He remained aboard the *Krishna* until September when he reported for basic flight training at NAS Pensacola. Following completion, he was designated a Naval Aviator and awarded his gold wings in January 1964.

Smith's first assignment was as an Air Intercept Control Instructor at Glynco, Georgia, until January 1965 when he shipped to Attack Squadron Forty-Four (VA-44) Hornets flying Douglas A-4D Skyhawks as a replacement pilot at NAS Cecil Field, Duval County, Florida. In August of 1965, carrier qualified, Smith reported to Attack Squadron Eighty-One (VA-81) "Sunliners," assigned as First Lieutenant and Personnel Officer. The squadron deployed to the Mediterranean from 24 August 1965 through 7 April 1966, as part of Carrier Air Group Eight (CVG-8) aboard the USS *Forrestal* (CVA-59). During this time, Smith volunteered for a tour in Vietnam.

Departing the ship upon its return to Virginia, Smith reported to VA-22 in May 1966 as Aircraft Division Officer and made his first deployment to Vietnam on 29 July as part of CVW-2 aboard the *Coral Sea*. It was during this deployment that Smith first attacked the Thanh Hoa Bridge. The *Coral Sea* returned stateside on 23 February 1967, and Smith remained with the squadron, deploying on a second WestPac/Vietnam tour on 11 November 1967 until 25 May 1968, this time aboard the USS *Ranger* (CVA-61). Smith left the squadron in July.

Smith spent the next two years assigned as a Production Test Pilot at the Naval Program Office (NAVPRO) at NAS Dallas, testing the new A-7 Corsair. In September 1970, he reported to Attack Squadron Hundred Seventy-Four (VA-174) "Hellrazors" at NAS Cecil Field for replacement pilot training.

In December 1970, Smith, having by now picked up the call sign "Snuffy," reported to VA-82 "Marauders" as Maintenance and later Operations Officer, and on 5 June 1972, he departed with the squadron aboard the *America* on his third Vietnam deployment, flying the A-7C Corsair. They arrived off Yankee Station on 21 July, and the unit suffered its first loss on 10 September, when a Corsair piloted by Lt. (jg) Steve Musselman was downed by a SAM. As Smith later recalled, "I believe he was listed as MIA vice POW because we all believed he had been killed as he was coming down in his chute. Since there was no proof of that, he was listed as MIA. When the POWs returned in 1973, we learned that he had never been seen in the prisons, thus was presumed dead. His actual 'condition' was not changed to KIA until much later."[7]

On 6 October, Smith took off in a flight of four Corsairs as the diversionary flights took off for their targets. Smith and Baldwin each carried one Walleye "Fat Albert" 2,000 lb. "smart" bomb while Sumner and Brister deployed standard Mk 84 2,000 lb. bombs.

The four aircraft split as they approached the target proceeding to the pre-briefed aim points thus allowing for a simultaneous roll in but from different directions. Smith and Baldwin rolled in together, pulled back the power, popped their speed brakes, and locked up the bridge on their scopes. After confirming that his wingman was "locked on" to the aimpoint, Smith then counted down "three ... two ... one ... launch." As planned, both walleyes and the four 2,000 pound bombs impacted the target nearly simultaneously. There was too much smoke to immediately assess damage, but later aerial photos confirmed that, after seven years, 871 air sorties, the loss of eleven aircraft and another 104 aircraft lost within seventy-five square miles of the bridge, the Thanh Hoa Bridge was down for good. Smith and the others were subsequently awarded the Distinguished Flying Cross for the mission.[8,9]

By this time, rumors of a cease fire were having an effect on operations and morale. As Commander Sumner stated to a reporter aboard the *America* in November. "They (North Vietnam) feel they are going to have a settlement soon. They're not worried about ammunition. They're shooting everything they've got.... The end is in sight, so they're going for broke."[10]

In an attempt to end North Vietnam's efforts to obstruct the peace talks in Paris, and "encourage" the North Vietnamese to return to the negotiating table, President Nixon ordered Operation Linebacker II. For eleven days, from 18–29 December, Navy and USAF tactical aircraft and B-52 bombers resumed round-the-clock bombing of targets in Hanoi and Haiphong.

The effort was successful, and on 27 January 1973, twelve days after Nixon announced the end of all offensive operations against North Vietnam, the Paris Peace Accords were signed ending the conflict and beginning the withdrawal of American forces in Vietnam. But the operation was not without cost. American losses during that eleven day period included twenty-six aircraft (USAF losses were fifteen B-52s, two F-4s, two F-111s, one EB-66 and one HH-53 search and rescue helicopter. Navy losses included two A-7s, two A-6s, one RA-5, and one F-4.) Ten American aviators were killed, eight captured, and eleven rescued.[11] The *America* suffered the loss of three killed, five MIAs and one POW.[12]

By the time Smith left the squadron in July 1973, he had flown 282 combat missions (Note: some of these were in Laos and a few were in the South) and had been awarded two Distinguished Flying Crosses. He also learned the danger of micromanagement of military operations by politicians from afar and the utter futility of waging a "sortie" war but against targets that resulted in little or no advantage to the U.S. These lessons would shape his thinking and decisions later in his career.[13]

Smith attended the Air Command and Staff School at Maxwell AFB, from August 1973 until July 1974, then returned to VA-174 for five months of replacement pilot training before joining Attack Squadron Eighty-Six (VA-86) Sidewinders at NAS Cecil Field as the executive officer. The squadron, attached to Air Wing Eight (CVW-8) deployed to the Caribbean and North Atlantic on 16 July 1975, aboard the USS *Nimitz* (CVN-68) on its maiden voyage, returning on 24 September.

Smith, now a full commander, took over command of the squadron from Cdr. Perry Gard on 22 April 1976, and deployed with the squadron to the Mediterranean the following 7 July, again aboard the *Nimitz*. He turned over command of the squadron to Cdr. Herbert W. Taylor on 2 June 1977, and departed for Prospective Commander Air Group (PCAG) at NAS Miramar in California, flying and familiarizing himself with the Navy's inventory of carrier aircraft including carrier qualification.

In September 1977, he took command of Carrier Air Wing Fifteen (CVW-15) while deployed at sea in the Western Pacific aboard the USS *Coral Sea* (CV-43). Shortly thereafter, *Coral Sea* returned from her deployment to her homeport at Alameda, California. Following a change-of-command in November 1978, Smith was given a staff assignment with the Navy Military Personnel Command (NAVMILPERSCOM) where he remained until assuming command of Light Attack Wing One at Cecil Field in February 1980.

In May of 1981, Smith underwent training in preparation for Surface Ship Command, and in January 1982, he assumed command of the USS *Kalamazoo* (AOR-6) a *Wichita*-class replenishment oiler commissioned by the U.S. Navy in 1973, and which carried fuel, weapons, and enough food to service 45,000 people for up to thirty days. It was a difficult time for the Navy, as Smith recalled: "The 'issue of the times' while I was in command was the serious drug problems we in the military were facing. Shortly after I took command we had a surprise unit sweep which meant that 100 percent of the crew provided a urine sample for testing. If my memory serves correctly, I recall that some 27 percent of the crew tested positive. It was about 'average' for the fleet in those days and, quite frankly, it was a scary situation. Here we are, a working oiler with heavy rigs, operating in very close proximity to other ships while connected alongside doing underway refueling.... It was about this time that our CNO, Adm. Tom Heyward made his 'not on my watch' speech which was followed by new guidance and the authority necessary for Commanding Officers to deal with the drug problem in an effective way. During my time on *Kalamazoo*, I believe we must have booted at least 25–30 sailors out of the Navy because they simply refused to comply with the rules.... That said, we were a good ship and worked very hard to meet our commitments."

Another staff assignment followed when, from August 1983 until January 1984, Smith served as Training and Readiness Officer on the staff of Commander—Naval Air Forces, Atlantic (COMNAVAIRLANT).

On 2 February 1984, Smith assumed command of the USS *America* (CV-66) from Capt. Denis T. Schwaab while *America* remained in port at Norfolk completing maintenance and upkeep tasks and conducting carrier qualifications.

America took to sea on 6 February 1984, and conducted training until 20 February, visiting Ft. Lauderdale, Florida, then returning to sea on 24 February to resume training. Following a visit to St. Thomas, she returned to Norfolk on 22 March to prepare for deployment.

Upon departing Norfolk on 24 April, *America* took part in Operation Ocean Venture, a regional security naval exercise conducted in the area of Puerto Rico, then proceeded to Caracas, Venezuela, before joining the Sixth Fleet for operations in the Mediterranean, followed by operations in the Indian Ocean with the Seventh Fleet, relieving the USS *Kitty Hawk* (CV-63) on 21 March, and remained on station until returning to the Sixth Fleet in late August. She transited the Suez Canal on 2 September, and participated in NATO Exercise Display Determination.

Captain Smith on the bridge of USS *America* (courtesy Leighton Smith).

Relieved by the USS *Dwight D. Eisenhower* (CVN-69) at Augusta Bay, Sicily, on 27 October, *America* arrived home at Norfolk on 14 November, and conducted carrier qualifications in the Virginia Capes from 29 November through 17 December. She entered the Norfolk Naval Shipyard on 18 January 1985, where she remained until 13 May, when she set out for sea trials in the Virginia Capes.

Following his relief by Capt. Richard C. Allen on 2 July 1985, Smith left the *America*, assigned to the Strategic Studies Group as a CNO Fellow at the Naval War College, Newport, Rhode Island. Among a group of officers personally selected by the CNO, Smith worked on a proposal to integrate various government agencies (State, Defense, Commerce) responses to given problems, rather than pursuing individual departmental objectives. As the senior officer of those in the "SSG," Smith was selected to present the proposal to Adm. James Watkins, the Chief of Naval Operations and Adm. William J. Crowe, Jr., the Chairman of the Joint Chiefs of Staff.[14]

Having been selected for Flag rank earlier that year, in June of 1996, Smith was assigned to the Office of the Chief of Naval Operations (OPNAV) at the Pentagon as Director Tactical Readiness, where he remained until February 1988.

In March 1988, he took command of Carrier Battle Group Six based at Mayport, Florida. "My CARGRU experience was 'interesting,' but quite frankly I was bored. I liked the action of being in the cockpit, the thrill of being the ship CO and responsible for everything, and I do mean everything! Now I was relegated to watching the young guys doing what I very much wanted to do. I did get in some flying but, in those days, the flag officers were encouraged to let the young guys bag the traps and get the flight time!"

In August 1989, Smith returned to staff work, assigned as the Director of Operations (J-3) on the staff of the Commander in Chief, U.S. Army-Europe (CINCUSEUR) based in Stuttgart, Germany, under General Galvin. "Gen. Jack Galvin was the very best warrior statesman I ever knew. Colin Powell was a great statesman but I never saw the warrior part of him rise to the level of Jack Galvin. We got along famously and I learned a great deal about joint warfare and leadership from him."

Smith returned to the Pentagon as a newly-promoted Vice Admiral in June 1991, once again assigned to the Office of the Chief of Naval Operations (OPNAV) this time as Deputy Chief of Naval Operations for Plans, Policy and Operations. In 1992, Admiral Smith was a major contributor to Navy staff reorganization and the development of *From the Sea*, a study outlining the Navy's strategy for the 21st century. A major premise of the paper is the idea that as the U.S. withdraws from overseas bases, Naval Forces will become even more relevant in meeting American forward presence requirements.[15]

Promoted to a four-star Admiral in April 1994, Smith was appointed Commander in Chief U.S. Naval Forces-Europe (CINCUSNAVEUR), a position that both his uncle, Page Smith, and Bush Bringle had had years before, and concurrently as Commander in Chief, Allied Forces Southern Europe (CINCSOUTH), a NATO command. It would not be an easy command.

Following the death of President Josip Broz Tito on 4 May 1980, combined with the decline of Communism in the late 1980s, ethnic tensions had grown in the Socialist Federal Republic of Yugoslavia to the point that by June 1991, with the declaration of independence by Slovenia and Croatia and the dissolution of the Yugoslavian state, the region broke out in a series of conflicts, later known collectively as the Yugoslav Wars (March 1991–June 1999). What resulted for the next several years was mass murder, genocide and ethnic cleansing as factions fought for control of territory. A U.N. Peacekeeping force (UNPROFOR) proved ineffective in keeping the peace.

In November 1995, the Presidents of Bosnia-Herzegovina, Serbia and Croatia met and concluded the Dayton Accords, bringing a cease fire and ending years of violence. It was signed in Paris on 14 December 1995.

On 20 December, Smith assumed the additional duty of Commander-Implementation Force (IFOR) a NATO-led multinational peacekeeping force in Bosnia and Herzegovina under the codename Operation Joint Endeavor. Smith would command 54,000 troops from thirty-four countries under NATO command and control. His goal, as he saw it, was to implement the Dayton Peace Accords by establishing stability, preventing a reoccurrence of atrocities, and keeping the warring factions separated. "When I first went into Bosnia I would be greeted by some of the citizens with 'Thank you for bringing peace to our country.' I always replied the same way: 'I cannot bring peace to your country. The only thing I can do is establish an environment in which peace can flourish. Your countrymen are the only ones who can bring peace.'"[16]

In a 1999 PBS interview, Smith characterized it as "the biggest damn mess in the world. Absolutely, completely unworkable! You had two political organizations, the United Nations and NATO, and they wouldn't talk to each other.... I was completely dismayed at the fact that [when] we attacked the leadership in Bosnia, the military guys in Bosnia, there were no efforts to get the United Nations and NATO to agree ... it was an impossible situation."[17]

Headquartered first in Zagreb, and later from December 1995 in Sarajevo, Smith found himself in conflict with the U.S. Ambassador, Richard Holbrooke, over their differences as to what was the scope and nature of his mission. As Holbrooke later stated: "I was a maximalist. I wanted the NATO force to do as much as possible. Most of the people in uniform, particularly at the higher ranks, and particularly those who were scarred by the Vietnam experience, were minimalists who wanted to do as little as possible. So issue after issue, we disagreed."[18]

Holbrooke was dissatisfied with the IFOR's efforts to arrest war criminals, which Smith believed exceeded his mandate as IFOR Commander. Smith recalled: "The rules of engagement were quite clear. I did not have the authority to arrest anyone. I had the authority to detain.... If we came across these guys in the routine course of carrying out our responsibilities, we ... were obligated to detain indicted war criminals and turn them over to the tribunal. And that's precisely the orders that we were operating under.... Out of all of the senior military officers of the countries involved that I talked with, and I talked to a lot of them, chiefs of defense staff, not one single one, not a single one, was in favor of going down that road, because all of us felt that it was a very dangerous path, during that period of time; it was an unknown path. We could not guarantee success, and there were likely to be substantial causalities, which would have created a very difficult environment for the peace force to continue its work."[19]

Adm. Leighton Smith as Commander of the NATO-led Multi-National Peacekeeping Force in Bosnia, 1995 (courtesy Leighton Smith).

Smith felt making arrests was a police function and outside the scope of his military mission and it could be counter-productive to his peace-keeping function, but he continued to get pressure from politicians to expand his mission. "If you want me to go after the war criminals—and I do not think that's a good idea right now—if you want me to go after them, give me the order, get the hell out of my way, and stand by for the consequences ... Gen. John Shalikashvili, the chairman of our Joint Chiefs of Staff and Gen. George Joulwan, SACEUR and CINCEUR, my bosses, both of them, were clear and unequivocal: 'Soldiers do not make good policemen. This is not a good idea. Don't send these guys on police missions. They are not policemen.'"[20]

Early in 1996, Smith traveled to Washington, D.C., and met with the CNO, Admiral Mike Boorda. "I knew that Mike needed to move some 'flags' around and I also knew that I was not likely to get another position so I told him that I thought it would be good for me to retire right after the elections, scheduled to be held in November 1996. He agreed so that was what I thought would be the date."

On 16 May 1996, Boorda committed suicide following a media investigation into the unauthorized wearing of combat "V" devices on two ribbons. In the interim, Smith returned to Bosnia. "I went back to Bosnia and, sometime in late May or early June (Secretary of Defense) Bill Perry came to Europe. I think we met up near Garmish, Germany. He brought George Joulwan, my boss, the deputy USAREUR and a couple of other folks. One issue brought up by Perry, again being very naive, was freedom of movement. Perry wanted to know why there was not freedom of movement all over Bosnia. My response was something like 'Mr. Secretary, you won't like the answer you are about to get but it is the truth. There won't be real freedom of movement in this country in your, or my, lifetime....' He was definitely *not* happy about that answer. We also discussed the election and timing thereof. The meeting ended with dinner and then I left for Zagreb because I had a scheduled meeting with President Tudjman. The next day, as we were preparing to leave to see Tudjman, my Executive Assistant, Capt. Rusty Petrea, came into my office and said he had gotten a call from Tudjman's office asking why I was being fired. That blew me away, so I made a couple of quick calls and learned that Perry's PAO had made a statement on the flight back to the States that 'Admiral Smith would be relieved sooner rather than later, as in a matter of weeks, not months.' Turns out that Perry had decided he wanted continuity in IFOR for the election. In other words, he wanted to get my relief, who had already been named, in place *before* the elections so that he would be able to be more effective after the election if there were problems, which we expected."

On 1 July 1996, Bosnia's first free elections since the end of the war were held in Mostar, and on 6 June, the Secretary of Defense's office announced "Adm. Leighton W. Smith will be replaced as commander of NATO-led troops in Bosnia."[21]

On 31 July 1996, Adm. T. Joseph Lopez relieved Adm. Leighton Smith as the Commander of IFOR. Asked whether Smith had been fired, a Pentagon spokesman, Navy Capt. Michael Doubleday, said, "No indeed. Absolutely not!" "That's a relief in command," White House spokesman Michael McCurry said, "a change of command that had been projected for some time."[22]

Smith retired from the Navy on 1 October 1996, after thirty-four years of service. His awards include two Defense Distinguished Service Medals, the Navy Distinguished Service Medal, three Legion of Merits, two Distinguished Flying Crosses, two Meritorious Service Medals, and twenty-nine Air Medals. He has also received the Order of Merit of the Republic of Hungary, the French Order of National Merit with the rank of Grand Officer and, on 5 March 1997, was made an Honorary Knight of the British Empire in a private audience with Her Majesty the Queen.

Since retiring, Smith has served as a Senior Fellow at the Center for Naval Analyses, a federally funded research and development firm located in Alexandria, Virginia, as well as Chairman of the Naval Aviation Museum Foundation and Chairman of the Naval Academy Alumni Association Board of Trustees. He is president of his own consulting firm, and serves on the Board of Directors of several major corporations. In 2007, Admiral Smith was named a "Distinguished Graduate" of the Naval Academy by the Naval Academy Alumni Association.

Notes

1. *From Thanh Hoa to Sarajevo: The Odyssey of Adm. Leighton W. Smith*, U.S. Naval Institute—Naval History and Heritage Command http://www.navalhistory.org/2010/11/23/from-thanh-hoa-to-sarajevo-the-odyssey-of-admiral-leighton-w-smith

2. Boyne, Walter J. "Breaking the Dragon's Jaw." *Air Force Magazine*, August 2011, vol. 94, no. 8.

3. Mersky, Peter. *US Navy A-7 Corsair II Units of the Vietnam War*. London: Osprey Publishing, 2004.

4. Ibid.

5. Interview with Leighton W. Smith—30 December 2012.

6. Chappel, John. "Serving His Country: 'You Can Do This.'" *The Pilot*, Southern Pines, North Carolina, 30 May 2010.

7. Interview with Leighton W. Smith—30 December 2012.

8. Mersky, Peter. *U.S. Navy A-7 Corsair II Units of the Vietnam War*. London: Osprey Publishing, 2004.

9. Boyne, Walter J. "Breaking the Dragon's Jaw."

10. "Navy Pilots Cautious with Peace Imminent." (AP) *Geneva Times*, 2 November 1972.

11. Nalty, Bernard C. *Air War Over South Vietnam: 1969–1975*. Washington, D.C.: Center of Air Force History, 1995.

12. USS *America* Museum http://ussamerica-museumfoundation.org/linebacker2.html

13. Hattendorf, John B. and Elleman, Bruce A. *Nineteen-Gun Salute: Case Studies of Operational, Strategic, and Diplomatic Naval Leadership During the 20th and Early 21st Centuries*. Washington, D.C.: Government Printing Office, 2010.

14. Ibid.

15. *From the Sea* http://www.globalsecurity.org/military/library/policy/navy/fts.htm

16. Interview with Leighton W. Smith—January 2012.

17. PBS *Frontline* "Give War a Chance. 11 May 1999. http://www.pbs.org/wgbh/pages/frontline/shows/military/etc/script.html

18. Ibid.

19. Ibid.

20. Ibid.

21. *New York Times*, 6 June 1996.

22. Demick, Barbara, and Michael E. Ruane. "U.S. Admiral Commanding NATO in Bosnia to Step Down—Leighton W. Smith Jr., Has Been Criticized as Too Cautious. Officials Say His Departure Is Routine." *The Inquirer* (Philadelphia), 7 June 1996.

Capt. Richard C. "Sweetpea" Allen (July 1985–February 1987)

When our citizens are abused or attacked anywhere in the world, we will respond in self-defense. Today we have done what we had to do. If necessary, we shall do it again.—President Ronald W. Reagan, 14 April 1986

In the early hours of 15 April 1986 Captain Richard C. Allen stood on the Captain's Bridge of the USS *America*, looking down to the flight deck as Air Wing One's (CVW-1) combat aircraft were prepared for strike operations against a foreign power. He knew that out in the same waters of the Gulf of Sidra, aircraft from the carriers *Saratoga,* and *Coral Sea* were undergoing similar preparations.

On 15 April 1986, under the code name Operation El Dorado Canyon, the United States launched air strikes against ground targets inside Libya. The stated objective was to send a message and reduce Libya's ability to support and train terrorists, by targeting and destroying five key objectives.[1]

Relations between the United States and Libya, never strong, had been steadily deteriorating since the 1960s, with accusations that the government of Colonel Muammar al–Qaddafi supported and sponsored terrorist activity and engaged in weapons smuggling and espionage. In 1973, Qaddafi claimed the entire Gulf of Sidra, sixty-two nautical miles extending to 32°30'N, as Libyan territorial waters.

The conflict climaxed early in 1986. On 7 January, President Reagan ordered all Americans to depart Libya and terminated diplomatic relations between the United States and Libya. At the same time, he ordered a second carrier battle group to the Mediterranean and ordered the Joint Chiefs of Staff to begin the feasibility of military operations against Libya. Declaring, as per international law, a twelve-nautical-mile (22 km; 14 mi) limit to territorial waters, the United States sent a naval task force into the Gulf of Sidra to challenge Qaddafi's proclaimed "Line of Death."

Freedom of Navigation operations, code-named Attain Document began in late January, lasting from 26–30 January and again from 12–15 February 1986, with American surface ships and aircraft reinforcing U.S. Secretary Of State George Shultz's assertion that there would be no restrictions on U.S. naval operations in international waters. Although there were approximately 130 intercepts of Libyan fighters in the airspace over the Gulf of Sidra, there were no incidents in the first two phases.[2]

Capt. Richard C. "Sweetpea" Allen (official U.S. Navy photograph).

USS *America*, with Air Wing One (CVW-1) embarked, departed Norfolk on 10 March for deployment in the Mediterranean accompanied by her battle group, and they arrived in the Gulf in time to participate in Attain Document III (23–29 March).

The U.S. Sixth Fleet sent a force into the gulf that included three carriers; USS *America* (CV-66), USS *Coral Sea* (CV-43) and USS *Saratoga* (CV-60) as well as five cruisers, six frigates, twelve destroyers, with the USS *Detroit* (AOE-4) and the USS *Savannah* (AOR-4). The support ships would supply the battle group arriving in the Gulf with fuel, ammunition and combat material. Designated Task Force 60, the battle group was under the command of Vice Adm. Frank B. Kelso.

On Sunday, 23 March, aircraft from the three U.S. aircraft carriers crossed over the "Line of Death" and began operations in the Gulf. The following day, 24 March, at 6:00 a.m. local time, the USS *Ticonderoga* (CG-47) accompanied by the destroyers USS *Scott* (DDG-995) and the USS *Caron* (DD-970) moved south of the 32°30' navigational line with fighter aircraft overhead providing cover.

In the air above flying Combat Air Patrol (CAP) were F-14A Tomcat fighter-interceptors of Fighter Squadron 102 (VF-102), the "Diamondbacks," off the *America*. Also in the air was another *America* aircraft, an EA-6B "Prowler" from VMAQ-2, a Marine Tactical Electronic Warfare Squadron.[3]

At 1:52 p.m. two SA-5 Gammon Surface to Air Missiles (SAMs) were launched from a missile base at Sirte, on Libya's northern coast, targeting two of the Tomcats of VF-102, but they missed their target, and fell into the sea. The Tomcats had been intercepting a Libyan MiG-25 Foxbat interceptor which had strayed too close to the battle group.

At 6:45 p.m. two additional SA-5s and a SA-2 Guideline SAM were fired from Sirte at Tomcats engaged in turning back two additional Libyan Mig–25s, and a sixth missile was fired at 7:14 p.m. Out of patience, Kelso ordered that all enemy military units departing Libyan waters or airspace were to be considered hostile.[4]

Alerted to several Libyan missile patrol boats approaching the battle group, Admiral Kelso ordered his aircraft to intercept. The *Saratoga* launched A-7E Corsair II fighters from VA-83 Rampagers, armed with High Speed Anti-Radiation Missiles (HARM) missiles, and A-6E Intruders armed with Harpoon missiles and Rockeye Mk-20 cluster-bombs from VA-85 Black Falcons, as well as Electronic Attack EA-6B Prowlers from VAQ-132 Scorpions (Electronic Attack Squadron 132).

The *America* launched A-6E Intruders from VA-34 "Blue Blasters" and EA-6B "Prowlers" from VMAQ-2 "Playboys" and the *Coral Sea* launched A-6Es from VA-55 "Warhorses" and EA-6Bs from VAQ-135 "Black Ravens."[5]

At approximately 8:30 p.m. local time, a Libyan La Combattante II G Fast Attack Craft Missile (FACM) patrol boat departed from the port of Misratah and approached the surface action group. It was engaged first by two

A-6s from VA-34 which damaged the craft with Harpoon missiles, followed by A6-Es from VA-85 which fired Rockeye Mk-20 cluster bombs, which sank the Combattante.[6]

At 9:00 p.m. the base at Sirte reactivated its target acquisition radar and was attacked by two A-7E Corsairs from VA-83 which launched two AGM-88 High-speed Anti-Radiation Missiles (HARMs), tactical air-to-surface missiles designed to home in on electronic transmissions coming from surface-to-air radar systems. It was the first use of the missile in combat. The transmissions ceased.

At 10:30 p.m. an A-6 from VA-85 attacked a Nanuchka II class guided-missile Corvette that had departed Bengazi. It fired Rockeyes, which heavily damaged the Corvette, forcing the craft to seek the cover of a neutral freighter in order to return to Bengazi.[7]

The following morning, 25 March, at 12:47 a.m., the target acquisition radar came on again in Sirte. Again, two A-7E Corsairs of VA-83 off the *Saratoga* fired two more HARMs, silencing the site permanently.

A second Nanuchka Corvette was attacked at 8:00 a.m. by an A-6E from VA-55, causing heavy damage with Rockeyes. A second A-6E from VA-85 launched a Harpoon missile which disabled the ship.[8]

With the boat dead in the water and on fire, Americans made no effort to interfere with Libyan rescue operations as the crew boarded inflatable rafts. No further efforts were made by the Libyans to interfere with American navigation in the gulf, and having demonstrated national resolve, after seventy-five consecutive hours of operation, U.S. forces withdrew at 3:00 p.m. on 27 March. Not a single American was killed in the operation.

The U.S. held Libya responsible for the 2 April 1986 bombing of TWA flight 840 over Argos, Greece, in which four Americans were among those killed. Qaddafi publically congratulated the terrorists and promised the escalation of violence against American targets.[9]

Again, on 5 April, terrorists bombed the La Belle Discotheque in West Berlin, in which one U.S. soldier and two others were killed and more than two hundred other people, including fifty U.S. servicemen, were wounded. The attack was blamed on Libyan terrorists. The United States claimed "exact, precise, and irrefutable" evidence of Libyan involvement. President Reagan authorized a retaliatory strike on Libya, codenamed Operation El Dorado Canyon.[10]

The plan, one of more than thirty developed in England, called for twenty-four U.S. Air Force F-111 Aardvarks from the 48th Tactical Fighter Wing (TFW) Royal Air Force (RAF) Base Lakenheath along with five EF-

111 Ravens from the 42nd Electronic Combat Squadron, 20th TFW at RAF Heyford to take off from England and transit a 6,400 mile round trip flight with between 8–12 aerial refueling. Four Aardvarks and one Raven turned back at the first refueling point. The task was complicated by France, Italy, Spain and Germany's refusal to allow transit through their airspace, necessitating a 1,300 mile detour each way through a narrow air corridor over Gibraltar into the Mediterranean. Upon their approach over Libya, they would be joined by fourteen Intruders and twelve Super Hornets and Corsairs launched from the carriers *Coral Sea* and *America*.[11]

It was an ambitious venture with many potential complications. The timing of the mission had to be precise so that the two strike forces, one Air Force, one Navy, more than 3,000 miles apart, could attack simultaneously. The Aardvarks and Ravens would be required to refuel at night in radio silence, and the crews would be fatigued from the thirteen-hour round trip flight. Additionally, crews untested in combat would be flying into an alerted and prepared enemy air defense. It was the longest, most demanding air combat mission in history.[12]

There were five primary targets; the Air Force F-111s would attack the Sidi Balal Naval Training Base, believed to be a terrorist training facility, the Azziziyah Barracks, a command center for Libyan Intelligence and the site of one of Qaddafi's five residences, and Okba Ben Nafi Air Base, the former Wheelus Air Force Base, all in Tripoli. Navy assets would attack a terrorist training camp at the Al Jamahiriyya Barracks and the military airfield at Benina Airport, both in Benghazi. Naval assets would also provide air defense suppression.

Now Captain Allen once again stood on the bridge watching as crews from VA-72 and VA-46, his Corsair squadrons, and VF-102 and their F-14 Tomcats prepared to launch attack aircraft against Libyan targets. Six of his A-7E Corsairs and a Marine EA-6B Prowler, assisted by eight F/A 18 Hornets off the *Coral Sea* attacked Libyan missile defenses. Seven of his A-6E Intruders from VA-34 "Blue Blasters" would attack the Jamahiriyya Barracks while eight Intruders from VA-55 "Warhorses" off the *Coral Sea* attacked the Benina Airfield. Additionally, four of *America's* Tomcats flew CAP, protecting the F-111s over Tripoli even as four Hornets from the *Coral Sea* protected the air over Benghazi.[13]

The raid, which began at 2:00 a.m. Libyan time, lasted only twelve minutes and dropped more than sixty tons of munitions. The results were mixed, with some missed targets resulting in collateral damage to residential neighborhoods, including, ironically, a near miss of the French Embassy in Tripoli. One American F-111, "Karma 52," was shot down by a Libyan SAM over the Gulf of Sidra, resulting in the loss of Air Force Maj. Fernando Luis Ribas-Dominicci and Capt. Paul Lorence.

Captain Allen must have felt a great sense of relief as all of *America's* aircraft returned safely to ship. It was not the first time he sailed in harm's way, nor would it be his last.

Richard Charles Allen was born to Everett and Eleanor (Scharmer) Allen at Rice Lake in Northern Wisconsin on 8 November 1939. He graduated Menomonie High School in 1957 and attended Stout State College before enlisting in the U.S. Naval Reserve as a Naval Aviation Cadet (NAVCAD) class of 24–59 in July 1959. He underwent training at the following Florida naval air/air auxiliary stations; NAS Pensacola (Pre-Flight), NAAS Saufley (Primary), NAAS Whiting (Basic) and NAAS Saufley (Carrier Qualifications) where he qualified aboard the aircraft carrier USS *Antietam* (CVS-36) in July 1960 flying a T-28 Trojan Trainer. He completed advanced training at NAAS Kingsville, Texas, and carrier qualified again on the *Antietam* in 1960 in a F9F-8B Cougar jet fighter. He was commissioned an Ensign and designated a Naval Aviator on 20 December 1960.[14]

After attending Escape and Evasion/Survival training at Stead AFB, Nevada, until 21 February, he was ordered to Attack Squadron VA-44 "Hornets" for A-4 "Skyhawk" replacement pilot training until 30 July 1961 and then joined fleet squadron VA-34 ("Blue Blasters") home-based at NAS Oceana, for a three-year tour during which he made two Mediterranean deployments aboard the USS *Saratoga* (CVA-60).

Allen had not yet joined the squadron in April 1961 when VA-34's A4D-2 Skyhawks had operated from the USS *Essex* (CV-9) in the Caribbean Sea during the Bay of Pigs invasion. From 26 October through 8 November 1962, during the Cuban missile crisis, the entire squadron flew aboard USS *Enterprise* (CVN-65) to augment the assigned air wing. VA-34 flew numerous missions in support of the Cuban quarantine, later transferring to the USS *Independence* (CV-62) until her return to the States on 26 November.[15]

On 5 July 1963 his appointment in the U.S. Naval Reserve was terminated and the next day he was augmented into the regular U.S. Navy. He married Margaret Perry Fricks Hall in Jacksonville, Florida, on 9 November 1963.

In July 1964, newly promoted to Lieutenant, Allen was ordered to VA-42 ("Green Pawns") and transitioned to A-6 Intruders home based at Naval Air Station Oceana, Virginia. The Intruder was the Navy's first true all-weather, carrier based jet attack aircraft. The cockpit used an unusual double pane windscreen and a side-by-side seating arrangement in which the pilot sat in the left seat, while the bombardier/navigator sat to the right and slightly lower. This additional crew member had separate responsibilities, using a unique cathode ray tube (CRT) display that provided a synthetic display of terrain ahead, the bombardier/navigator was able to guide the pilot in making a low level attack in all weather conditions.

From October 1967 until June 1969, he served with VA-75 ("Sunday Punchers") flying Intruders aboard the *Kitty Hawk* (CV-63) and the *Saratoga* (CV-60). During combat cruises aboard these carriers, November 1969 through June 1970, Allen, now a lieutenant commander, flew seventy-two missions against targets in North Vietnam.

He next attended the Naval Postgraduate School in Monterey, California, where he earned a Bachelor of Science degree in Engineering Science in June 1971.

Due to a loss of visual acuity he was re-designated as a Naval Flight Officer on 20 August 1971, and served with Commander Medium Attack Wing One as an A-6 bombardier/navigator until the following May when he reported to VA-65 (the world famous "Fighting Tigers") as Operations Officer aboard the USS *Independence* (CVA-62) homeported at Norfolk, Virginia.

His early time with the squadron was while the *Independence* was in dry-dock, but was present for President Nixon's address from the ship's deck on Armed Forces Day in May 1973. The ship subsequently sailed on a North Atlantic-Mediterranean-Indian Ocean cruise in June of that year. While deployed in the Mediterranean in October, *Independence* was attached to Task Force 60.1 which along with Task Force 60.2 was standing by to assist with the possible evacuation of civilians during the Yom Kipper War, a conflict between Israel and an Arab States Coalition led by Egypt and Syria that lasted for nineteen days (6–25 October 1973).

Leaving the squadron in January 1974, Allen next attended the Armed Forces Staff College after which he reported (in July) to VA-85 "Black Falcons," an A-6 squadron, as Executive Officer, arriving in time to provide air cover for the evacuation of Americans and foreign nationals from the island of Cyprus following a coup that overthrew the government.

He assumed command of the squadron on 7 November 1975. The following year he became the first naval officer to exceed 3,000 A-6 flight hours, remaining in command until 25 February 1977.

In December 1978, while serving as an Air-to-Surface Weapons Program Coordinator in the Office of the Chief of Naval Operations (CNO) he was selected as the first Naval Flight Officer for Carrier Air Wing command and in May 1979 he took command of Carrier Air Wing Six (CVW-6) aboard the USS *Independence*, and then served on the U.S. Sixth Fleet staff as Assistant Chief of Staff—Operations, home ported in Gaeta, Italy, until March 1982.[16]

After attending commanding officer training, Allen was given command of USS *Detroit* (AOE-4), a combat logistics force ship, at Norfolk, Virginia, on 8 March 1983. Allen returned to a combat zone when the *Detroit* deployed to the Mediterranean on 20 October 1983. On its third day at sea, the *Detroit* learned that two trucks loaded with explosives and driven by members of the Islamic Jihad, had driven into the U.S. Marine barracks at the Beirut Airport in Lebanon, killing 241 American servicemen and 58 soldiers of the French 1st Parachute Chasseur Regiment, as well as six civilians. For the Marines, it was the bloodiest single day since Iwo Jima.[17]

The *Detroit* was assigned as the principal combat logistics force ship supporting Allied units of the Multi-National Peacekeeping Force during the early stages of what became known as the Lebanese Civil War. A Multi-National Force (MNF) of American, French and Italian troops had been in place in Lebanon since 29 September1983, following the assassination of Lebanese President Bachir Gemayel. The 1,400 (later increased to 1,800) Marines of 2nd Battalion, 8th Marine Regiment were relieved in October by the 3rd Battalion 8th Marines. Their stated mission was to help provide stability for the new Lebanese government.

Violence intensified following the barracks bombing, and political pressure, as well as losses which would eventually total 265 servicemen, resulted in President Reagan ordering the withdrawal of 1,700 Marines beginning on 7 February 1984. Several hundred civilians were evacuated from Beirut between 10–12 February, and the last Marines boarded Navy vessels on 26 February, preceded by the Italians on 20 February, and followed by the French on 31 March.

During its seven month deployment, the *Detroit* set a ship's record of 301 replenishments consisting of 156,000 barrels of fuel, 2,100 tons of munitions, 250 tons of dry stores, and 250 tons of refrigerated stores, despite a fuel fire while moored at Souda Bay, Crete, on 9 January 1984. The *Detroit* returned to Norfolk on 2 May.

Following a year of shore duty as Director of Joint Operations on the staff of Commander-in-Chief, Atlantic from July 1984 until May 1985, Allen assumed command of the USS *America* (CV 66) on 2 July 1985. During his tour, *America* completed the first-ever aircraft carrier operations in the restricted waters off Vestford, Norway.

As a selectee for Flag rank, Captain Allen was assigned as Director for Operations, U.S. Atlantic Command in June 1987 and was promoted to Rear Admiral (Lower Half) on 1 February 1988. In July 1989 he assumed the position of Commander Carrier Group Six (COMCARDIV SIX) aboard the USS *Forrestal* (CV-59). In his concurrent position as Commander of Task Group 4.1, he led counter-drug operations in the Caribbean.

In January 1991, Allen was assigned to the office of the Chief of Naval Operations (CNO), and was promoted to Rear Admiral on 1 March of that year. He served first as Assistant Deputy Chief of Naval Operations, then in February 1992 as Director of the Assessment Division.

Promoted to Vice Admiral on 18 March 1994, Allen was appointed Commander Naval Air Force U.S. Atlantic Fleet (COMNAVAIRLANT) at Norfolk, Virginia. In that position, he headed a five-member Honor Review Board investigating allegations of cheating at the U.S. Naval Academy.

In December 1992, third-year midshipmen were suspected of cheating on an engineering final exam by having advance knowledge of the questions. Within days, the Naval Academy ordered an inquiry by agents of the Naval Criminal Investigative Services (NCIS) which implicated twenty-eight midshipmen of whom six were convicted by student honor boards and expelled.[18]

However, new information provided by the expelled students and others, combined with congressional pressure, resulted in a second investigation conducted by the Naval Inspector General. After interviews of more than eight hundred midshipmen, and Academy staff, the Inspector General, Vice Adm. David M. Bennett, implicated 133 midshipmen in the cheating scandal. A review by a panel of three retired admirals, all former Naval Academy Superintendents or Commandants dismissed charges for three midshipmen, referred several for disciplinary action, and sent the remainder of the cases to the Honor Review Board, headed by Admiral Allen.

Working twelve-hour days, six days a week, the board conducted 106 individual hearings in which the accused midshipmen could review the evidence against them, call witnesses in their defense and offer rebuttals. Although allowed legal counsel, they were required to represent themselves in the hearings. The board's recommendation was to expel twenty-nine midshipmen, discipline forty-two others and acquit the remaining thirty-five.

Allen was present at the pier on 24 February 1996, when the *America*, returning from a six month deployment to the Mediterranean, tied up at Norfolk for the last time, bringing its thirty-one year career to a close. Allen could identify with the occasion, as his own thirty-seven year career was in its last days. Less than a month later, on 15 March 1996, Allen retired from the Navy with the rank of Vice Admiral.[19]

His personal awards include the Distinguished Service Medal (two awards), Defense Superior Service Medal, Legion of Merit (three awards), Distinguished Flying Cross (two awards), Defense Meritorious Service medal (two awards), Air Medal (two individual and several strike flight), Joint Service Commendation Medal, Navy Commendation Medal with combat "V," Navy Achievement Medal with Combat "V," and several unit, service and campaign awards.

In addition he was selected as East Coast Intruder of the year in 1972, and received the Navy League's 1986 John Paul Jones Award for Inspirational Leadership. He was appointed to the position of President of the Association of Naval Aviation on 22 June 1998.

Allen passed away on 24 May 2009, after a long battle with cancer. Following a memorial service, held at Campbell Memorial Presbyterian Church in Weems, Virginia, on Wednesday, 27 May, he was buried at Arlington National Cemetery with full military honors including a Navy jet "flyover." In remembering Allen, a close friend recalled, "He insisted that we call him by his favorite nickname, 'Sweetpea,' which I found very difficult. As a veteran of the Marine Corps, I just couldn't look an admiral in the face and call him 'Sweetpea!' But that's just the kind of man he was—part ironclad hero and part softhearted friend."[20]

Note: For readers who wish to learn more about the operational capabilities of the "Intruder" and the airmen who flew them, the authors suggest they read the book, *The Flight of the Intruder*, written by former A-6 pilot Stephen Coonts.

Notes

1. Leefloor, Elizabeth. *Party Like It's 1986: Operation El Dorado Canyon*, 22 March 2011. http://www.redicecreations.com/article.php?id=14676
2. Operation Attain Document—Global Security.Org http://www.globalsecurity.org/military/ops/attain_document.htm
3. USS *America* Virtual Museum http://ussamerica-museumfoundation.org/index.html
4. Sweetman, Jack. *American Naval History: An Illustrated Chronology of the United States Navy and Marine Corps 1775–Present*. Annapolis, MD: Naval Institute Press, 2002.

5. Grossnick, Roy A. *Dictionary of American Naval Aviation Squadrons,* Vol. 1 Naval Historical Center, September 1994.

6. Ibid.

7. Symonds, Craig, and William J. Clipson. *Naval Institute Historical Atlas of the U.S. Navy.* Annapolis, MD: Naval Institute Press, 2001.

8. Grossnick, Roy A. *Dictionary of American Naval Aviation Squadrons,* Vol. 1. Naval Historical Center, September 1994.

9. Sweetman, Jack. *American Naval History: An Illustrated Chronology of the United States Navy and Marine Corps 1775–Present.* Annapolis, MD: Naval Institute Press, 2002.

10. Endicott, Judy G. "Short of War—USAF Contingency Operations." USAF Historical Studies Office, Operation El Dorado Canyon. http://www.afhso.af.mil/topics/factsheets/factsheet.asp?id=18650

11. Boyne, Walter J. "El Dorado Canyon." *Air Force Magazine,* March 1999, Vol. 82, No. 3.

12. Ibid.

13. Stanik, Joseph T. *El Dorado Canyon: Reagan's Undeclared War with Qaddafi.* Annapolis, MD: Naval Institute Press, 2003.

14. Transcript of Naval Service for Rear Admiral Richard Charles Allen—U.S. Navy NMPC-2 Pers–48, 17 October 1988.

15. VA-34 History—Department of the Navy, Naval Historical Center, Washington Navy Yard, Washington D.C., 20374.

16. Transcript of Naval Service for Rear Admiral Richard Charles Allen—U.S. Navy NMPC-2 Pers–48, 17 October 1988.

17. USS *Detroit* http://www.combatindex.com/hardware/detail/sea/aoe4_data.html.

18. Schmitt, Eric. "Expulsions Urged in Navy Cheating Case," *New York Times,* 1 April 1994.

19. Dorsey, Jack. "Fleet's Top Aviator to Fold His Wings. Vice-Admiral Richard C. 'Sweetpea' Allen Retires Today." *The Virginian Pilot (Norfolk),* 15 March 1996.

20. Carlson, Richard W. "Danger Zone: The Week at Home and Abroad," *Charleston (SC) Mercury,* 22 September 2009.

Capt. James Lair
(February 1987–August 1988)

"The finest group of individuals our Nation has ever assembled."—
Admiral Lair commenting on the crew of the USS *America.*

On 12 May 1975, at approximately 2:10 p.m. local time, the SS *Mayaguez,* a 500-foot container ship of American registry was seized in international waters by gunboats of the Khmer Rouge as it steamed along the Cambodian coast, en route to the port of Sattahip, Thailand.

In Washington, D.C., where there was an eleven hour time difference, President Ford awoke to the news of the seizure and ordered a meeting of the National Security Council (NSC) for 10:00 a.m. and placed American forces in the Western Pacific (WESTPAC) on alert.

The recent fall of the governments in South Vietnam and Cambodia had left the United States with no diplomatic avenues to pursue. Memories of the seizure of the USS *Pueblo* seven years earlier in January 1968 by North Korea created an additional imperative to act swiftly. Following a press conference announcing the seizure at 1:50 p.m. Washington time, President Ford ordered a naval force, consisting of the aircraft carrier USS *Coral Sea* (CVA-43), destroyer escort USS *Harold E. Holt* (DE-1074) and the guided missile destroyer USS *Henry B. Wilson* (DDG-7), into the area. The USS *Coral Sea* was just entering the Indian Ocean en route to Perth, Australia, for a ceremony commemorating the Battle of Coral Sea. She was ordered to reverse course and proceed full speed toward the Gulf of Thailand.

Aboard the *Coral Sea*, pilots of Attack Squadron Twenty-Two (VA-22) "Fighting Redcocks," part of Air Wing 15 (CVW-15) were nearing the end of their seven-month deployment, having departed NAS Lemoore on 5 December 1974. The squadron had taken part in the evacuation of Saigon the previous April during Operation Frequent Wind, flying cover for helicopters. Many of the squadron's pilots were veterans of the Vietnam War and now they were again preparing their A-7 Corsairs to fly combat missions. Among them was the squadron's 35-year-old Operations Officer, Lt. Cdr. Jim Lair, known to the junior officers as "The Maj." possibly in reference to his time as a Marine.

James A. Lair was born in Westchester, a suburb of Los Angeles, on New Year's Day 1940, the older of two children of George and Agnes Lair. His father had served as a Naval officer in both the Second World War and in Korea, and from a young age Lair wanted to serve as an officer in the military.

Shortly after graduating from Mount Carmel High School, Lair enlisted in the U.S. Marine Corps

Captain James Lair (official U.S. Navy photograph).

Reserve as a rifleman on 25 October 1957, at the age of seventeen. He served with the 14th Rifle Company at Santa Monica, California, until he entered the Navy in June 1960, through the Naval Aviation Cadet Program at Loyola University. He earned his wings and was commissioned an ensign in December 1961.[1]

Lair was assigned to replacement pilot training with Sea Control Squadron Forty-One (VS-41) "Shamrocks," an anti-submarine operations training squadron and he reported to NAS North Island, near San Diego, California. The Navy hoped to counter the growing presence of a large Soviet submarine fleet in the Western Pacific by developing anti-submarine warfare (ASW) aircraft, and Lair was trained to fly the Grumman S-2 Tracker, the first purpose-built single airframe ASW aircraft to enter naval service. Lair completed his carrier qualification (CARQUALS) in April 1962.

Following completion of training, Lair was sent to San Diego, California, assigned to Anti-Submarine Squadron Thirty-Eight (VS-38) "Red Griffins" aboard the USS *Bennington* (CVS-20) a World War II–era *Essex*-class anti-submarine aircraft carrier. VS-38 was the Navy's first carrier-based ASW Squadron. The *Bennington* departed San Diego on her fifth WESTPAC deployment on 6 January 1962, and Lair joined her at port in Hong Kong in May.[2]

While assigned to the *Bennington* as a Landing Signal Officer (LSO), Lair made three Western Pacific (WESTPAC) deployments and flew the S-2E Tracker and later the A4-B Skyhawk. His first deployment from 6 January through 25 July 1962, the fifth WESTPAC deployment for the ship, was primarily operating in the South China Sea, but also supported U.S. operations in Laos.

In May 1963, *Bennington*'s home port moved from San Diego to Long Beach, California, and in August she sailed to Seattle for "Seafair 63" then continued north to Juneau and Kodiak, Alaska, the first carrier to operate in the North Pacific since World War II. As Lair wryly recalled, "We went up in the summer ... obviously."[3]

The Bennington deployed on her sixth WESTPAC deployment from 19 February until 11 September 1964, sailing to Pearl Harbor, Yokosuka, Sasebo, Hong Kong, and Manila Bay. Returning to Long Beach, *Bennington* was dispatched to Eureka, in Humboldt County, California, during Christmas 1964 to provide disaster relief from severe flooding with water levels that exceeded thirty feet. The *Bennington* remained offshore in heavy seas and the twenty Marine helicopters she carried were invaluable in providing assistance and emergency supplies to the stricken residents.[4]

The foul weather and mountainous terrain made flight operations extremely hazardous, and on the morning of 26 December, a Sikorsky H-34 Choctaw helicopter of Marine Medium Helicopter Squadron Three Hundred Sixty-Three (HMM-363) "Lucky Red Lions" off the *Bennington* and piloted by Marine Capt. Richard Gleason headed up the Eel River in heavy rain on a rescue mission. Aboard was the co-pilot 1st Lt. William L. Arbogast, crew chief Cpl. Joseph W. Brinkley, a Navy Photographer 1st Class Alonzo Slaughter and a civilian guide, Ervin A. Hadley. Shortly after spotting a group of 45 refugees and marking their position, there were four loud explosions, the aircraft lost power and crashed into the Eel River.

Gleason recalled: "We were losing power, and I saw that we weren't going to clear the river. We hit and the cockpit filled with water immediately as the plane went under. The water was too muddy to see the instrument panel and I remember thinking for an instant that this was the closest I ever came to death." Unable to locate his co-pilot, he exited the window and swam 25 feet to the surface in the icy water. Gleason survived with injuries, but the other four aboard the aircraft perished in the water.[5]

In March of 1965, Bennington again departed Long Beach on her seventh WESTPAC deployment. Lair departed the ship midway through the deployment while the *Bennington* was in port in Japan.

Lair reported to the Naval Postgraduate School in Monterey, California, in December 1966 and he graduated in June 1968 with a Bachelor's Degree in International Relations.

The war in Vietnam was continuing to hold America's attention in 1968 as troop levels rose to their highest level when President Johnson approved raising the maximum number of troops in Vietnam to 549,500. It was also the deadliest year with 16,592 Americans killed and almost 28,000 Allied soldiers killed, primarily ARVN troops. The TET Offensive in January and February would be followed by the first peace talks in Paris in May and an end to the bombing of North Vietnam at the end of October reflecting America's ambiguity towards the war in Vietnam.

Following his transition training to the Douglas A-4C Skyhawk, a delta-winged carrier capable attack fighter, Lair was assigned to Attack Squadron One Hundred Twelve (VA-112) "Broncos" stationed at NAS Lemoore and under the command of Cdr. Tommy Gatewood. The squadron and Lair deployed to Vietnam as part of Air Wing Sixteen (CVW-16) aboard the USS *Ticonderoga* (CV-14) on 1 February 1969.[6]

The fourth U.S. naval warship to bear the name, the USS *Ticonderoga*, an *Essex*-class World War II era aircraft carrier, had an illustrious service record for both World War II and in Vietnam where she launched the first airstrikes into North Vietnam.

On the afternoon of 2 August 1964, possibly in response to earlier attack by American supported South Vietnamese patrol boats on coastal installations in the Gulf of Tonkin, North Vietnam attacked the American destroyer USS *Maddox* (DD-731) as it sailed along the coast of North Vietnam, collecting intelligence but disputably in international waters. Three Soviet built P-4 motor torpedo boats attacked the *Maddox* without effect, all torpedoes missing. The Maddox returned fire, damaging one boat. In response to reports of the attack, the *Ticonderoga* launched four, rocket-armed F-8E Crusaders to the assist the *Maddox*. Arriving on scene, they launched Zuni rockets and strafed the North Vietnamese craft with 20 mm cannons, with the result of one patrol boat dead in the water and on fire with the other two damaged.[7]

Two days later, on the evening of 4 August, the *Ticonderoga* again received a request for assistance, this time from the USS *Turner Joy* (DD-951) operating in support of the *Maddox*. Believing themselves under attack, the *Turner Joy* took evasive maneuvers, engaged targets, and requested air assistance and again the *Ticonderoga* launched aircraft. Reports at the time claimed two patrol boats sunk and two damaged. Subsequent intelligence and study calls into question whether any attack actually occurred on 4 August.[8]

However, in response to the actual attack on 2 August and the suspected attack on 4 August, President Johnson ordered Seventh Fleet carrier forces to launch retaliatory strikes. On 5 August, attack aircraft from the *Ticonderoga* and USS *Constellation* (CVA 64) destroyed oil storage facilities at Vinh and damaged or sank about thirty enemy naval vessels in port or along the coast, the first of what would be thousands of attacks on the North Vietnamese mainland. Two days later, the U.S. Congress overwhelmingly passed the Gulf of Tonkin Resolution allowing President Johnson the authority to deploy American military forces against North Vietnam.

On 4 March 1969, the *Ticonderoga* was back in Vietnam on her fifth consecutive combat cruise. Aboard was Air Wing Sixteen (CVW-16), recently transferred from the USS *Oriskany* (CVA-34). Coming on line at "Yankee Station" (17°30'N and 108°30'E) approximately 190 km east of Dong Hoi, North Vietnam, *Bennington*'s mission was primarily interdicting communist supply lines and making airstrikes against enemy positions.

At approximately 1:34 p.m. on 15 April, *Deep Sea 129*, an unarmed

Navy Reconnaissance EC-121 Warning Star of VQ-1, out of Atsugi, Japan, was shot down by two North Korean MiG-17s roughly 100 nautical miles off the North Korean peninsula killing all 31 Americans aboard.[9]

In response, the *Ticonderoga* was ordered north to the Sea of Japan as part of Task Force 71 (TF-71) a carrier task force comprised of the *Ticonderoga*, USS *Enterprise* (CVA9[N]-65), USS *Ranger* (CVA-61) and USS *Hornet* (CVA-12). They remained in the area, protecting reconnaissance aircraft in the area until the crisis abated. Involved in a war in Southeast Asia, the United States had little enthusiasm for entering a second war with North Korea, and America's response to the shoot-down was "restrained." On 27 April, the *Ticonderoga* departed for Subic Bay, P.I. for maintenance and upkeep.[10]

The *Ticonderoga* returned to Yankee Station on 8 May and resumed interdiction operations, then sailed to Sasebo and Hong Kong, before returning to the line on 26 June for 37 more days of air operations. She then rejoined TF-71 in the Sea of Japan for the remainder of her deployment. She departed Subic Bay on 4 September, arriving in San Diego on 18 September. On 10 October 1969, Attack Squadron One Hundred Twelve was disestablished.

After transitioning to the Vought A-7E Corsair II, Lair was assigned to Attack Squadron One Hundred Ninety-Five (VA-195) "Dam Busters," so named for its destruction of the Hwa Chon Dam in North Korea on 1 May 1951. As part of Air Wing Eleven (CVW-11) aboard the USS *Kitty Hawk* (CVA-63) the squadron returned to Vietnam in November 1970. It was the squadron's sixth combat deployment to Vietnam and they would conduct operations there until 17 July 1971. Targeting rail yards, power plants and lines of communication and transportation, the squadron set records for combat sorties flown and ordnance dropped. During his two combat cruises, Lair flew more than two hundred combat missions over Vietnam.

Lair was sent to the School of Command and Staff at the Naval War College, receiving an M.S. in International Relations from George Washington University in June 1972. After a tour as an Instructor Pilot (IP) with VA-122 "Flying Eagles" at NAS Lemoore, Lair, now a lieutenant commander, was assigned as Operations Officer for Attack Squadron Twenty-Two (VA-22) "Fighting Redcocks" as part of Air Wing Fifteen (CVW-15) aboard the USS *Coral Sea* (CVA-43).

On 5 December 1974, the squadron departed San Francisco Bay on a WESTPAC deployment aboard the *Coral Sea* and reached the Philippines on

29 December. She then commenced a schedule of air wing refresher qualifications and training, interspersed with periods of maintenance at Subic Bay in February and March.

Although the Paris Peace Accords between the United States and North Vietnam had been signed on 27 January 1973, and the last U.S. combat troops had departed South Vietnam on 11 August, the war was not over for the Vietnamese. In mid–April 1975, as Northern forces overran the South, the *Coral Sea*, as well as the USS *Enterprise* (CVA (N)-65), USS *Midway* (CV-41) USS *Hancock* (CVA-19) and the USS *Okinawa* (LPH-3) were diverted to the South China Sea.

The *Coral Sea* was on stand-by during evacuation of the Cambodian capital of Phnom Penh on 12 April 1975 during Operation Eagle Pull. Over the following two weeks, the carrier operated off the Vietnamese coast as the North Vietnamese forces inexorably moved south.

On 29–30 April, Operation Frequent Wind, the evacuation of hundreds of Americans and Vietnamese from Saigon was initiated and aircraft of VA-22 helped provide air cover for the evacuation helicopters. The last American helicopter to lift off the roof of the United States Embassy was escorted by a "Fighting Redcocks" A-7E.[11]

As Lair later recalled: "Our mission was to provide cover for the U.S. ships off of Saigon and escort Marine Helicopters evacuating personnel from the U.S. Embassy. I was on the first mission of the day at about 1:00 p.m. We proceeded to the area off the coast of Saigon and were amazed at the massive fleet of refugee boats fleeing South Vietnam. Nothing very eventful happened. I spent the rest of the day and night monitoring the evacuation. A Corsair from VA-22 flew that last helicopter escort mission from the U.S. Embassy."[12]

The *Coral Sea* remained in the area until 2 May, when she departed the South China Sea for a port call in Singapore. The carrier was en route to Perth, Australia, to participate in a ceremony commemorating the Battle of Coral Sea when it was ordered to reverse course after being advised of the seizure of an American merchant vessel in international waters by Cambodian forces.

Lair, VA-22's operations officer, was one of the first to be made aware of the situation.

"I was the Operations Officer of VA-22 which was one of the two A7E light attack squadrons on *Coral Sea*. Early, somewhere between 4:00–5:00 a.m. on the morning of the 13th, I got a call from my Commanding Officer to report to the Admiral's Conference Room for a meeting regarding the recovery of the U.S. Merchant Ship *Mayaguez*. This was the first that I'd heard of the incident.

"The Admiral's meeting included personnel from VF-111/51, VA-22/94 and VA-95 (A-6 Intruder Squadron). The briefing focused on the safety of the crew and how to prevent the ship from being taken into a Cambodian port. We didn't want another *Pueblo* style incident. From what I can recall, there was very little intelligence on the location of the crew. It was unknown whether they were still aboard the ship, already on the Cambodian mainland, or on Koh Tang Island. Planning proceeded forward with several options for the Admiral (Commander Task Force 77) to provide to higher authority for consideration."

Early on 15 May, protective airstrikes were flown from the carrier against the Cambodian mainland naval and air installations, and Lair was strike leader for the first launch of the day.

"We were briefed that the Air Force Special Ops HH/CH-53s were inserting Marines onto Koh Tang Island to rescue the crew of the *Mayaguez*. We launched and proceeded to Koh Tang Island. There was no one that we could contact to provide accurate information for air support. As we found out later, the inserting helicopters had met heavy gunfire and some had been shot down which caused some problems on the ground. I was then scheduled to be the Strike Lead for the third launch of the day. We were briefed on what had occurred with the insertion earlier in the day and that our mission was to check in with the Air Force Airborne Battlefield Command and Control Center (ABCCC) aircraft (EC-130) and receive our assignments.

"We launched with two A-7s from VA-22 and one A-7 from VA-94. Launch was normal, rendezvous normal and we checked in with the ABCCC. The Carrier Air Wing Commander flying an A-6 Intruder (VA-95) spotted a high speed 'swift boat,' supposedly Khmer Rouge, heading to the vicinity of the *Mayaguez*. At this time, I didn't know that the crew of the *Mayaguez* had been released and returned to their ship. My flight was contacted by the ABCCC to proceed to the position of the 'swift boat' and await further instructions.

"The 'swift boat' was a former U.S. Navy Patrol Boat River (PBR) that had been captured by the Khmer Rouge with the fall of Cambodia earlier in the year. We arrived over the 'swift boat' and estimated that it was doing in excess of 25–30 mph and was still heading toward the *Mayaguez*. At this time we were given clearance to destroy the swift boat. We first dropped our cluster bombs but because of the time of fall of the weapons, the swift boat outran the pattern. Secondly the swift boat was maneuvering aggressively which further complicated the weapons' delivery accuracy. It appeared that the only solution was a low angle strafing tactic.

"The A-7E had a General Electric M61 Gatling Gun with a rate of fire of 4,000–6,000 rounds per minute. The A-7E also carried 1,000 rounds of 20 mm ammunition. I began the strafing run aiming at the stern of the boat so that if it turned either direction I could compensate. I started the run at approximately 1,000 feet of altitude and used about a ten degree dive angle. The in range firing cue appeared on the Heads Up Display at approximately 700 feet above the water. I started firing and could see the rounds impacting the boat. I ceased firing at approximately two hundred feet above the water. I made a hard turn and saw that the boat was sinking. I reported the results and returned to the *Coral Sea*.

"Upon return to the *Coral Sea*, we were briefed that the crew had safety returned to the *Mayaguez* and the ship was preparing to get underway and proceed to Thailand with their cargo. The remainder of the day was spent monitoring the activities that were taking place on the island of Koh Tang. We discussed that we were running out of daylight and needed to get the Marines off the island. We had learned from the evacuation of Saigon that night extractions can be challenging to say the least.

"Finally about 6:00–7:00 p.m. it was decided that the HH/CH-53s would begin the extraction. I don't remember if one or two helicopters came to *Coral Sea*. It was interesting in listening to the ship briefing the Air Force pilots about the lighting configuration that an aircraft carrier has at night. The Air Force pilots did a great job. The Marines that they brought to *Coral Sea* were beat to say the least. The next day, 16 May, there was much discussion with the Task Force Commander concerning available options for recovering the bodies of the Marines and Air Force personnel that we left behind the previous day. The outcome was that none of the bodies were recovered.

The *Coral Sea* departed the area on 17 May and proceeded to Subic Bay, where the Air Force Helicopters and Marines were off loaded. The *Coral Sea* then proceeded to Perth, Australia, for the Coral Sea Days."[13]

VA-22 returned to its home base at NAS Lemoore on 1 July 1975, and Lair remained with the squadron until August of 1976 when he transferred to Attack Squadron One Hundred Forty-Six (VA-146) "Blue Diamonds" as the executive officer (XO). During his time with the squadron, Lair made two WESTPAC deployments.

The first deployment, on 12 April 1977, was the squadron's fourteenth deployment in a twenty-year period, and they sailed to NAS Cubi Point, Philippines aboard the USS *Constellation* (CV-64) as part of Air Wing Nine (CVW-9).

The *Constellation*, a *Kitty-Hawk* class carrier launched in 1960, is the third ship of the line to be named after the "new constellation of stars" that graced the first flag of the new United States. The first USS *Constellation*, a three-masted square-rigged frigate launched on 27 March 1794, was the first ship to be commissioned into the United States Navy; the first put to sea; and the first to engage, defeat, and capture an enemy vessel.[14]

Arriving in June 1977, the squadron conducted Anti-Submarine Warfare (ASW) operations, before returning to NAS Lemoore in November.

After only eleven months ashore, VA-146 returned to sea with the *Constellation* on 26 September 1978, again deploying to the Western Pacific and making port calls in Korea and Japan as well as participating in Copethunder 77, a simulated combat airpower employment exercise, sponsored by the Pacific Air Forces at Clark AFB in the Philippines. In November, Commander Lair assumed command of VA-146.

On 27 December 1978, *Constellation* and her escorts were directed to sail toward Singapore in response to the internal crisis in Iran which threatened U.S. interests in the Arabian Gulf, but on 2 January 1979, they were ordered to remain on station in the South China Sea and not enter the Indian Ocean for fear of escalating tensions. With the departure of the Shah of Iran into exile on 16 January, the crisis abated to the degree that the *Constellation* and her escort ships were released from contingency operations on 28 January. Two days later, on 30 January, all non-essential American personnel and their dependents were ordered to evacuate Iran.[15]

An outbreak of violence between North and South Yemen on 7 March 1979, toward the end of her deployment resulted in President Carter ordering the USS *Constellation* to make a high speed transit to the Indian Ocean from the Philippines, and the *Constellation* and her airwing remained in the area for 47 days until relieved by the USS *Midway* (CV-41). In mid–April the *Constellation* departed for Diego Garcia, then returned to the Philippines before returning to Lemoore on 17 May, heralded by a 23-plane flyover by the "Blue Diamonds." Twice extended on her deployment, her service earned the award of the Navy and Marine Corps Expeditionary Medal.[16]

Upon returning to Lemoore, VA-146 received twelve new A-7E's equipped with newly developed Forward Looking Infrared Receiver (FLIR) technology for evaluation, and the rest of the year was focused on developing operational tactics for its utilization.

On 26 February 1980, the squadron again deployed aboard the "Connie" for the West Pacific. The following day, Lair flew off her deck for the last time, en route to NAS Miramar and a new assignment as a tactical air analyst in the Office of the Chief of Naval Operations (CNO). During that assignment, Lair developed a five-year defense plan, and was promoted to captain in March 1981.

In July, he was assigned as commanding officer of Air Wing Six (CVW-6) aboard the USS *Independence* (CV-62) and he reported aboard shortly after she returned from her deployment in the Mediterranean and Indian Oceans.

The *Independence* again deployed to the Mediterranean in June 1982 and provided critical support to the Lebanon Contingency Force of 800 U.S. Marines, part of the multinational peacekeeping force in Lebanon. In late June, in an unprecedented accumulation of U.S. Naval airpower, the *Independence*, along with the USS *Forrestal* (CV-59) battle groups joined the USS *Dwight D. Eisenhower* (CVN-69) and USS *John F. Kennedy* (CV-67) for operations in the eastern Mediterranean lasting for several days, before relieving the two carriers.[17]

Although a veteran of two hundred combat sorties, and present at major conflicts throughout his career, it was ironically an accident that came close to closing his career. As Lair recalled the event: "On 15 October 1982, at approximately 8:30 Zulu time, I and three others ejected from a Lockheed S-3A Viking of Anti-Submarine Squadron Twenty-Eight (VS-28) Mavericks on the flight deck of USS *Independence* about fifty miles east of Beirut, Lebanon, in the Eastern Mediterranean. We were operating in support of the U.S. Marines ashore during the Lebanon Crisis of 1982–1983. I was Commander, Carrier Air Wing Six at the time and wanted to fly to Naval Air Station Sigonella, Italy, to visit the Air Wing Six beach detachment and thank the personnel at Sigonella for their support during our current deployment.

"Our flight was the only scheduled flying for the day. I was the pilot and the VS-28 Operations Officer was the copilot with the squadron commander in the right rear seat and another officer in the left rear seat. We were spotted on one of the waist catapults as normal, tensioned out as normal. I did the normal instruments and controls check before saluting the catapult officer and we were a go for launch. After I saluted the catapult officer, there was a slight delay which was normal but this time the aircraft started down the catapult track at a very slow speed compared to the normal catapult shot acceleration. The catapult officer sensed something was wrong and signaled for a catapult suspend by crossing his arms below the waist.

"For a pilot this meant nothing until the catapult was in fact suspended and the catapult officer walked out in front of the aircraft and signaled a throttle back. In this case the aircraft had broken the hold back fitting and was moving down the cat very slowly. I looked at the airspeed indicator and remember seeing fifty knots. I realized that there was a malfunction and we were not going to reach the required safe flying speed at the end of the shot. I also remember hearing a UHF radio call—'Eject/Eject/Eject' which I later found out was the Air Boss. As the aircraft approached the end of the flight deck, either I or the copilot initiated the ejection using the alternate ejection handle between the legs.

"On all launches and landings the S-3 ejection switch was in the command ejection position. This meant that if any of the four crew members initiated the ejection all four would go. If it were out of the command ejection position, if the pilot or copilot initiated an ejection all four would go but if one of the back-seaters initiated an ejection only that person would eject. This was for safety reasons.

"The ejection system functioned as advertised. The entire sequence for all four seats to fire takes only four seconds, so that there is no seat-to-seat collision between the seats at the top of the seat travel. Once the seat fires it's only three-fourths of a second to travel approximately 240 feet and get seat/man separation and an open chute.

"It was a hellava ride. I landed close to the port side of the ship. I hit the water hard because I only got about a one-half swing in my chute before hitting the water. We were picked up by Air Wing helicopters and returned to the ship in about twenty minutes. The cause of the catapult malfunction was human error related to some maintenance that was performed on the catapult the night before without the proper personnel being informed that it was 'not operational.' It was an exciting day to say the least. I injured my back, knees and shoulders because of the 'hard landing' in the water."[18]

In November 1982, Lair assumed command of the USS *Caloosahatchee* (AO-98) a World War II–era *Cimarron*-class fleet oiler. He supported operations in Grenada in October and November 1983 and deployed to the Mediterranean from April until October 1984. Following staff assignments as Executive Assistant to the Navy Assistant Chief of Staff, and as Assistant Chief of Staff to Commander Naval Air Force—Atlantic (COMNAVAIRLANT) Lair was given command of the USS *America* (CV-66), assuming command on 28 February 1987, relieving Capt. Richard C. Allen.

America had arrived back at Norfolk Naval Shipyard on 20 November 1986, for a fifteen-month comprehensive overhaul, the longest overhaul during her career. Extensive modifications were necessary to allow her to operate the F/A-18C Hornet, the A-7E Corsair II's replacement aircraft. As such, the majority of Lair's time in command was overseeing the transition. The remaining months of 1988 were spent conducting training exercises, and in August 1988, Lair relinquished command to Capt. John J. Coonan, Jr., and was appointed to a one-year tour of duty as Chief of Staff to the Commander of the Sixth Fleet. In September of 1989, Lair returned to the Office of the Chief of Naval Operations, this time as Director of Tactical Readiness.

In June of 1991, Lair, newly promoted to Rear Admiral (Lower Half) the previous April, assumed command of Carrier Strike Group Two (CSG-2) at Norfolk, Virginia, commanding Carrier Strike Force–Sixth Fleet, and embarked aboard the USS *John F. Kennedy* (CV-67). The *Kennedy* was newly returned in March from airstrike missions during Operation Desert Storm (16 January–28 February) in which she had launched a total of 114 strikes during the 42 days of conflict, expending 3.5 million tons of ordnance. She returned in March to be upgraded and refitted to accommodate the F/A-18C Hornet.[19]

In February 1992, Lair was presented with his second star, and on 6 March 1992, the *Kennedy* got a new skipper, Capt. Timothy R. Beard. Most of the time was spent training and qualifying the crew and air wing for the next deployment.

In the summer of 1992, the U.S. Navy decided to group escorts more consistently with aircraft carriers. Instead of routinely changing the cruisers, destroyers, and frigates assigned to each carrier battle group, each of the Navy's 12 carrier battle groups were to consist of an aircraft carrier; an embarked carrier air wing; cruiser, destroyer, and frigate units; and two nuclear-powered attack submarines.

For the *Kennedy*, the group would consist of Carrier Air Wing Three (CAW-3), the guided missile cruisers USS *Wainwright* (CG-28), USS *Leyte Gulf* (CG-55) and USS *Gettysburg* (CG-64), Destroyer Squadron Forty, guided missile frigates USS *Halyburton* (FFG-40) and USS *McInerney* (FFG-8), the frigate USS *Capodano* (FF-1093), the oiler USS *Kalamazoo* (AOR-6), the ammunition ship USS *Santa Barbara* (AE-28), and two nuclear submarines; USS *Seahorse* (SSN-669) and USS *Albuquerque* (SSN-706).[20]

On 7 October 1992, *Kennedy* got underway on its fourteenth Mediterranean deployment, transiting the Strait of Gibraltar on 18 October, and entering the Messina Strait on the 21st. During the next months, the ship would host Secretary of Defense Dick Cheney, conduct training and planning for Operation Seawind with the Egyptian Navy and Air Force, and African Eagle with Moroccan forces.

On 21 January, the *Kennedy* began conducting flight operations in the eastern Mediterranean, lasting until 28 January, when the carrier began its transit out of the region. As the situation following the breakup of Yugoslavia deteriorated into war in Bosnia and Herzegovina, on 25 February, *Kennedy* began monitoring airdrops over Bosnia-Herzegovina in conjunction with Operation Provide Promise, a military operation aimed at protecting and providing humanitarian aid to Kurds fleeing their homes in Northern Iraq. She continued that duty until 25 March when she was relieved by the USS *Theodore Roosevelt* (CVN-71). After disembarking her air squadrons on 6 April 1993, *Kennedy* docked at Norfolk the following day.

On 25 June 1993, as the *Kennedy* prepared for dry dock and a $491,000,000 comprehensive overhaul, Lair was relieved by Rear Adm. John J. Mazach, a former skipper of the USS *America*, as commander of Carrier Group Two in a ceremony at Norfolk Naval Base aboard the *Kennedy*.

Mazach had left his position as Deputy Director of Plans and Policy for the U.S. European Command in Stuttgart, Germany, while Lair was transferred to Stuttgart to finish his career as Director of Operations, U.S. European Command. His responsibilities included the training and deployment of all U.S. forces in Europe, Northern Iraq, and most of Africa.

Lair retired with the rank of Rear Admiral in 1995 with over 8,000 flight hours and 1,410 carrier landings. His personal awards include the Defense Distinguished Service Medal, four Legions of Merit, a Defense Meritorious Service Medal, a Meritorious Service Medal, two Individual Air Medals, twenty-two Strike Flight Air Medals, four Navy Commendation Medals with the Combat "V" and various campaign awards.[21]

Looking back, Lair reflects, "After a lengthy military career, and upon leaving, you come to realize that, first, there's no going back and you quickly realize that you're departing the finest group of individuals our Nation has ever assembled. You were part of this magnificent team and you and this team would go to the gates of hell for each other. There's not one civilian organization or company where this mindset is present."[22]

Capt. James Lair on the America

"I took command of USS *America* (CV-66) in February 1987 from Capt. Richard 'Sweetpea' Allen. The ship was in dry dock at the Norfolk

Naval Shipyard. *America* was the only carrier to go through a comprehensive overhaul (eighteen months) versus a Service Life Extension in lieu of Procurement (SLEP) which could take three years. This was a challenging period because it demanded total coordination/cooperation between the shipyard, the ship and the Commander Naval Air Forces Atlantic Fleet. Without this cooperation, the completion date would be in jeopardy and more importantly the ability of the carrier to be fully operational on the required date could also be in jeopardy.

"Every piece of rotating machinery in the engineering spaces was removed for overhaul. A completely new combat detection center was being designed and installed. All the catapult/arresting gear equipment was removed and overhauled. The crew was removed from the ship and berthed on a former liberty ship moored astern of *America*. This was a smart idea as it made access to the ship easy and kept the crew together as a team.

"The next year was intense. It required the entire ship to 'come to life.' At times it appeared we'd never get there but thanks to the superb leadership, dedication and super effort of the entire crew, *America* was ready for sea on schedule. It was a once in a lifetime experience to be on the bridge hearing the announcement 'underway' as we departed the Norfolk Naval Shipyard on a cold, wintery February morning, under our own power headed down the James River to the Virginia Capes operating area.

"From February through April 1988, *America* went through numerous examinations that included flight deck certification, fleet refresher training (that focused on damage control and seamanship), and the most difficult, the operations propulsion plant examination (OPPE). *America*'s crew as usual met all the above challenges and was certified fully operational in April 1988.

"In May 1988, *America* was selected to participate in New York City's Fleet Week. We were the first aircraft carrier to visit New York City in fifty years. I thought it was most fitting that *America*, the ship named after our country was most appropriate. It was a magnificent sight sailing up the Hudson River with the Statue of Liberty directly on the bow and Ellis Island to the left. It reminded me of what the great people that fled oppression and came to America with only what they could carry onboard the ships must have thought as they first saw Lady Liberty. The city of New York opened its 'arms' to our crew. The mayor, Ed Koch gave us the symbolic key to the city. George Steinbrenner gave us free admission to Yankee Stadium. The crew was overwhelmed with the 'heroes' welcome the city gave us.

"The end of my time in command was near. I received orders to be the Chief of Staff, Commander U.S. Sixth Fleet. On a bright day in August 1988, I was relieved as the Seventeenth Commanding Officer of the USS *America*. As I departed the ship for a final time, I knew that the Navy had given me the opportunity to be a part of, and work alongside, the greatest group of individuals I'd ever been a part of. It was truly an honor and privilege to be the Commanding Officer of the only ship to be named after our wonderful nation, the USS *America*."

Notes

1. Interviews with James A. Lair, October–December 2012.
2. USS *Bennington* History—http://www.uss-bennington.org/home.php.
3. Interviews with James A. Lair, October–December 2012.
4. http://www.uss-bennington.org/stz-Eureka_Dec-64_1.html.
5. Wingo, Hal. "Rescue by Copter and Bo'sun's Chair." *Life Magazine*, 8 January 1965.
6. Grossnick, Roy A. *Dictionary of American Naval Aviation Squadrons*, Vol. 1. Naval Historical Center, Dept. of the Navy, 1994.
7. Gulf of Tonkin Crisis, August 1964—Naval History and Heritage Command, Dept. of the Navy http://www.history.navy.mil/faqs/faq120-1.htm.
8. Ibid.
9. U.S. Naval Institute/Naval History and Heritage Command, Naval History Blog: http://www.navalhistory.org/2010/04/15/15-april-1969-deep-sea-129-shootdown
10. Brecher, Michael, and Jonathan Wilkenfeld. *A Study in Crisis*. Ann Arbor: University of Michigan Press, 1997.
11. A-4 Skyhawk Assn. website VA-22 Fighting Redcocks http://a4skyhawk.org/3e/va22/va22.htm
12. Interviews with James A. Lair, October-December 2012.
13. Ibid.
14. http://www.ussconstellation.org/constellation_history.html.
15. VA-146 http://www.vfa146.navy.mil/history.htm.
16. Ibid.
17. *Independence* website http://navysite.de/cvn/cv62.htm.
18. Interviews with James A. Lair, October-December 2012.
19. USS *John F. Kennedy* http://www.history.navy.mil/danfs/j3/john_f_kennedy.htm
20. Ibid.
21. Golden Eagles Website http://epnaao.com/BIOS_files/REGULARS/Lair-percent 20James percent20A.pdf
22. Interview with James A. Lair, February 2013.

Capt. John J. Coonan, Jr.
(August 1988–October 1989)

"My dream began as a 12 year old.... My heroes were the test pilots who daily flew the latest jet fighters and explored their capabilities and limitations. One of the proudest days in my life was earning my wings of gold."—John J. Coonan, Jr., PBS broadcast 2001

Captain John J. Coonan, Jr., was born in Pawtucket, Rhode Island, on 30 November 1944. His father, who also retired as a Navy Captain, was deployed in the Southwest Pacific flying the PB4Y (Navy version of the B-24) and did not see his son until he was thirteen months old.

The elder Coonan would also fly amphibious PBY-5A Catalinas during World War II, and later command VP-5, VW-11 and Fleet Air Wing 6. He was stationed at NAS Quonset Point for several years in the early 1950s, and son "JJ," as he was called, grew up in Wickford and East Greenwich. The Coonan family returned to Rhode Island during his father's deployments, and young Coonan worked summers at Kennecott Copper in Rumford.

They moved fourteen times before his graduation from Bishop Kenny High School in Jacksonville in 1962.

Coonan graduated from the University of Virginia under the Regular NROTC Program in June 1966. He was designated a Naval Aviator on 29 September 1967. He flew the A-7 Corsair during a Vietnam deployment in VA-87 aboard the USS *Ticonderoga* (CVA-14), and a Mediterranean deployment aboard USS *Roosevelt* (CVA-42).

In a 2001 PBS TV interview Coonan said, "Flying off an aircraft carrier is without question the most challenging flying I have ever experienced. It's an adrenaline high each and every time. The sense of accomplishment when you successfully bring your aircraft back to a pitching deck in heavy weather is beyond description. Are we nervous?

Captain John J. Coonan (official U.S. Navy photograph).

Heck yes. Would we do it again and again? Absolutely! Aviation physiolo-
gists measured the pulse rate of Navy combat pilots and their pulse rate
was higher on final approach to the carrier after a mission than it was when
they were under fire in their bomb runs."

Following tours as an Aviation Assignment Officer with Commander,
Naval Military Personnel Command, he served in VA-81 and Light Attack
Wing One staff; he served as XO and then CO of the "Valions" of VA-15
from June 1980 until September 1981. While commanding VA-15, he was
selected as the first East Coast recipient (and only the second naval aviator
recipient) of the Vice Adm. James Stockdale Award for inspirational leadership.

He commanded Carrier Air Wing One from October 1983 through
March 1985 where he deployed aboard USS *America* (CV-66). Additional
commands included: Light Attack Wing One, USS *Mars* (AFS-1), and USS
America (CV-66) from August 1988 through October 1989.

Concerning his time aboard *America*, Coonan said: "We were at sea
for almost my entire tour and steamed the equivalent of three times around
the world."

Following a tour as Director, Program Planning and Assessment (J8)
at USCINCLANT, he assumed command of Naval Aviation Schools Command in April 1993. By the time he retired in 1997, he had accumulated
more than 4,500 flight hours (including more than 3,000 in the A-7 Corsair)
and logged over 1,000 carrier arrested landings.

He then joined the staff of the National Naval Aviation Museum Foundation in Pensacola, Florida. He served as Director of Development and
later Vice President of Education and Chief Operating Officer.

His most lasting contribution to aviation and to the foundation,
however, was his stewardship of the National Flight Academy, the premier
and one-of-a-kind scientific, technological, engineering and mathematics
(STEM) teaching facility in this country. He was selected to bring the con-
cept to reality and serve as the Academy's first Director. Unfortunately, he
succumbed to cancer in June 2009.

John J. Mazach, Vice Admiral, USN (Ret.), nominated Captain Coonan
for recognition by the Rhode Island Aviation Hall of Fame (RIAHOF). He
wrote:

"No one in the military is successful without a firm understanding of
leadership and how to lead. John Coonan realized his leadership qualities
early in his career and applied them often. As a Lieutenant Junior Grade
in his first attack squadron tour, JJ found out what combat flying over Viet

Nam at night was all about and never looked back. He was always a leader in the air (as well as on the ground) from his first combat tour all the way through his tour as the Air Wing One Commander on what would eventually be his ship, USS *America* (CV-66). His consummate leadership was recognized when he commanded Attack Squadron Fifteen in 1981. He became the first recipient of the James B. Stockdale Leadership Award, given annually to the Commanding Officer who best exemplifies the enduring inspirational leadership characteristics of Admiral Stockdale."

Retired Vice Adm. Gerry Hoewing, who heads up the National Naval Aviation Museum in Pensacola, seconded the nomination. "Captain Coonan not only distinguished himself with a tremendous career as an active duty Naval Aviator, but he was also the project manager and first Executive Director of the National Flight Academy ... the 'best in the world aviation-inspired learning adventure.'"[1]

Coonan's Near Miss

In the Spring of 2006 *Foundation* magazine published by the Naval Aviation Museum Foundation located in Pensacola, Florida, Captain Coonan described a 1981 event which could have created an international incident and prematurely ended his budding career. This is a summary of that story and is reprinted here with the permission of the Naval Aviation Museum Foundation and the Rhode Island Aviation Hall of Fame.

Coonan vs. Ivan

In 1981, during the Iranian Hostage Crisis, "JJ" Coonan was commanding VA-15, an A-7 squadron deployed aboard USS *Independence* (CV-62) to the Indian Ocean. Since they were constantly at sea, there were no land targets for maintaining their bombing proficiency. As a result, the air wing used the battle groups' surface combatants as targets.

During that period the Cold War had not yet thawed and it was common practice for the Soviets to shadow the battle group. A "tattletale" warship observed operations and reported the carrier's position. In this case the tattletale was a Soviet Krivak-class guided missile frigate.

One day the wing scheduled a war-at-sea exercise using one of the battle group's destroyers as the target. Coonan decided to qualify one of his pilots as a strike leader on this mission; each aircraft would carry six MK 76 practice bombs.

VA-15 had the newest version of the A-7E Corsair. It could be guided to its target from an airborne E-2C Hawkeye via Strike Attack Vectoring (SAV). This information could be seen on the A-7E's heads up display.

Immediately after launch Coonan was tasked by *Independence*'s Strike Ops to verify the location of the Soviet tattletale. He broke off to accomplish that task, and directed his strike-leader-in-training to proceed with the "attack." Coonan would catch up when he could.

Still about a mile in trail, he pulled up to observe the weapons delivery in the target ship's wake. Rolling on his back, Coonan saw the distinctive red deck of a Soviet ship and transmitted "Abort ... abort!" Too late.

"I then watched helplessly as twelve practice bombs with associated smoke charges cut across the wake of the Soviet *Krivak*. Ivan was not a happy camper! Almost immediately every threat warning indicator in my cockpit lit up!

"Waiting for the high warble of a missile launch, my heart beating a mile a minute, I made a defensive break down and away to an altitude that, trust me, was less than 200 feet. I exited stage right, thankful that there was no further action from the *Krivak*.

"With visions of the end of my career flashing before me, I gathered my chastened strike-leader and his wingman and headed back to the ship for recovery and what would be a long talk with the CAG and the embarked admiral," wrote Coonan.

"Apparently, the E-2 had broken lock on the battle group destroyer that was our target. In reacquiring the target, the E-2 crew had inadvertently locked on the Soviet tattletale.

"That said, my strike-leader-under-training should have been able to recognize that he had the wrong ship once he and his wingman reached the roll-in altitude to deliver the practice weapons. The *Krivak* was one of the more recognizable Soviet warships," Coonan observed.

"As I recall, we never heard any report from on high that Ivan had reported the 'attack' to his superiors.

"Apparently, the CO of the Soviet warship thought twice about advising his superiors that he had allowed aircraft from the carrier they were supposed to be monitoring to drop practice bombs near his ship.

"We lived to fly another day! And the would-be strike leader was back to square one," concluded Coonan.

Notes

1. The above article appeared in the special program for the 2010 edition of the RI-AHOF induction dinner for that event. It was researched and written by Frank Lennon, Rhode Island Aviation Hall of Fame. It is reprinted here per his permission.

Both "JJ" Coonan and his father were leaders and warriors during their war years. John J. Coonan Sr., as an Ensign U.S.N.R., was awarded the Distinguished Flying Cross "For heroism and extraordinary achievement in aerial flight as pilot of an airplane in action against enemy Japanese forces during the Aleutian Islands Campaign...." "JJ" received numerous awards during his naval career. They included the Defense Superior Service Medal, two Legions of Merit, four Meritorious Service Medals, Air Medals, the Navy Commendation Medal with Combat "V," and various campaign and unit ribbons.

As an aside, co-author Wise flew the PB4Y Privateer in an East coast squadron, Patrol Squadron Twenty Four during his initial tour, the last squadron to fly the veteran aircraft.

Capt. John J. Mazach
(October 1989–February 1991)

"We'd sail to Hell and back, with J. J. Mazach"—Sign hung off the ship upon the departure of Mazach as captain of USS *America*

On 15 January 1991, the USS *America* passed through the Suez Canal and on 16 January entered into the Red Sea. That same day, the UN-imposed deadline for Iraq's unconditional withdrawal from Kuwait expired. At 2:00 a.m. on 17 January, Operation Desert Shield became Operation Desert Storm.

The *America*, under the command of Capt. John J. Mazach, had suspected that they might be called to Southwest Asia for military action when, upon emerging from the Norfolk Naval Shipyard on 2 August 1990, following a four-

Captain John J. Mazach (official U.S. Navy photograph).

month Selected Restricted Availability (SRA), they received the news of Iraq's invasion of Kuwait. That suspicion must have grown, when on 28 December, just two months into a five month training cycle, the *America* was ordered to deploy in support of Operation Desert Shield.

At that time, the Combined Command Control Communication Cryptology and Intelligence (C4I) package installed aboard the *America* included the Navy Tactical Command System Afloat (NTCSA), the Contingency Tactical Action Planning System (CTAPS) along with advance tracking capabilities which were integrated for the first time and partnered with the Naval Tactical Data System (NTDS) which provided the ship with intelligence processing capabilities unmatched by any other ship in the fleet.

By 9 January 1991, the ship was through the Straits of Gibraltar into the Mediterranean. Once in the Red Sea, the *America* joined the carriers USS *Saratoga* (CV-60) and USS *John F. Kennedy* (CV-67) as part of Battle Force Red Sea. Embarked aboard the *America* was Carrier Air Wing One (CVW-1) which initially provided Combat Air Patrol (CAP) coverage for the battle force.

During the cruise over, Captain Mazach, as one of only two combat-experienced pilots aboard, the other being the CAG, met with the pilots, none of whom had combat experience, and tried to prepare them for the upcoming mission:

"During my briefings, which were really just 'talks' in ready room, I spoke to pilots prior to their commencing combat flights during Desert Storm. The CAG was Mike Bowman, who retired as a Vice Admiral, a close friend and also a Captain at the time. These discussions were aimed at trying to take some of the edge off launching into combat for the first time, which we did within twenty-four hours after transiting through the Suez Canal. We re-hashed their training and how these first flights should be confidence builders and the crews should do nothing different than they had been doing in training up to that point. We talked about taking care of each other while in the air and the importance of good, clear, although brief, communications.

"Battle Force Red Sea referred to the chain of command in the Red Sea where we were steaming. We had three carriers in the Red Sea and each had a Battle Group Commander embarked and the senior of the three acted as the Force Commander with the other two following his orders from a tactical standpoint. Battle Force Red Sea acted as single point of contact for the Desert Storm Air Commander.

"Carriers often deployed with Cruiser Destroyer Group Commanders

(CRUDESGRU) Commanders. These flag officers were surface warfare officers rather than aviators which were Carrier Group Commanders (CARGRU) Commanders. Deploying Battle Group Commanders are now called Carrier Strike Group Commanders with no distinction given to surface or aviation leadership. When I had *America*, our embarked flag officer was Rear Adm. Doug Katz who was a surface warfare trained officer and had commanded a Battleship as opposed to a carrier. He was CRUDESGRU 2. Carriers can only be commanded by aviators and the norm back then was to have a Carrier Group Commander deploy in the carrier since he was an aviator and almost always had previously commanded a carrier and thus brought additional experience with him. Not so aboard *America* in 1991!"[1]

On 19 February, CVW-1 flew its first air strike of the war, targeting an ammunition depot north of Baghdad and destroying it. The following night, in its first night strike, CVW-1 aircraft blew up an oil production facility. What followed was three weeks of almost continuous air operations, launch-

Captain Mazach (center) aboard the *America* with Rear Adm. Riley Mixson, Commander-Battle Force Red Sea (left), and Rear Adm. Doug Katz, COMCRUDES-GRU 2 (courtesy John J. Mazach).

ing attacks into Iraq against bridges, mobile Scud sites, oil production facilities and units of Iraq's elite Republican Guard.[2]

On Valentine's Day, 14 February, *America* entered the Persian Gulf and joined up with Battle Force Zulu, containing three other carrier groups. Along with the USS *Midway* (CV-41), USS *Ranger* (CV-61) and USS *Theodore Roosevelt* (CVN-71), she flew missions to attack Iraqi forces inside the Kuwait Theater of Operations (KTO). Targets in eastern Iraq were also attacked. *America* was the only carrier battle group to launch strikes in support of Operations Desert Shield and Desert Storm from both the Red Sea and Persian Gulf.[3]

With the initiation of the ground war on 24 February, *America* provided air support for coalition troops as they assaulted into Kuwait, targeting Iraqi tanks, artillery and troop concentrations. Within one hundred hours of the start of the ground assault, Kuwait was liberated and a cease-fire order was in place. The aircraft of CVW-1 were credited with the destruction of more than 380 tanks and armored vehicles.

By the time *America* sailed for home on 4 March, CVW-1 had flown 3,008 combat sorties and expended over 2,000 tons of ordnance without the loss of a single aircraft. After seventy-eight continuous days at sea, she made a six-day port call at the Red Sea coastal town of Hurghada, Egypt, then sailed through the Suez Canal, arriving home at Norfolk on 18 April.

For Mazach, it would be his last cruise aboard *America* as her captain. Earlier, on 8 February, he had turned over command of *America* to Capt. Kent. W. Ewing.

John James Mazach was born in Coffeyville, Kansas, during World War II on 10 January 1944. His father, a lieutenant in the Army Air Corps, was serving as an instructor pilot in the AT-6 Texan, a single-engine advanced trainer aircraft. Mazach grew up an only child in Bay Village, Ohio, then Nashville, Tennessee, where, following his graduation from high school, he attended Vanderbilt University. He played on the baseball team and was awarded an NROTC scholarship and appointed a Midshipman on 19 September 1963.

Following his graduation from Vanderbilt with a B.A. degree in History, Mazach was commissioned an ensign on 5 June 1966. He reported for Naval Air Basic Training at NAS Pensacola, Florida, then to NAS Chase Field, outside Beeville, Texas, for advanced training upon the completion of which, on 24 October 1967, he was designated a Naval Aviator and awarded his Gold Wings.

From October 1967 until June 1968, Mazach trained as a replacement pilot in Attack Squadron One Hundred Seventy-Four (VA-174) "Hell Razors" at NAS Cecil Field, Florida, training with A-7A/B Corsair II Light Attack jets. In June 1968, he was assigned as Flight Officer and eventually a Line (Maintenance) Officer with Attack Squadron Eighty-Seven (VA-87) "Golden Warriors" at Cecil Field.

"VA-87 was a brand new A-7B squadron in 1968 making all of us who were assigned to the squadron 'Plank Owners,' that is, original members of a new squadron. The CO was Cdr. Tom Dunlop. I joined the squadron as a first tour aviator straight out of Navy flight training. That's the same year I was married, and many of my squadron mates joined me in Nashville, as part of the wedding party. There were actually three of us in the squadron who had attended Vanderbilt University together as NROTC members of the class of 1966."[4]

The war in Southeast Asia was escalating as American military commitments increased, and on 1 February 1969, the squadron, attached to Air Wing Sixteen (CVW-16), departed San Diego bound for Vietnam aboard the USS *Ticonderoga* (CVA-14). Following brief visits to Pearl Harbor and Yokosuka, Japan, the *Ticonderoga* arrived off the coast of Vietnam at Yankee Station on 4 March. During the next four months, she would spend four periods on the line.

The squadron flew its first combat mission on 4 March against enemy targets in South Vietnam.[5]

Mazach recalled: "At that juncture in the air war in Vietnam, we were assigned to cover the southern part of the war zone and flew most of our combat missions into Laos and in support of the Tet offensive. We managed to get as far north as the Mu Gia Pass, a mountain pass in the Annamite Range between northern Vietnam and Laos, and a principal point of entry into the Ho Chi Minh Trail through Laos. We were also assigned some targets further north, but the majority of our work was with airborne Forward Air Controllers doing interdiction missions along the Ho Chi Minh Trail.

"This was the first deployment of the A-7B and while not a giant leap over the A model that preceded it, the airplane was a more accurate bomber and the FACs loved to work with

John Mazach, fighter pilot circa late 1960s (courtesy John J. Mazach).

us. Combat was new to everyone in the squadron, except the skipper, and we quickly learned to cope with getting shot at, mostly by 23 mm, 47 mm or 85 mm anti-aircraft artillery (AAA). SAMs were not plentiful down south so we rarely worried about them. The squadron was very young and we had twelve junior officers on their first fleet squadron tour which was far in excess of the norm of three or four and made for more gray hair for the skipper."

(Cdr. Tom Dunlop was KIA in Viet Nam as the Airwing Commander—CAG-14—in a subsequent tour).[6]

During her second period on the line, the *Ticonderoga* was ordered to the Sea of Japan in a show of force following the shoot down of a Navy EC-121 reconnaissance aircraft by the North Koreans on 16 April 1969. The crisis abated and the *Ticonderoga* sailed to Subic Bay for maintenance and upkeep arriving on 27 April. By 8 May, she was back on the line, flying interdiction missions. Her fourth period, beginning on 26 June, saw thirty-seven more days of air sorties against enemy targets.

"The deployment lasted nine months and while the airwing lost the Airwing Commander in an aircraft accident, as well as several other aircraft and pilots, VA-87 returned with all of our pilots and all but two of our aircraft. I lived in a stateroom aboard the *Ticonderoga* with my wingman who was a Lieutenant Commander and the Operations Officer for the squadron. I was a lieutenant junior grade at the time, and rooms were not plentiful on a small carrier so many of the department heads had to give up their single man rooms for two-man rooms. I was the schedules officer in the squadron so we accomplished a good deal of business in our stateroom. The OPS officer was a very experienced aviator, and although he had no prior combat experience, much of what I learned about flying I learned from him. He was a superb aviator."

The *Ticonderoga* finished her tour as part of Task Force Seventy-One (TF-71) in the Sea of Japan, and arrived in San Diego on 18 September, with the award of a third Navy Unit Commendation. Earlier, on 1 July, Mazach was promoted to full Lieutenant.

In December 1970, Mazach reported to the Bureau of Naval Personnel in Washington, D.C., serving as a detailer in the Aviation Assignment Section. "I was assigned to Washington, D.C., as an aviation assignment officer (detailer) and learned more in two and one half years about the Navy then I ever imagined. Going to D.C. as a Lieutenant is usually not a good thing as a flying job was a more sought after assignment. I mention this because when I returned to VA-105, an A-7E squadron, I had to 'double up and catch up' as far as flying skills were concerned."

Mazach was promoted early to Lieutenant Commander on 1 September 1972, and departed Washington in June 1973 to return to VA-174 for replacement pilot training this time in the A-7E, before reporting to Attack Squadron One Hundred Five (VA-105) "Gunslingers," in January 1974 as maintenance and operations officer.

"I was a very young Lieutenant Commander, having been promoted ahead of my contemporaries and I competed in the squadron with Department Heads much more experienced than I was. Mediterranean deployments were often intense periods of flying training type missions broken up by numerous port visits which often made staying current, or qualified in the airplane landing on the carrier, difficult."[7]

The squadron made two deployments to the Mediterranean aboard the USS *Saratoga* (CV-60), "The Fighting Cock," the first beginning on 27 September 1974, until 19 March 1975, as part of Air Wing Three (CVW-3) with Cdr. R. F. Moreau in command. "The squadron CO, the Air Wing Commander (CAG-3) and the Carrier CO were exceptional leaders and it was on this tour that I gained insight into what sorts of leadership styles work in different situations. Also, I began to understand more about how an aircraft carrier operates."

The ship made port calls to Spain, Italy, Turkey, and Monaco. "Many of the wives would follow the carrier from port to port for a period of time which was great, but, also made getting back to sea and flying day and night more of a challenge," Mazach recalled.

The second deployment under Cdr. J. E. Carpenter, who took command on 17 November 1975, departed on 6 January 1976, and returned home on 28 July.

Mazach was selected to attend the Air Command and Staff College and reported to Maxwell Air Force Base, Montgomery, Alabama, in May 1976 to further his Professional Military Education (PME). "There were only six Naval officers in the class and one was a well-known Seal named Dick Marcinko who later commanded Seal Team 6 as its first CO and then wrote books that were best sellers of sorts. That tour offered me a chance to learn a lot about the Air Force and Army and I made many friends whose paths I would cross again later in my career. One such friend was an Air Force Maj. Dick Myers, who went on to be named Chairman of the Joint Chiefs." Upon his graduation in June 1977, Mazach returned to VA-174 as a replacement pilot before rejoining the fleet.

In December of 1977, Mazach reported aboard Attack Squadron Fifteen (VA-15) "Valions" as the executive officer (XO) while the squadron was at sea, embarked as part of Carrier Air Wing Six (CVW-6) aboard the USS *America* (CV-66) on a Mediterranean deployment.

The *America* had departed Hampton Roads on 19 September, and alternated port calls along the coasts of Spain and Italy with operational exercises including "National Week" in February, before being relieved by the carrier *Forrestal* at Rota, Spain, and arriving home on 25 April 1978.

On 19 April 1979, Mazach relieved Cdr. Robert S. Smith, and took over as skipper of VA-15. "I had been XO for about sixteen months prior to taking command so I was ready. My XO was a close friend from my first squadron, VA-87, who had also served with me ashore in D.C. as a detailer in the Bureau of Naval Personnel, responsible for assignment of officers, and since we had just left that job, we were able to pretty much get the folks we wanted in the squadron. We had yet another VA-87 pilot there as well as some of the most talented officers and pilots I have ever served with. We were a very competitive group and the squadron deployed to the Mediterranean and won just about every readiness award that was available to us."[8]

On 20 June, Lt. Donna L. Spruill became the first female Navy pilot to carrier qualify in a fixed-wing aircraft. Lieutenant Spruill piloted a C-1A Trader to an arrested landing aboard the *Independence*. The squadron deployed to the Mediterranean again on 28 June 1979, this time aboard the USS *Independence* (CV-62). Three days later, on 1 July, Mazach was promoted to full Commander. "The opportunity to command a squadron is one that all Naval Aviators aspire to the most. My boss during the VA-15 tour as Commanding Officer was Carrier Air Wing Six (CAG-6) Dick "Sweetpea" Allen who was later CO of *America* and who I later relieved as Commander Naval Air Forces Atlantic. My tour as VA-15 CO was a blast and I learned a lot about leadership."[9]

On 26 June 1980, Mazach was relieved as VA-15 CO by Cdr. John J. Coonan, and he returned to Washington, assigned first as Assistant Head, then Head of Aviation-LCDR/Junior Officer Assignment Branch of the Naval Military Personnel Command, remaining there until he was assigned command of Carrier Air Wing Three (CVW-3) in February 1982.

After five months of PCAG training, Mazach took command of Air Wing Three on 29 July 1982, and following periods of carrier qualifications and maintenance, the air wing went to sea again on 26 April 1983, as part of Solid Shield 83 a joint operations exercise along the southeastern seaboard, then headed into the eastern Atlantic to participate in Ocean Safari, a NATO exercise held from 3–17 June 1983, that involved some ninety ships from ten nations. Ocean Safari simulated air strikes into Great Britain,

France, and West Germany, and following a port visit to Portsmouth, the *Kennedy* was back at Norfolk by 1 July.

After a short stay, the *Kennedy* departed Norfolk on 27 September with *Washington Post* military correspondent George C. Wilson aboard. Carrier qualifications were conducted off the coast of Virginia before she set sail for Rio de Janeiro, Brazil, on 2 October. Following a three-day port call, 13–16 October, the *Kennedy* departed for the Mediterranean. Mazach recalled: "As Commander Air Wing Three (CAG-3), I was embarked aboard the USS *John F Kennedy* and deployed to the Mediterranean Sea in 1983 for what was supposed to be a routine deployment. Our air wing was a bit 'different' in that John Lehman, who was Secretary of the Navy at the time, wanted to 'experiment' with the aircraft mix in the air wing, looking to create and deploy a long range strike capable wing. He replaced two squadrons of A-7s with an extra squadron of A-6s and additional A-6 tankers. Air wings at the time deployed with about twenty-four A-7s and twelve A-6s plus fighters and other air wing aircraft. We deployed with no A-7s and thirty-eight A-6s including tankers! It was an interesting challenge for an A-7 type CAG!"

While en route, on 23 October, a suicide bomber attacked the USMC Multi-National Force (MNF) Barracks at Beirut International Airport, killing 241 Marines. A subsequent car bomb killed 58 French paratroopers. The *Kennedy* arrived in the area on 28 October.[10]

CVW-3 took its first loss on 8 November, when an F-14A Tomcat of VF-31 crashed into the sea off the Lebanese coast, resulting in the death of the pilot, Lt. (jg) Cole O'Neil and his Radio Intercept Officer (RIO) Cdr. John C. Scull. Three days later, on 11 November, VF-31 lost a second F-14A when it went into the water. The pilot, Lt. David P. Jancarski, was injured exiting the aircraft, but the RIO, Lt. Cdr. Oliver L. Wright, escaped unhurt. Both pilots were fished out of the water by Sea Knight helicopters of HS-7.

On 24 November, the carrier's Grumman C-1A Trader, *Caroline II*, was lost at sea while on a ferry flight near Palma, Italy. Aviation Machinist Mate 2d Class Fernando Pena perished in the crash. That same day, the air wing, joined by aircraft of CVW-6, embarked aboard the USS *Independence* (CV-62), began flying air reconnaissance missions over Lebanon, gathering valuable intelligence to target Syrian positions for the gunfire support ships offshore.

The first air combat occurred on 3 December when two F-14s of VF-31, flown by Cdr. John C. Burch with Lt. John W. Miller as RIO, and by Lt. Gregory G. Streit with Lt. (jg) James E. McAloon as RIO, took fire from

Syrian SAM and AAA positions. A retaliatory strike was launched the following day: "We had two carriers in the eastern Mediterranean and we launched a strike in retaliation for the Syrians firing on our photo F-14s that were taking pictures for the theater commander. The strike was a coordinated strike with Carrier Air Wing Six on USS *Independence*."

CVW-3 aircraft included VA-85, which flew seven combat sorties, and VA-75 which flew three sorties, with other squadrons providing Combat Air Patrol (CAP), electronic countermeasures, and rescue operations. One A-6E Intruder from VA-85 was struck by a SAM and went down. The pilot, Lt. Mark A. Lange, died from injuries sustained in ejecting from the aircraft. Lt. Robert O. Goodman, the bomber/navigator, was captured by the Syrians and held until 3 January 1984. The Syrians released Lange's body to the U.S. Embassy in Beirut on 7 December. CAG-6, Cdr. Edward K. Andrews, safely ejected from his A-7E Corsair and was recovered by Christian Lebanese fishermen, and returned to the *Independence*.

"As it turned out, there was no element of surprise in the strike as there were calls made from outside the ships participating prior to the strike launching that were intercepted alerting the Syrians that we were coming and they were manned and ready. Much written about the strike and many lessons learned. I was the lead for my strike group just as was the CAG from the other strike group leading his group. I was just luckier than he was. It was during this tour that I was promoted to Captain ahead of my contemporaries and this tour was also the tour I couldn't seem to finish as I kept getting extended because of the possibility of additional hostilities in the area, which thankfully never happened."[11]

Except for a brief visit to Naples, the *Kennedy* remained on station, conducting air strikes against enemy artillery positions in support of the MNF until relieved by the USS *Saratoga* (CV-60) on 18 April and she departed for home, arriving at Norfolk on 2 May 1984. Mazach departed CAG-3 on 6 May 1984. (On 3 January 2013, CVW-3 made Naval history when Capt. Sara A. Joyner, USN, assumed command to become the first woman to lead a U.S. Navy carrier air wing.)

Mazach was next assigned as training officer at Commander, Naval Air Force—U.S. Atlantic Fleet, followed by a three month assignment (January-April 1986) to the Surface Warfare Officers School Command. "The Surface Warfare School was actually called Senior Officer Ship Materiel Readiness Course (SOSMRC) and was designed for aviators, and others, who were headed for command of a deep draft vessel for the first time. It was held back in mid- to late 80s in Idaho Falls, Idaho (part of the Nuclear

Reactor Site training facility) and finished up in Newport, Rhode Island, at Navy's Surface Officer Training School. The course concentrated on steam propulsion systems and other engineering subjects then switched to rules of the road and ship handling at Newport."

On 24 May 1986, Captain Mazach relieved Capt. David E. Frost, and assumed command of the USS *Seattle* (AOE-3), a Sacramento Class fast combat support ship. She deployed to the Mediterranean in August 1987 through February 1988. "It was my first opportunity to command a ship and for me, an aviator by trade, a chance to be exposed to ship command prior to a possible carrier command at a later date. It was for me, a tour that required a steep learning curve on how to maintain the ship and her crew. We deployed with Carrier Group Two embarked aboard the USS *Coral Sea* to the Mediterranean and provided fuel, ammo, and food to the battle group while deployed. This meant many hours steaming alongside a carrier or a cruiser or destroyer (sometimes one on each side) some 120 feet away, at thirteen knots, while transferring goods and fuel for hours at a time. A good tour for learning the art of ship driving, but, in my case, a real challenge in keeping the ship at the proper level of readiness as she was an old ship, but, very capable if you took care of her."[12]

On 15 February 1988, Mazach was relieved by Capt. James K. Tolbert, and was assigned as Chief of Staff for the Commander Cruiser/Destroyer Group Eight. "This billet is for a Naval Aviator post command officer, and I went there because I did not screen for command of an aircraft carrier on my first opportunity. Obviously disappointed, I went to the job with mixed emotions feeling that my career was ending. I worked directly for the Commander Cruiser Destroyer Group Eight, a Surface Officer who was at the time Rear Adm. Mike Boorda. I ran the staff and helped in administering to a large number of destroyers, cruisers and battleships that were assigned to the group when not deployed. When the group deployed we had our own ships and we were embarked aboard a carrier, the USS *Theodore Roosevelt* (CVN-71) on her first deployment, working for a different Admiral but a real hero, Rear Adm. Dave Robinson. In retrospect, the tour was probably the most beneficial I could have ever experienced. I learned more about surface ships and their 'care and feeding' then any aviator could. Mike Boorda was a prince to work for and later became CNO. We were very close and I feel sure he watched over me and my career before his untimely departure from this earth."

On 14 October 1989, Mazach was present at another change-of-command ceremony, as this time, he relieved Capt. John J. Coonan to

Change of Command ceremony October 1989, with Captain John J. Mazack (right) relieving Capt. John J. Coonan (courtesy John J. Mazach).

become the nineteenth Skipper of the USS *America*. "Timing is everything it is often said, and mine was superb in that after taking command of *America* in Monaco from my dear friend John Coonan and bringing the ship and air wing home, the ship went into the shipyard and stayed there until we started workups for our next deployment which was accelerated due to the events brewing in the Persian Gulf.

"As it turned out, we deployed on New Year's Day 1991 and steamed through the Mediterranean and into the Suez Canal with no stops. When we entered the Red Sea on 16 January, we were told to take station and be prepared to launch strikes into Iraq by 2:00 a.m. the following day. Desert Storm had begun. On the way over to the war, I was informed that I had been selected to the rank of Rear Admiral and, much to my chagrin, would have to leave the ship while the war continued without me. My tour on *America* was the most satisfying of any tour I had. I worked with some of the finest sailors and officers the Navy had to offer."

On 8 February 1991, at 10:00 a.m., in an informal ceremony adjacent to the carrier's island, Mazach turned over command of the *America* to

Capt. Kent W. Ewing as she steamed across the Red Sea. As the ship was at war, much of the pomp and ceremony was absent; however, Rear Adm. D. J. Katz, Commander, Cruiser-Destroyer Group Two, presented Captain Mazach the Legion of Merit Medal. The crew also found a way to express their feelings.[13]

Upon his departure from the *America*, Mazach was appointed Deputy Director for Plans and Policy with the United States European Command (USEUCOM), whose commander simultaneously served as Deputy to the Supreme Allied Commander, Europe (SACEUR) within NATO. Mazach recalled: "I departed America at sea during Desert Storm and eventually ended up In Stuttgart, Germany, for my first joint tour as a brand new one star Admiral. USEUCOM was the U.S. component to the Supreme Allied Commander Europe (SACEUR), a NATO Command. I worked as the Deputy J-5

A farewell from the crew (John J. Mazach).

for Air Force Maj. Gen. John Davey who was an absolute joy to work for, in an area that I had no experience whatsoever! We worked for a four–Star Air Force General, Jim McCarthy, and the command had been very busy with Desert Storm, and was just unwinding when I came onboard. I worked with Navy Admirals, Marine Generals as well as Army and Air Force general officers and a total mix of officers on their staffs. We all lived on base at Patch Barracks which had been a German tank base during World War II. I got to meet a lot of foreign Army, Navy, Air Force and Marines while a part of the J-5 and gained a great deal of experience. The leaders of the Army, Air force and Navy in Europe all worked for USEUCOM."

In June of 1993, Mazach took over command of Carrier Group Two (CARGRUTWO). The previous summer, the decision was made to more permanently affiliate escorts with the carriers they escorted and each of the twelve carrier battle groups would now consist of an aircraft carrier with an embarked carrier air wing, cruiser, destroyer, and frigate units; and two nuclear-powered attack submarines. For CARGRUTWO, this consisted of Carrier Air Wing Three (CVW-3) Destroyer Squadron Forty; the nuclear submarines USS *Seahorse* and USS *Albuquerque*; the guided-missile cruisers USS *Wainwright*, USS *Leyte Gulf*, and USS *Gettysburg*; and the carrier USS *John F. Kennedy*, which served as the battle group's flagship.[14]

"I took command of Carrier Group Two when I returned to the states from Stuttgart. Carrier Groups, not unlike Cruiser Destroyer Groups, are normally embarked in a carrier. When I was Chief of Staff at Cruiser Destroyer Group Eight, we deployed in *Theodore Roosevelt*. The chief of Staff of a Cruiser-Destroyer Group is always an aviator since the Admiral is a Surface Warrior. Aviation expertise and experience is needed at one of the two leadership positions. The Chief of Staff of a Carrier Group, which is always commanded by an aviator, is always a Surface Officer and is normally responsible for the ships in the Battle Group that are not carriers.

"Because of ships' schedules, we never deployed but we were able to do workups and short at-sea assignments to keep the staff's skills honed. A group staff is made up of mostly officers and a few enlisted support folks. The type of officers are varied, by design, including submarine types, surface types, aviators, supply types as well as communicators and systems types. Taking a group to sea involves many moving parts, from care and feeding of each ship (obviously each ship has a skipper and a full crew, but the Battle Group staff represents those individual ships to the group commander) to the port calls and schedules that change often on deployment. It was a great tour to learn about warfare at sea, both from a surface perspective and a submarine perspective, as I was already well versed on the aviation perspective."[15]

On 1 September 1994, Mazach was designated Rear Admiral (upper half) and was assigned as Director, Strategy and Policy Division in the Office of the Chief of Naval Operations (CNO).

"It was my first Pentagon tour. My shop, N51, worked on all of the policy issues for the CNO. The CNO while I was the N51 was Adm. Mike Boorda, with whom I had served under when I was his Chief of Staff at CRUDESGRU 8. The Vice Chief of Naval Operations at the time was a longtime friend and classmate from high school, Adm. Joe Prueher.

"As Director, I was a member of the Total Force Policy Board which meant I was the active duty contingent to the Naval Reserve Command. We also coordinated Navy Nuclear Weapons policy and wrote all of the briefs for support of the National Maritime Strategy, the National Military Strategy and the National Defense Strategy."

On 7 March 1996, Rear Admiral Mazach was designated a Vice Admiral and later that month, on 15 March 1996, he was appointed as Commander Naval Air Force, U.S. Atlantic Fleet (COMNAVAIRLANT). "I went to Norfolk right from the Pentagon and took command from my former CAG, and USS *America* CO, Vice Adm. Dick 'Sweetpea' Allen. Certainly at the time, it was the finest shore command in the Navy for an aviator. I say at the time, because, not too many years after I left in 1998, the Navy decided to make one Type Commander the lead dog and Commander Naval Air Forces Pacific Fleet (COMNAVAIRPAC) became the three star leader and assumed the title of Commander Naval Air Forces. COMNAVAIRLANT became a two-star billet working for COMNAVAIRFOR on the west coast.

"I had always chosen my aide from a group of very talented young officers who were above average F-18 Hornet pilots so I could take them flying when I flew and they could keep me out of trouble. I always flew single seat Hornets and when we flew we had two airplanes, one for the aide and one for the admiral! I flew with fleet squadrons and learned much about what was really going on in the fleet as a result, which was very valuable to me.

"My Chief of staff was in charge of a staff that was made up of enlisted, civilian and officers from all walks of life in the Navy (aviation maintenance, ship maintenance, supply, IT support, admin support, safety, and of course operational support.) The AIRLANT Staff took care of all things aviation on the east coast, deployed or based in home port, including the aircraft carriers assigned at that time to Commander In Chief Atlantic Fleet who was my four-star boss in Norfolk."[16]

Even as his career was coming to a close, Mazach, now a Vice Admiral knew that maintaining a knowledgeable and experienced work force was a key in accomplishing the Navy's mission.

"Probably one of the hardest things to do with a staff the size I had as COMNAVAIRLANT was to keep a good pulse on the real needs of the sailors and officers who manned the ships and airplanes that my command was responsible for. Retention of both officers and enlisted was much more difficult back in the mid-nineties then it is now and I worked hard with my Pacific counterpart, Vice Adm. Mike Bowman, who had been the CAG on *America* when I was CO, to make the Navy a place where folks wanted to stay and do good things. I think we had a good deal of success!"

Vice Adm. J. J. Mazach retired from the Navy on 31 December 1998, ending a naval career spanning more than thirty-two years. His awards include the Distinguished Service Medal, Defense Superior Service Medal, Legion of Merit (3 awards), Distinguished Flying Cross, Bronze Star, Air Medal with numeral 8, Navy Commendation Medal with Combat "V," and numerous campaign and commendation medals.

Mazach retired to Jacksonville, Florida, and promptly went to work for the Northrop Grumman Corporation. "My first day at work in a civilian job was at the same place as my first day at work in the fleet, Cecil Field Naval Air Station. We had spent many years there in the Navy and had many friends still there. It was almost like coming home."

Perhaps his sailors' affection for their skipper was best summed up by the banner that hung from the fantail as Mazach departed the *America* back in 1991; "We'd sail to Hell and Back with J. J. Mazach."

Notes

1. Interview with John J. Mazach, 3 March 2013.
2. USS *America* (CV-66) Virtual Museum http://ussamerica-museumfoundation. org/index.html.
3. "Carrier Air Wing One (CVW 1)." Global Security.org. http://www.globalsecurity. org/military/agency/navy/cvw1.htm.
4. Interview with John J. Mazach, 17 March 2013.
5. *Dictionary of American Naval Aviation Squadrons—Volume 1.*
6. Interview with John J. Mazach, 17 March 2013.
7. Ibid.
8. Ibid.
9. Interview with John J. Mazach, 27 March 2013.
10. Ibid.
11. Interview with John J. Mazach, 27 March 2013.
12. Ibid.

13. *America* (CV 66)—Naval Cruise Book—Class of 1991.
14. Polmar, Norman. *The Naval Institute Guide to the Ships and Aircraft of the U.S. Fleet,* 15th ed. Annapolis, Maryland: Naval Institute Press, 1993.
15. Interview with John J. Mazach, 5 April 2013.
16. Ibid.

Capt. Kent W. Ewing
(February 1991–August 1992)

> There were two ejections in my naval career. Some say I got mine and someone else's!—Captain Kent Ewing commenting on successfully surviving two ejections from the A-7E jet aircraft

If it can be said that being a combat pilot is "in the blood," then certainly that would apply to Capt. Kent Ewing. He was born in the midst of World War II, on 1 June 1943, the oldest of six children. His father was an Army Air Force Instructor Pilot at Goodfellow Field, outside San Angelo, Texas, who taught student pilots in the North American Aviation T-6 Texan, a single-engine advanced trainer aircraft used to train pilots of the United States Army Air Forces.

In April 1944, he moved with his pregnant mother to Eureka, Illinois, his father's hometown, when his father was sent overseas to Foggia, Italy, to fly B-17 bombers. His twin brothers were born on 20 June 1944, the year their father completed his fifty missions. "Eureka was the home of Eureka College, Ronald Reagan's Alma Mater, as well as my parents and all my aunts and uncles."

"Dad was a career USAF officer, who retired as the Senior Project Officer on the C-141 Starlifter aircraft in 1968. Post war, we lived at Warner Robbins AFB, Georgia, then we moved to Alexandria, Virginia,

Capt. Kent W. Ewing (courtesy Kent Ewing).

when dad was assigned duty at the Pentagon. From my first through tenth grade we lived in Oakwood, Ohio, a suburb of Dayton, while Dad did three tours of duty with the Air Force Institute of Technology (AFIT) and Flight Test Directorate at Wright Patterson AFB. AFIT is the Air Force's graduate school of engineering and management as well as its institution for technical professional continuing education."[1]

Young Ewing took to flying early on, encouraged by his father. "Growing up, we always had some kind of an airplane while my dad was alive. My early years in Dayton were wonderful! I flew Waco's and an old Seabee with dad from ages 10–15, and flew in the Aero Club at Eglin AFB."

When Ewing was in the tenth grade, his father was transferred to Eglin AFB, near Valparaiso, Florida, as project officer on the F-105 Thunderchief fighter-bomber. Not impressed with the academic opportunities available at Choctawatchee High School, his father enrolled him at the Georgia Military Academy, Atlanta, Georgia, for his junior and senior year. "I made good grades, made many lifelong friends and received appointments to the USCG academy, Merchant Marine academy, and earned standby appointments for Annapolis and West Point."[2]

Instead, Ewing attended the University of California—Los Angeles (UCLA) on an NROTC scholarship. "I got my private pilot's license while at UCLA under the Flight Introduction Program, offered by the Navy. This gave me a leg up later during flight school. I soloed in a T-34 Mentor (a military version of the Beechcraft Model 35 Bonanza) at the Aero Club at Norton AFB, San Bernardino, when I was nineteen, and I spent four wonderful years at UCLA."

In June 1965, Ewing graduated from UCLA with a B.S. in Economics, was commissioned an Ensign in the U.S. Navy and was ordered to report to Pensacola Naval Air Station, Florida, for flight training. Following initial training at NAS Saufley Field and primary flight training at NAS Whiting Field, Milton, Florida, flying the T-28 Trojan, Ewing was sent to NAS Corpus Christi in Texas for advanced flight training. "The chief of staff there interviewed me and told me my grades were such that they wanted me to go into jets. Foolishly, I turned them down because I wanted to fly the 'spad,' the huge single engine single seat A-1 Skyraider attack aircraft. They were already being given to the Vietnamese and the USAF, and the last Navy squadrons were transitioning to jets, but I was a dumb Ensign."

In August 1966, Ewing was designated a Naval Aviator and his father, now a colonel at Wright Patterson AFB, attended the ceremony and pinned on his wings of gold. Ewing was ordered back to Whiting Field as a Selectively Retained Graduate (SERGRAD) instructor pilot with Training Squadron Three (VT-3).

"I married my long time love, Ann Graves, in a double wedding with her sister and my brother in San Bernardino, California, and then we headed off to Whiting in our 1964 Porsche with a huge bag on the luggage rack. I had a wonderful time there flying four sorties a day. The war was on in Southeast Asia, and we were pumping out Marine helicopter pilots headed for Vietnam. The CO told me he was a spad pilot and he would get me orders to an A-1 squadron, but it never happened. I finally saw the light, went to Kingsville and transitioned to jets."

Upon reporting to NAAS Kingsville, outside Kingsville, Texas, in January 1969, Ewing was assigned to Training Squadron Twenty One (VT-21) "Redhawks," transitioning to the F-9F8 Cougar, a swept-wing carrier-based jet fighter, which was a variant of the F-9F Panther.

After carrier qualification aboard the USS *Lexington* (CV-16), Ewing was assigned to Attack Squadron Hundred Twenty Five (VA-125) "Rough Raiders" in April 1969, at NAS Lemoore, California, for Replacement Air Group (RAG) training. Currently designated as Fleet Replacement Squadron (FRS) the training is designed to prepare new and transitioning aviators for service with the fleet.

"I was fast-tracked through the RAG. We carrier qualified aboard the USS *Bennington*. This was my first night traps (landings). After ten day traps and six night traps, the Landing Signal Officer (LSO) told me I was doing so well that they were labeling me as a 'mustpump.' I did not know what that meant, except that they said I was going to get two more day and two more night traps. Great, I thought. I got to fly an aircraft home to Lemoore, which was walking in 'tall cotton' for a LTJG!"

The war in Vietnam was in full-swing, and the need for aviators was high, and "mustpump" was naval slang for "expedited replacement."

"Within a week, around the end of August 1969, Ann drove me to Travis Air Force Base and I was 'mustpumped' to VA-164, which was embarked with Air Wing 21 aboard the USS *Hancock* (CVA 19). I flew from Travis, near Fairfield, California, to NAS Cubi Point, Subic Bay in the Philippines. I then flew on a Carrier Onboard Delivery (COD) aircraft out to the USS *Hancock* (CVA-19), arriving in early September. My first flight with VA-164 was in combat."[3]

Assigned to Attack Squadron Hundred Sixty Four, "Ghost Riders," as part of Carrier Wing Twenty One (CVW-21), Ewing deployed twice to Vietnam aboard the *Hancock*, arriving at the beginning of the first deployment in September 1969 through 24 July 1970, and a second from 22 October 1970, through 3 June 1971. In all, Ewing flew two hundred combat missions, including Operation Freedom Bait, airstrikes against North Vietnamese anti-aircraft and missile sites south of the 19th parallel in response to attacks on unarmed RF-4 reconnaissance aircraft on 21–22 November. He also flew a diversionary attack on Haiphong Harbor to cover a covert, and ultimately unsuccessful, rescue of POWs from Son Tay Prison. Additionally, the squadron was involved with interdiction missions along the Ho Chi Minh trail, and received the Meritorious Unit Commendation from the Secretary of the Navy.[4]

The *Hancock* alternated duty at Yankee Station with two other carriers, the USS *Ranger* (CV-61) and USS *Kitty Hawk* (CV-63), until being relieved by the USS *Midway* (CV-41) on 10 May 1971.

Shortly after returning to NAS Lemoore in June 1971, Ewing received orders to report to the Pacific Missile Range at the Naval Air Missile Test Center (NAMTC), (currently the Naval Air Warfare Center-NAWC) at Point Mugu, California. Located adjoining Mugu Beach, reputed to be where Juan Cabrillo landed on 10 October 1542, the center was established in 1946 as a hub for missile research and development.

"At Point Mugu, I was introduced to the world of projects and testing. I flew the A-4, A-7, A-6, OV-10, T-28 and a leased Cessna 310 during my duty there and had many laser designator/laser 'Bulldog' missile projects. It was great duty, and while assigned there, my second application to test pilot school was accepted. In June 1973, we drove to Patuxent River Maryland, towing the '64 Porsche behind a 1972 Cadillac, at the height of the Jimmy Carter fuel crisis. We were rationed ten gallons at every stop!"

Ewing reported to NAS Patuxent River and was enrolled in the U.S. Naval Test Pilot School (TPS), the first class to take the twelve month course of instruction, extended from nine months, and he graduated in May 1974. Alumni of the Navy TPS include astronauts Alan Shepard, Scott Carpenter, Jim Lovell, Wally Schirra, John Young, John Glenn, Pete Conrad, Alan Bean, Mark Kelly, Richard Gordon, and Sunita Williams.

"The Navy Test Pilot's School was the most rigorous academic endeavor I ever attempted—one full year of flying, test writing, report writing, and Master Degree level aerodynamics. Luckily, the class had a bunch of smarter than me folks who helped me through the math, as the flying and report writing came easily. I flew all the aircraft on the school ramp: F-8 Crusader, T-38 Talon, A-4 Skyhawk, T-28 Trojan, OV-1 Mohawk, U-6A Beaver, U-1A Otter, and sail planes. To graduate we had to complete a full Naval Preliminary Evaluation of an aircraft we had never flown before, which included four flights or six hours, whichever came first. I wrote an eighty-five-page report on the F-4J Phantom as my graduation exercise.

"I stayed on there for three years, testing mostly out of control spins and departures in the T-34C turbo Mentor, the TA-7 Corsair II, and the TA-4J Skyhawk. I was the only Navy Test Pilot on the TAV8A two-seat Harrier project. I took it aboard all the aviation amphibs and carrier certified the USS *Franklin D. Roosevelt* (CVA 42) for Harriers so they could make their Mediterranean deployment with a Harrier squadron as part of the air wing. I made the first Harrier night carrier landing in May 1976."[5]

Ewing departed Patuxent River in October 1976, and following attendance at the United States Navy Strike Fighter Tactics Instructor program (SFTI program), more popularly known as Top Gun in November and December 1976, at the former Naval Air Station Miramar in California, he reported to VA-174 "Hellrazors" in January 1977 for RAG training. The squadron's skipper was Cdr. John S. McCain III, son and grandson of admirals and a future U.S. Senator and Presidential candidate.

"After three years and 650 accident free testing hours as a test pilot, I was ordered back to the fleet, headed for my Department Head tour in VA 86, aboard the USS *Nimitz*. During that transition, I interviewed and took a five-day physical with NASA. I was among the first group to be interviewed for the Space Shuttle program. I went to Houston, and then on to RAG training, before reporting to VA 86."

In May 1977, Ewing reported to Attack Squadron Eighty Six (VA-86) "Sidewinders" at NAS Cecil Field, and the squadron embarked on 1 December as part of Air Wing Eight (CVW-8) aboard the USS *Nimitz* (CVN-68) for a deployment to the North Atlantic and Mediterranean that official records describe as "uneventful." It was anything but uneventful for the squadron's thirty-five-year-old Maintenance Officer, Lieutenant Commander Ewing.

On 17 January 1978, he and another of the squadron's A-7E Corsairs were engaged in simulated combat with two F-14 Tomcats of VF-84.

"It was a cold, rainy, windy day over the Tyrrhenian Sea, part of the Mediterranean Sea off the western coast of Italy. *Nimitz* was coming out of a port visit to Naples, and had rounded Stromboli Island. The sea and the weather were awful. We were all suited up in our survival suits, when flight operations were cancelled. Two hours or so later, the weather improved and we were immediately sent to flight quarters. This time, I was in such a rush I did NOT put on my 'poopy suit' (cold weather survival gear). This was a bad mistake.

"I was flying wing on the squadron XO, Cdr. Bernie Smith, on an air to air mission against two F14s from VF 84. I took on a high side sidewinder shot on one of them, and flew very close to the aft end of an F-14 in full zone 5 afterburner, while pulling about twenty units angle of attack. In other words I was fairly loaded up as I was taking my 'pretend' shot. The next thing I knew my airplane was catapulted/thrown/ launched into a spin at about 14,000 feet.

"I wasn't overly worried. I had been there before. I was the spin guru from Patuxent, right? Well this one went flat, a very flat upright spin with rather fast rotation. This was very unusual for an A7, which usually pops right out of uncontrolled flight when you just let go of the stick and 'wind your watch' while it recovers!

"Not that day! She spun right on down. I was supposed to eject at 10,000 feet but I rode it to about 4,800, then pulled the lower handle, looked up to see a good chute of orange and white and then looked between my boots to see the A7 still spinning right below me into the water!

I survived the ejection, now what? I wondered. I went into the 48-degree waters of the North Tyrrhenian Sea with twenty-five plus knots of wind and about 15–18 foot waves. I had never been colder. My raft did not inflate so I was floating using my survival vest/horse collar floatation and trying to keep my hands from freezing. I was barely able to pop the flare for the helo to see me and the wind direction. After 30–45 minutes in the water, the core temperature got pretty well down there. The helicopter rescue was led by my combat experienced XO and when I was finally back aboard, I was barely able to talk or walk due to cold. An accident investigation found that the aircraft was bent from having run off the runway at Cecil Field the year before and had high angle of attack anomalies, so it of course did not act like a regular (not wrecked and repaired) A7 Corsair II. I flew the next day. My neck was stiff, but I climbed back on the horse."[6]

That same January, Ewing received a telegram from NASA advising him that he had not been selected for the Space Shuttle Program. The *Nimitz* returned to her homeport of Norfolk, Virginia, on 20 July 1978.

"I found out on my return that I had been selected for the program, but the list had changed and I had been replaced with a female mission specialist, Judy Resnick, who later died on her third trip into space when the shuttle Challenger exploded shortly after liftoff.

"I went to a Society of Experimental Test Pilots (SETP) convention in Los Angeles in September 1978, and met Ms. Resnik, who informed me that I WAS on the original pilot list, but NASA HQ had done the 'PC' (politically correct) thing and put her and an African-American on the list. She was really upset and told me to 'call George Abbey and tell him that I should be selected on the next round.' I said, 'No, they only get one shot.' I had already screened for Command so I pursued a Navy career instead of a career as a NASA astronaut."

In July 1979, Ewing transferred to Attack Squadron Sixty Six (VA-66) "Waldos" at NAS Cecil Field and reported in as the squadron's new executive officer. On 4 November 1979, a group of Islamist students and militants supporting the Iranian Revolution took over the American Embassy in Tehran, taking fifty-two Americans hostage, initiating a stand-off between the United States and Iran that would last 444 days, and become known as the Iranian Hostage Crisis.

On 15 April 1980, VA-66 deployed to the Indian Ocean as part of Air Wing Seven (CVW-7) aboard the nuclear carrier USS *Dwight D. Eisenhower* (CVN-69) in response to the Iran hostage crisis, with Rear Adm. Byron Fuller the embarked flag. She relieved the USS *Nimitz* three days after the failed attempt to rescue the Iranian hostages, Operation Eagle Claw, on 24 April 1980, which resulted in the deaths of eight American servicemen, one Iranian civilian, and the destruction of two aircraft.[7]

Due to continuing tensions in the area, *Eisenhower* remained on station off the coast of Iran for over eight months. It was during this period that Commander Ewing experienced his second ejection.

On 11 October 1980, Ewing relieved Cdr. Frank H. Gerwe, Jr., as skipper of VA-66. Nine days later, on 20 October 1980, Ewing was leading a flight of A-7s over the Arabian Sea:

> I was Commanding Officer of the "Waldos," leading a four plane flight with two "nuggets" on their first flight in the squadron. I was leading the nuggets through some formation acrobatics and at the top of a barrel roll, at about 14,500 feet, I felt the engine surge and quit, actually throwing me forward into the straps a bit.
>
> I rolled upright, deployed the Ram Air Turbine (RAT) to maintain electrical power and went into the relight procedure. I never got any fuel flow as I glided at 220 knots and I knew it was not going to relight, so I told the "wingies" I would be stepping out, and to get their cameras out to film the ejection. I lowered my seat, took off the kneeboard, glided to 5,000 feet, and made a picture perfect controlled ejection using the face curtain actuator.
>
> I landed into a flat calm sea with sea snakes and sharks aplenty. My major worry was getting fouled in the chute as it almost came down on top of me. I immediately got into the raft as there were sharks all around me. I told the helicopter crew not to put a guy in the water, however, they did anyway. He

came swimming up to me with a knife in his teeth. He said he had to deflate the raft.

Uneventful hoist and fly back to the ship. This time I flew again five days later after recovering from some windblast damage stretching the muscles of my left eye. Engine failure was probably due to a main fuel pump failure.

After a total of 254 days at sea, *Eisenhower* returned to Norfolk on 22 December 1980.

"We flew off the *Eisenhower* on 21 December 1980, headed for home to Cecil Field, where we were treated to a great homecoming by the squadron wives and future *America* CO, Capt. Leighton "Snuffy" Smith, ComLatWing One. Present were the Mayors of the cities around Jax (Jacksonville).

"As CO of the Waldos, I deployed for work ups to Roosevelt Roads in March of '81, then to NAS Fallon in Nevada from April through May '81."

NAS Fallon is home to the Naval Fighter Weapons School (Top Gun), and the surrounding area contains 84,000 acres of bombing and electronic warfare ranges. It is the Navy's premier air-to-air and air-to-ground training facility.

"I was back aboard 'Ike' in June 1981 for our work ups; then we sailed to St .Thomas for a port visit over the July 4th holiday."

Ewing made a second deployment aboard *Eisenhower* with VA-66, this time to the North Atlantic, from 20 August through 7 October 1981. "We sailed north of the Arctic Circle on a NATO operation and I made a zero/zero landing in the fog off of Norway when the ship was suddenly caught in heavy fog. I could not have landed were it not for the ACLS Mode I system working perfectly. We returned to Cecil Field from 6 October through 28, then we were back aboard 'Ike' until 23 November, then spent Thanksgiving and Christmas at home."

Shortly after departing on a third deployment on 5 January 1982, for a cruise to the Mediterranean, Ewing was relieved by Cdr. Richard D. Lichtermann, II on 5 February 1982.

"My last flight as CO of VA-66 was on 28 January 1982, with the last of my 344 traps on the *Eisenhower*. The change of command took place on board *Eisenhower* while in port at Naples, Italy. Ann flew over and Captain Clexton, captain of the *Eisenhower*, was the guest speaker. My XO, Cdr. David Lichtermann, one of the finest Naval Officers I have ever known, took command of VA 66.

"Ann and I visited Gaeta, Italy, before flying back home as it would be our next duty station, assigned as the Chief of Staff for Aviation on the Commander Sixth Fleet staff, based on board USS *Puget Sound* home ported in Gaeta, Italy. It was a NATO refueling site between Rome and Naples.

"We rented out the Jacksonville home, packed up and reported in. I served as the aviation advisor to Vice Adm. Bill Rowden, Commander Sixth Fleet. We reported aboard around the time of the Red Brigade kidnapping of Brig. Gen. James Dozier. It was a scary time. All staff officers above the rank of Commander were issued a gun permit and a 9 mm pistol for personal protection. I was less than comfortable for our six-year-old daughter to go to school there. She started first grade at the small school in Gaeta, and her Italian got to be pretty good! We lived in a villa in Formia and Ann and Alexis and many of the staff wives followed the ship from port to port and visited many Mediterranean sites. Regretfully, I never got them to Israel, because there was too much terrorism."[8]

In May 1982, Vice Adm. William Rowden, was responsible for the operational control of all naval task forces, battle groups, amphibious forces, support ships, land-based surveillance aircraft and submarines operating in the Mediterranean Sea.

"My main memories of staff duty consist of the many exercises we held in the Gulf of Sirta, asserting our rights for Freedom of Navigation (FON Ops) and 'tweaking' Ghadaffi at every opportunity. During this time, the Embassy and the Marine Barracks were blown up in Lebanon and the Israelis shot down over eighty Syrian (Russian) fighters using F-15 and F-16 aircraft. My job was to keep count on those aerial victories and all the goings on in Libya, Lebanon, and Israel. It was a turbulent time in the Mediterranean area of operations."

In December 1982, Ewing was assigned as a special assistant for aviation to Adm. Bill Crowe, who was CINC South, a four-star NATO billet, headquartered in Naples, Italy!!

"It was my Christmas present from Vice Admiral Rowden. Admiral Crowe was in the process of having the four-star command in Naples assume the position as Commander In Chief—U.S. Naval Forces Europe (CINCUSNAVEUR), reporting to Gen. Bernie Rodgers at SHAPE HQ in Brussels. So I commuted from 'home' in Formia for the next six months to serve one of the best admirals in the U.S. Navy. Crowe later became CINCPAC and then Chairman of the Joint Chiefs under Ronald Reagan. Admiral Crowe, a submariner, benefitted from my aviation knowledge and appreciated the commute I was making. He and his wife, Shirley, made Italian social life a pleasure for Ann and me."

On 23 March 1984, Ewing took command of Carrier Air Wing Seventeen (CVW-17), headquartered at NAS Oceana, Virginia. The air wing flew down to Mayport, Florida, for its first deployment aboard the USS *Saratoga* (CV-60) and departed for the Mediterranean on 2 April 1984.

"I had received orders to take command of Carrier Air Wing Eight, embarked in USS *Nimitz*. Ann was six months pregnant with Taylor, while we hunted for a house in Virginia Beach. Interest rates were 14 percent, nothing was on the market, but we found our house on Linkhorn Bay and I started pre–CAG training at VF-101 at Oceana, flying the F-14. The schedule looked ideal because CVW-8 and the *Nimitz* were just commencing their pre-deployment work ups. There would be time for Ann to have a baby and me to fix up the house before I deployed. It was not to be. While I was finishing up carrier qualification in the F14, I received verbal orders to Air Wing Seventeen (CVW-17) and the *Saratoga* to relieve the CAG there early and be ready for possible early deployment .

"I assumed command of CVW-17, and it was a really interesting conglomeration of squadrons that had not jelled during workups. It included the last two fighter squadrons to transition from F-4 to F-14s (VF-74 and VF-103), a Marine A-6 Intruder squadron (VMAW-533), a Marine EA-6B Prowler command, VAW-125 flying the E-2C Hawkeye, attack squadrons VA-81 and VA-83 flying the A-7 Corsair II, VS-30 in the S-3, and HS-11 in the SH-3 Helo.

"We made a fairly typical deployment to Mediterranean and by the time we 'in chopped' to Sixth fleet we were ready for any tasking. We did the normal FON operations off Libya and planned strikes into Lebanon, but we never executed them.

"I made my 1,000th carrier landing in an A-7E from VA-81 in the same sortie that Capt. Jack Ready, the Saratoga's commanding officer, made his. We celebrated the occasion with Rear Adm. Jerry Tuttle, our embarked Battle Group Commander, also holder of more than 1,000 traps.

"We returned home on 20 October 1984, and I worked up the air wing for the next CAG to take on deployment. Admiral Crowe made room in his busy schedule between CINCPAC and Chairman, Joint Chiefs, to be my guest speaker when I turned over the Air Wing in August 1985."[9]

Ewing next reported for duty as the Tactical Air Analyst in the Office of Program Appraisal (OPA) on the staff of the Secretary of the Navy, John Lehman, at the Pentagon, Washington, D.C.

"It was an interesting time in our Navy, as John Lehman was building the six hundred ship Navy! I almost actually enjoyed going to work at the Pentagon, or the 'world's largest adult day care center' as it was known to many. I worked for two aviator admirals, both future four-star admirals, Rear Adm. Bud Edney and Rear Adm. Jerry Johnson, both of whom were highly respected.

"In 1986, the Navy was booming. That was the year that *Top Gun*, the movie and *Hunt for Red October*, the book, were released and there were 35,000 applications to Annapolis. The most significant event was my being consulted once again as an Aviation expert to Admiral Crowe, then Chairman of the JCS. His exec called me in for a private meeting with the Chairman to assist in the planning for Operation El Dorado Canyon which was the April 1986 raid on Libya. We discussed rules of engagement (ROE), names of leaders of the three carriers, etc. I reminded the Chairman that he had actually met the CO of *Saratoga* and the CAG at my change of command in Mayport."

During his time at the Pentagon, Ewing attended a semester as a Fellow at the International Relations course at the John F. Kennedy School of Government at Harvard University.

Following his Pentagon assignment, Ewing reported to Newport, Rhode Island, to attend the Senior Officers Ship Material Readiness Course (SOSMRC) in preparation for taking command of a naval vessel. The five-month course of instruction was designed to provide prospective commanding and executive officers with core knowledge and skills to include damage control procedures and equipment operation, materiel self-assessment and shipboard safety requirements, to better prepare them for their upcoming command.[10]

"We moved the family back into our home in Virginia Beach and I reported for a five-month course in Newport, Rhode Island. This was 'black shoe' (sea-going as opposed to 'brown shoe'/naval aviator) country. We had a very enjoyable time there as I prepared for Deep Draft Command of the USS *Sylvania*, and I left there feeling well prepared."

The USS *Sylvania* (AFS-2) was a *Mars*-class Combat Stores Ship with the mission of resupplying the fleet while underway and was a pioneer in the use of helicopters for "vertical replenishment" (VERTREP) which significantly reduced the time necessary for alongside replenishment. She carried two UH-46 Sea Knight helicopters and her cargo capacity of 7,300 tons included provisions, supplies, ammunition and aviation fuel, all but the fuel deliverable by air.

On 24 October 1987, Ewing relieved Capt. Hugh D. Wisely to take command of the *Sylvania* and in January 1988, the ship deployed to the Mediterranean.

"I assumed command on a sunny Saturday, pier side in Miami, Florida. What followed was routine work ups, a Board of Inspection Survey, which I recall was a really tough inspection, and our Mediterranean Deployment. We serviced two battle groups and the Mediterranean Amphibious Ready Group (ARG) during our deployment.

"Due to the mission to carry fresh food to the ships underway, we made many port visits. I learned much about ship handling, with and without tugboats. We experienced a wonderful Easter port visit to the port of Malaga during the Semana Santa (Holy Week) celebration there."

On 5 May 1989, Ewing turned over command of *Sylvania* to Capt. William H. Kennedy, but he remained at Norfolk, taking the assignment as Assistant Chief of Staff for Operations and Readiness on the staff of Commander Naval Air Forces Atlantic (COMNAVAIRLANT), reporting to Vice Adm. Jack Ready.

COMNAVAIRLANT exercised administrative control (ADCON), and in some cases operational control (OPCON) of ships, submarines, aircraft, and fleet marines assigned to the Atlantic Fleet, as well as the material readiness, administration, training, and inspection of units/squadrons under his command, and was additionally responsible for providing operationally ready air squadrons and aircraft carriers to the fleet.

"I turned over command of *Sylvania* to Bill Kennedy in port at Norfolk. We were celebrating the ship's 25th anniversary and I invited as many of former COs as could attend. The guest speaker was Commander Naval Air Forces Atlantic, Vice Adm. Jack Ready, my former CO of *Saratoga* when I was the CAG, and future boss. I reported to the staff of CNAL while awaiting screening for Carrier Command."

As it turned out, Ewing would assume command of one of the nation's mightiest warships at sea, while the nation was at war. On 8 February 1991, at 10:00 a.m., in an informal ceremony, Capt. J.J. Mazach turned over command of the carrier USS *America* to Ewing, the twentieth man to command her.

"The Change of Command ceremony took place in Khakis on the flight deck while in the Red Sea. We were ordered to join three other carriers in the Persian Sea as the fourth carrier and we entered the Strait of Hormuz on 13 February 1991. Two days later, on 15 February, we made our first launch in support of General Schwarzkopf's mighty end run into Iraq and we launched thirty aircraft up at dawn. During the recovery, an A-6 Intruder had total hydraulic failure resulting in no brakes and no nose wheel steering. Both crew ejected as the nose dropped over the 'crotch.' I now had a 'hood

Captain Ewing signing 500-pound bombs for delivery into Iraq, February 1991 (courtesy Kent Ewing).

ornament' with twenty plus aircraft waiting to land, refuel, rearm and get back to the war. Within twenty minutes, we shoved it into the gulf and recovered the rest of the air wing."[11]

Less than a month earlier, at 2:00 a.m. on 17 January 1991, Operation Desert Shield had transitioned into Operation Desert Storm, and the United States had initiated air strikes into Iraq.

"I got to fly two combat missions in the S-3 aircraft, the first time to look at the burning oil wells set afire by Sadaam, and on the second, I got to see the 'Highway to Hell' from Kuwait north into Iraq."

The *America* remained in the region through the beginning of the ground war on 24 February and the ceasefire four days later on 28 February.

"We were visited by Adm. Bud Edney, the Commander-in-Chief Atlantic Fleet (CINCLANTFLT) who was getting briefed on the war effort. He asked me if we could turn the *America* around in seven months, versus the normal eighteen months, in order to get the carrier deployment schedule back on track. I said, 'Sure,' but the biggest problem would be one of morale, which could be mitigated if *America* was the ship chosen for Fleet Week and the 'mother of all parades' being planned by Mayor Dinkins! He said he could most likely make that happen, and he did!

"At one point, during February, we had a four carrier formation in the Persian Gulf Battle Group with USS *Midway* and USS *Ranger* in front with USS *America* and USS *Theodore Roosevelt* bringing up the rear, which required some very precise ship handling and made for a great photo. I had never seen four aircraft carriers in formation, either before or since. It also made America the only carrier to operate on both sides of the Arabian Peninsula.

"Going home, we made a fast transit up the Red Sea doing twenty-five knots in the fog and at night in order to make the northbound convoy for the Suez Canal. It was my first Suez Canal transit."

After transiting the Suez Canal, *America* sailed for home, returning to Pier 12 at Norfolk on 18 April 1991. By the time the USS *America* departed the Persian Gulf, she had conducted 3,008 sorties and dropped over 2,000 tons of ordnance without the combat loss of a single aircraft.[12]

"It was the greatest homecoming I have ever experienced with over 25,000 folks on the pier. Ann had been managing all the details such as arranging places to stay for those coming from out of town. We could not hear the docking pilots on the hand-held radios because the crowd and bands were so loud! It was a wonderful day, and it made up for eggs that were dropped on the USS *Hancock* when we came home while sailing under the Golden Gate Bridge in 1970."

Good to his promise, Admiral Edney arranged for the *America* to represent the fleet during Fleet Week in New York City.

"We had the shortest yard period on record! We bribed all the yard-birds with pictures and war memorabilia so they would work hard and fast. We told them about Fleet Week and that President Bush would be on board.

"We sailed out of Norfolk at the end of May looking really sharp, and we flew on twenty-five airplanes and then headed for Fleet Week in New York City. We arrived at Sandy Hook/Verrazano Bridge on 31 May, and anchored out with USS *Wisconsin* while waiting for the cruise ships to clear the piers. It seemed the whole city worked to accommodate all the military for the parade.

"On Sunday, 2 June, we moved the *America* from anchorage to Pier 42, one pier north of the USS *Intrepid* Museum. We had over 25,000 visitors per day while we were pier side.

"On Monday, 10 June, the ship and many of the sailors and officers were interviewed starting at 7:30 a.m. with Joan Lunden from Good Morning America. After my interview, we boarded the Captain's Gig and sailed down the Hudson to the Marina near the World Trade Center and we docked next to Donald Trump's mega yacht.

"I was taken to the parade formation site to lead over five hundred *America* sailors up Broadway. Cag Bowman and I led the troops. We walked behind Secretary of Defense Dick Cheney and Generals Colin Powell and Norman Schwarzkopf and their staffs. It was the greatest ticker tape parade ever."

Following Operation Coming Home in New York City, *America* took to the sea again in August, this time on an eight-week deployment to the North Atlantic, to participate in the NATO exercise Northstar 91.

"We sailed with Rear Adm. Fred Lewis, Commander Carrier Group Four and his staff embarked, and the Vice Admiral in command of the Second Fleet embarked in the USS *Mount Whitney* (LCC-20) in the Battle Group.

"The exercise was to operate a carrier battle group in the Vest Fjord, off Bodo, Norway, and practice Anti-Submarine Warfare (ASW) operations to test the theory that the walls of the Fjord would prevent Soviet anti-ship missiles from targeting the carrier.

"We had tight operating parameters, but the *America* was used to tight operations following the Desert Storm operations in the Persian Sea. We were opposed by two U.S. nuclear submarines and one nuclear submarine from Great Britain, as well as some Dutch diesel boats. We set up some really innovative ASW operations, to include darkening the ship which hadn't been done since World War II, and it seemed to work. We were in the fjord for 4–6 days, operating day and night operations and were never touched by a submarine. Next, we operated in an even smaller fjord down south, the first and last time ever. All of the crew received 'Blue Nose' certificates for operating above the Arctic Circle."

The *America* returned home in October and immediately began preparations for their "turnaround" deployment, including a boiler/engineering operation inspection.

"We sailed out to sea on 28–31 October for the boiler trials. This is when the 'Perfect Storm' formed up and hit us. Forty to fifty foot seas, but luckily we had not planned for any flight operations. We had two helicopters onboard, and we triple lashed them down behind the island and kept her fair to the wind and seas, to avoid heavy rolls.

"The night of 29 October, we were called by a U.S. Coast Guard C-130 to see if we could assist in a rescue of the *Anna Christina*, a 105-year old, three-masted schooner that was foundering about 100–150 miles to the East of our position, in the middle of the storm in seventy-foot seas!

"I said, 'Sure, but I'm not going to steam to the East.' We were the 'Lilly Pad' for two SH-60 USCG helos from Elizabeth City that landed at about midnight, refueled, and headed East. They were gone for about 3–4 hours and rescued nine people one at a time from the schooner, then returned to our ship really low on fuel. We gave the victims food, refueled the helicopters, and they took the crew to shore.

"This did not make the newspapers, as the fishing fleet up north got all the news coverage, however the helicopter pilots got Air Medals and DFCs, and some of my crew were also awarded medals. I was made an honorary Coast Guardsman."

On 2 December 1991, *America* departed on her second deployment in a year, bound for the Mediterranean, Indian Ocean, Red Sea, and the Persian Gulf, becoming the first carrier to redeploy to the region, following the Gulf War.

"We left sometime around the first week in December bound for the Mediterranean Sea and to the Persian Gulf. We made port in Naples for Christmas. There were three USSR ships in the harbor; two combatants and one merchant. I watched at noon on 25 December 1991, as the Hammer and Sickle flag went down and the white, red and blue Russian flag went up on the three ships! I said out loud 'We just won the Cold War.' My chiefs went to the nearest warship and got me one of the Soviet Union flags and presented it to me later at my farewell party."

Following port visits in Athens, Greece, Antalya, Turkey, and Haifa, Israel, *America* transited the Suez Canal into the Persian Gulf. Prepared for difficulties, the cruise was uneventful. Following regional exercises, *America* transited back through the Suez Canal, returning home on 6 June 1992.

"The ship went into dry dock and a major yard period and plans were made for my change of command which would occur while we were in the ship yard, that is, a high security environment resulting in lots of extra things to consider but we pulled it off. It was a great ceremony with Vice Adm. Tony Less, Commander, Naval Air Forces—Atlantic (CNAL), as the speaker. It was a great end to the best job I would ever have."

Ewing's final assignment was to the staff of the Chief of Naval Operations at the Pentagon in OP 80, responsible for generating a budget for the entire U.S. Navy.

"My immediate boss was Rear Adm. Dave Oliver, who, although a brilliant attack submariner, thought we only needed seven to nine carriers! His

Together on Dependents Day Cruise in 1992 were three commanders of USS *America*: RADM Laurie Heyworth (USN, Ret.), first CO; Captain Ewing; and RADM By Fuller (USN, Ret.), 10th CO (courtesy Kent Ewing).

boss was Vice Adm. Bill Owens who had arrived from the Sixth Fleet, where he had embarked in *America* less than a year before. The entire Navy was being run by nuclear submariners who had little to zero knowledge of carrier battle group operations. It was a scary time especially after Bill Clinton became President.

"I watched as Les Aspin, the newly appointed Secretary of Defense (SECDEF) and four of his Capitol Hill staff took $50 Billion out of the Defense budget between 20 January and mid–March! That is when I put in my retirement papers. I left the Pentagon on April Fool's Day 1993 and I never looked back. It was the best move I ever made. I now believe I should have walked off the *America* into retirement."

Captain Ewing retired from the Navy after a twenty-eight year career, with service in three wars and 220 combat missions. His combat decorations include the Bronze Star Medal, fifteen Air Medals (Strike/Flight) and three Navy Commendation Medals with combat "V."

With 6,000 military flight hours and 1,120 carrier landings on eighteen different aircraft carriers, Captain Ewing transitioned easily into civilian life where he has added 9,500 flight hours, flying with Leitch, Inc., the Eclipse Aircraft Corporation, the Beechcraft Pilot Training Group, and ATAC, ATSI (two Civil Aviation Advisory Organizations under contract to the Government). He is type rated in the L39, the Douglas A4, the Hawker Hunter, and the Eclipse 500. Ewing says of his retirement, "After 47 years, I'm still married to my beautiful Ann and I still drive that 1964 Porsche."

Notes

1. Interview with Kent Ewing, 17 May 2013.
2. Ibid.
3. Interview with Kent Ewing, 26 May 2013.
4. Gargus, John. *The Son Tay Raid: American POWs in Vietnam Were Not Forgotten.* College Station: Texas A&M University Press, 2010.
5. Interview with Kent Ewing, 17 May 2013.
6. Ibid.
7. Iran–U.S. Hostage Crisis http://www.historyguy.com/iran-us_hostage_crisis.html #.UafsyqPn_IU.
8. Interview with Kent Ewing, 4 June 2013.
9. Ibid.
10. Naval Surface Force Public Affairs" http://www.navy.mil/submit/display.asp?story_id=50963
11. Interview with Kent Ewing, 21 June 2013.
12. USS America CV-66 http://militarysnooze.tripod.com/america.htm.

Capt. William W. Copeland, Jr.
(August 1992–February 1994)

I squeezed off my AIM-9 Sidewinder at the lead MiG.... The Winder hit the MiG at the wing root, severing both wings from the aircraft; we were at 500 feet above the ground so the MiG went in right away...."[1]

William W. Copeland, Jr., was born in Buenos Aires, Argentina, in 1944. The son of a career Foreign Service Officer, he entered the Navy in 1965 through the Aviation Officer Candidate Program. He graduated from Virginia Polytechnic Institute (Bachelor of Science in Electrical Engineering) and was commissioned in 1967. He received Master of Science degrees from the University of Southern California in 1980, and from the Naval War College in 1985.

Designated a Naval Aviator in 1968, he reported to Fighter Squadron One Fifty One flying the F-4 Phantom and in 1970 joined Fighter Squadron Fifty One for their transition from the F-8 Crusader to the F-4 Phantom. The squadron had become known as MiG killers when squadron pilots shot down two North Vietnamese MiG-21s in 1968 and four MiG-17s in 1971. Copeland and his flight leader bagged two more MiG-17s in 1972 during the squadron's deployment aboard the USS *Coral Sea* (CVA-43).[2] He recalled the shoot-down as follows:

Capt. William W. Copeland, Jr. (official U.S. Navy photograph).

"On 11 June 1972, a Sunday morning, I was launched in an F-4B with Don Bouchoux my RIO, and Commander (Tooter) Teague, skipper, as my flight lead. We were the MiG Cap for the strike group holding between the Thanh Hoa area and Hanoi. I had lost my radios. I looked up and the fight was on when I spotted four MiG-17s. I broke hard to the outside to place nose-to-tail separation from the lead MiGs. I always told myself, when given a choice, shoot the leader first. I squeezed off an AIM-9 Sidewinder at the lead MiG that was preparing to "gun" Tooter and his RIO Ralph Howell. The winder hit the MiG at the wingroot, severing both wings from the aircraft; we were at five hundred feet above the ground so the MiG went in right away.

"Tooter fired several winders at the MiG leader's wingman, scoring a kill himself. I started to chase the other two MiGs who were running North, but decided I could not leave my skipper alone. I came back with him, and we proceeded back out to the coast. Along this journey, at a very low altitude, I got hit with small arms fire. We spoke about ejecting, but decided to stay with the jet until we got feet wet.

"Upon going feet wet, we shut down the burning engine, and again decided not to eject. Though the fire light was out, the boat would not take us as they saw us steaming black smoke. Upon holding for the returning airwing to land, the black smoke dissipated, and we were permitted to land. It was a hot day, so we needed a little 'afterburner' in the groove. When we hit the deck, we were covered with foam—the fire had been so intense that it had welded the sparrow missile to the fuselage. Why it never cooked off, God only knows. The aircraft never flew again! Today it is on a pedestal in front of a VFW club in Olean, New York."[3]

Following instructor duty at the Navy Fighter Weapons School (Top Gun) from 1972 to 1975 he returned to Fighter Squadron One Fifty One embarked aboard the USS *Midway* (CV 41) homeported in Yokosuka, Japan. In 1978 he attended the United States Test Pilot School at Edwards Air Force base and upon completion reported to the Naval Air Test Center, Patuxent River, Maryland.

Copeland joined Fighter Squadron One Hundred Two in July 1981 as Executive Officer and assumed command in November 1982. In March 1984, he joined Commander Task Force Sixty Staff in Naples, Italy. He was assigned to the Senior Course at the Naval War College in Newport, Rhode Island, in August 1984 and in 1985 became the F-14 Program Coordinator within the office of the Deputy Chief of Naval Operations for Air Warfare. Copeland was ordered to command Carrier Air Wing One on board USS *America* (CV 66) from July 1986 to February 1988. He assumed command of the USS *San Diego* (AFS 6) from October 1988 to April 1990, and served as the Current Operations Officer (J33) for the Operations Director at the U.S. Atlantic Command from May 1990 to May 1992. He then took over the helm of the USS *America* from August 1992 to February 1994. He attended the Senior Officer National Security at Harvard University, and was subsequently the Deputy Director for Operations at U.S. Central Command, MacDill Air Force base, Tampa, Florida, from September 1994 to March 1997. Copeland next attended the National Strategy Leadership Course at Johns Hopkins University from April through May 1997, and assumed command of Carrier Group Eight in August 1997.[4]

Military Awards

During his naval aviation career Copeland accumulated over three hundred combat missions, 1,300 carrier arrested landings, and five thousand flight hours in thirty different types of aircraft, including the F-14 (Tomcat), F-15 (Eagle), F-16 (Falcon), F-17 (Thunder), and F-18 (Hornet). His personal awards include the Silver Star, two Defense Superior Service Medals, two Legion of Merit Medals, a Meritorious Service Medal, Sixteen Air Medals, One Air Medal Gold Star, Navy Commendation Medal with Combat "V" and four Gold Stars in lieu of subsequent awards, the Navy Achievement Medal and numerous commendations, campaign medals and ribbons.[5]

Copeland retired from Naval service as a Rear Admiral in 2000. After retirement he worked at Sun Microsystems Federal, Inc., specializing in business development and account management until 2009. Presently, he is President of WWC Consulting, LLC, working as an Executive Coach who advises CEOs and their teams how to become more effective leaders.[6]

Notes

1. Correspondence with Rear Adm. William W. Copeland, Jr., USN (Ret.), January 2013.
2. Official Biography of Rear Adm. William W. Copeland, Jr., USN (Ret.), Navy History and Heritage Command, Washington, D.C.
3. Correspondence with Rear Adm. William W. Copeland, Jr., USN (Ret.), January 2013.
4. Official Biography of Rear Adm. William W. Copeland, Jr., USN (Ret.), Navy History and Heritage Command, Washington, D.C.
5. Ibid.
6. Winstoncopeland.com/about us

Capt. Ralph E. Suggs
(February 1994–September 1995)

> My family has a long history of military service, dating back to the Civil War, World War I, World War II and Korea. It was expected that we would serve our country in some capacity.—Suggs commenting in the *North Carolina State University Magazine* on his upbringing.

Ralph E. "Benny" Suggs, a native of Whiteville, North Carolina, graduated from North Carolina State University in May 1969. He was commissioned an Ensign through the Naval Aviation Officer Candidate Program in February 1970, and earned his Naval Aviator wings in Kingsville, Texas, in May 1971 following advanced jet training.[1]

Upon completion of A-6 Intruder replacement pilot training in Attack Squadron Forty-Two, Suggs reported to Attack Squadron Seventy-Five, where he served as Squadron First Lieutenant, Line Division Officer, NATOPS

Officer, and Landing Signal Officer (LSO). After two Mediterranean deployments in USS *Saratoga* (CV-60. He returned to Attack Squadron Forty-
Two as an instructor Pilot and Carrier Qualification Phase Head. Upon
completion of A-7E cross training in April 1979, he was assigned to Carrier
Air Wing Six as Air Wing LSO, and deployed in USS *Independence* (CV-
62). Following six months at the Armed Forces Staff College in Norfolk,
Virginia, and a brief reassignment to Attack Squadron Forty-Two, Suggs
joined Attack Squadron Thirty-Five, then deployed to the Mediterranean
in the USS *Nimitz* (CV-68). He served fourteen months as the Squadron's
Operations Officer and made successive deployments in USS *Carl Vinson*
(CV-70), during her Caribbean shakedown cruise, and in USS *Nimitz*, once
again to the Mediterranean. Following his next assignment as Attack
Squadron Thirty-Five's Maintenance Officer, he was assigned to Medium
Attack Wing One as Readiness Officer in June 1984. In November 1984 he
was selected as Flag Secretary to the Commander-in-Chief, U.S. Atlantic
Fleet, a billet he held until 1986.[2]

After a brief period of A-6 refresher training with Attack Squadron
Forty-Two, Suggs reported in June 1986 to Attack Squadron Fifty-Five as
Executive Officer. He subsequently assumed squadron command in December 1987 while deployed aboard the USS *Coral Sea* (CV-43) in the Mediterranean.[3]

On 25 March 1986 Attack Squadron Fifty-Five participated in an attack on a Libyan Nanuchka II guided
missile patrol boat with Rockeye cluster bombs in response to hostile fire
from the patrol craft. The boat was
heavily damaged and was subsequently sunk by a Harpoon strike by
Attack Squadron Eighty-Five Intruders from the USS *Saratoga* (CV 60).
On 14–15 April six of the VF-55 Intruders attacked Benina Airfield at
Benghazi and destroyed numerous
parked aircraft and surrounding hangars, support facilities, aircraft aprons,
and other airfield equipment and
vehicles. (The strike was in response
to the involvement of Libyan trained

Capt. Ralph E. Suggs (official U.S.
Navy photograph).

terrorists in a specific incident: the Berlin disco bombing in which American servicemen were killed.)[4]

While serving as its Executive and Commanding Officer, VF-55 earned the following recognitions: Commander Naval Air Force, U.S. Atlantic Fleet, Battle Efficiency Award; Rear Adm. Clarence Wade McClusky Award; Chief of Naval Operations Safety Award; Navy Meritorious Unit Commendation; Pratt and Whitney Operational Excellence Award; Commander, Carrier Air Wing Thirteen Excellence Award; and, Commander, Medium Attack Wing One nomination for the Admiral Arleigh Burke Fleet Trophy.[5]

Captain Suggs assumed command of USS *San Diego* (AFS 6) in 1991 and subsequently commanded USS *America* (CV 66) from 1993–1995. While in command of *America*, he participated in NATO Combat Operation Deliberate Force (Bosnia) and Operation Uphold Democracy (Haiti).

Ashore, Suggs attended the Armed Forces Staff College in 1980, served as Flag Secretary to the Commander in Chief, U.S. Atlantic Fleet, from November 1984 to 1986 and as Executive Assistant to the Deputy Commander in Chief, U.S. Naval Forces Europe from February 1989 to February 1991.

Following command of USS *America* (CV 66), Captain Suggs was selected for the Chief of Naval Operations' Strategic Studies Group at the Naval War College, Newport, Rhode Island. He was promoted to Rear Admiral in May 1996 and was assigned as Director for Operations, Plans, & Policy, U.S. Atlantic Fleet, in June 1996. He then served as Commander Carrier Group Six/Commander *Stennis* Battle Group in December 1997.

Rear Admiral Suggs' awards and decorations include four Legion of Merit Medals, Defense Meritorious Service Medal, Meritorious Service Medal, and two Navy Commendation Medals. Upon his retirement in 2000, Admiral Suggs had flown over 3,600 jet flight hours of which 2,800 were in the A-6 Intruder and had logged over 800 carrier landings.[6]

After retirement Admiral Suggs worked for Harley Davidson in Wisconsin as Director of Field Service Operations. As of this writing he is now Executive Director of the North Carolina State Alumni Association.[7]

Notes

1. Official Biography of Rear Admiral Ralph E. Suggs USN, (Ret.), Navy History and Heritage Command, Washington, D.C.

2. Ibid.

3. Ibid.

4. Grossnick, Roy A. *Dictionary of American Naval Aviation Squadrons; The History of VA, VAH, VAK, VAL, VAP and VFA Squadrons* (Volume 1). Washington, D.C.: Naval History Center, Department of the Navy, 1995.

5. Official Biography of Rear Admiral Ralph E. Suggs, USN (Ret), Navy History and Heritage Command, Washington, D.C.

6. Ibid.

7. Joe Hice, Jr., blog: "Benny Suggs, A Lasting Impression."

Capt. Robert E. Besal
(September 1995–September 1996)

Bob, I think I've found your plane.—Diver Joe Kistel informing Bob Besal that he had located the aircraft underwater from which Besal had ejected almost 38 years earlier

Bob Besal believes in miracles! He experienced one in 1974, and returned to revisit the miracle almost 38 years later, twenty miles off the coast of St. Augustine, Florida.

Capt. Robert E. Besal (official U.S. Navy photograph).

In July 2012, Joe Kistel, executive director of Think It, Sink It, Reef It (TISIRI) a Marine Conservation Company, was leading a team of divers when they discovered the wreckage of a Navy A-7 jet fighter lying on the seabed eighty feet below the surface, off the coast of St. Augustine. TISIRI specializes in, among other things, artificial reefs. The wreckage had become part of a productive ecosystem and artificial reef, and sea bass, scorpion, trigger and octopus now called the broken metal structure home.[1]

Kistel made several dives, returning to the wreckage to explore, and he located a data plate on the wreckage, which ultimately led to identifying the pilot, a 24-year-old Lieutenant junior grade, Robert Besal, attached at the time to Attack Squadron Eighty-Two (VA-82) Marauders. The Vought A-7C Corsair had been lost in a training exercise in 1974 in a mid-air collision. Incredibly, the pilot had survived, was alive, a retired admiral teaching Aviation Maintenance Technology at Trident Technical College in Charleston, South Carolina. Kistel located and contacted Besal.

Besal recalled: "I was scheduled to fly in a four-plane formation on 2 December 1974. As the most junior pilot in the flight, my position was number two, the flight leader's wingman. Leading the flight was my commanding officer, Cdr. Peter Schoeffel, a very experienced aviator, and with whom I had learned to fly the A-7 when I was in training with VA-174. Our flight proceeded normally from NAS Cecil into the offshore skies near St. Augustine. During the tactical maneuvering portion of the training mission, we were performing simulated formation dive-bombing roll-ins.

"As we pulled out from one dive, I separated too far from the flight leader, and added power to rejoin in correct position. Closing the lead aircraft rapidly in a climbing turn, I became disoriented as to his flight path and with considerable overtaking speed, I miscalculated my clearance of his plane, striking my tail against his fuselage. The impact broke off the tail of my aircraft, and it became uncontrollable, pitching over and spiraling downward. Heeding the radio calls of the two other flight members to abandon the plane, I ejected at 15,000 feet, and began a long, cold, parachute descent to the Atlantic."[2]

Schoeffel was able to guide his plane back to Cecil Field Naval Air Station. Besal found himself alone in the cold Atlantic Ocean, floating in the frigid water with an air temperature of forty degrees. It was overcast, and rainy, and he shot pencil flares, desperately trying to get the attention of a nearby helicopter.

"Fortunately, something went right for me that morning, and after bobbing in the cold ocean for about a half hour, I was plucked from the water by a Navy SH-3 Sea Knight helicopter which just happened to be in the area on a training mission. That they found me in the waves and swells that morning is my own personal miracle."[3]

Even more of a miracle, when one considers that the helicopter was operating in the area on a routine water indoctrination flight and the crew was trained in search and rescue operations. Not many can claim to have survived a mid-air collision over water.[4]

On 22 September 2012, under blue skies and white clouds on a calm sea, Besal and his wife Jenny sailed with Kistel to the site of the downed aircraft and, not a diver, Besal waited above while divers brought up artifacts. Besal reflected on an event that might have too early ended what turned out to be a distinguished thirty year career in Naval aviation. "I was blessed," Besal later recalled; "I was fortunate no one else was hurt."

Robert E. Besal was born in Chicago, the eldest of six boys and three girls born to Robert J. and Helen Besal. His father, a World War II Army Air Forces veteran, was a leader in the lighting industry and Besal's family moved from Chicago to Cincinnati, Ohio, and eventually Atlanta, Georgia.

"Since my earliest memory, I had been consumed with flying, and all things aviation. My mother often related an anecdote to me about when I found a small wheel from a baby stroller in the alley behind our first home, and when my father asked what I was going to do with it, I without hesitation informed him that I was going to 'build an airplane.'

"I was extremely blessed to live among pilots, mostly Naval Aviators, throughout my early years, and I hung on their every word when they spoke of their aviation experiences. When I was eleven years old, I received my first airplane ride in a World War II-vintage trainer. This adventure was the gift of a neighbor who lived five doors away in Hinsdale, Illinois. Capt. Charles S. Downey had just finished restoring his Meyers OTW biplane, which was adorned with 'FLY NAVY' across the bottom wings, and gold Naval Aviator wings on the tail. Chuck was, is, and likely always will be the youngest person to earn his Navy wings—two weeks before his nineteenth birthday. He served with true distinction in the Pacific flying Curtiss SB2C Helldivers in VB-80, flying combat missions against the Japanese forces from the decks of USS *Ticonderoga* and USS *Hancock*. He later served as commanding officer of two Naval Reserve squadrons based at NAS Glenview. When Chuck handed me a leather helmet and goggles that morning, he sparked a fire in me that has never gone out."[5]

In high school, Besal learned about the NROTC and focused his energy toward earning a Navy scholarship. His efforts were rewarded with acceptance into the NROTC unit at Auburn University in Alabama.

"The Navy Unit became the real center of my college life, and I enjoyed every moment of it. The instructors became my role models. I devoured the Naval Science courses, and enjoyed making many friendships of future officers. One in particular, my classmate, Charles B. Askey, would become a strong friend. Charlie and I both commanded the NROTC Battalion, cruised together for summer midshipman training, graduated and roomed together through flight training, earned carrier qualification together aboard USS *Lexington*, and received our Navy wings together. Charlie served as my best man, and we subsequently cruised together aboard the USS *Saratoga* in Carrier Air Wing Three."

It was while he was a midshipman at Auburn that Besal first walked the decks of *America*; "My first-class summer training cruise was aboard *America*. We left from Pier 12 in Norfolk in July 1971 for six weeks of the ship's Mediterranean Deployment. I was assigned to the embarked helicopter unit, HC-2 DET 66. Because the detachment was short one pilot, the Officer-in Charge elected to let me fly as co-pilot on the daily flight schedule. On 10 July 1971, I made my first flight from *America*'s deck in an HH-2D Seasprite."

Upon his graduation from Auburn in June 1972, and his commissioning as an ensign in the Navy Reserve, Besal reported to the Naval Aviation Schools Command at NAS Pensacola, Florida, for three weeks of aviation indoctrination, then to Training Squadron One (VT-1) Eaglets at Saufley Field for Primary School in the *Beech T-34B Mentor*.

In August 1972, Besal was reassigned to Training Squadron Nineteen (VT-19) Attack Frogs, a basic jet training squadron at NAS Meridian, Mississippi. He flew the North American T-2A and T-2B Buckeye, the Navy's intermediate training aircraft, intended to introduce Naval Aviators and Naval Flight Officers to jet aircraft. Classes included basic jet familiarization, radio operations, precision aerobatics, formation flying, night flying, air-to-air gunnery, and carrier qualification.

In May 1973, Besal moved to Training Squadron Seven (VT-7) "Eagles," still at Meridian, to learn the fundamentals of strike aviation in the Douglas TA-4J Skyhawk. This second phase of flight training included manual Air-to-Ground Bombing, Tactical Formation, Air Combat Maneuvering and Operational Navigation at low altitude. Again, students performed Field Carrier Landing Practice (FCLP) in preparation for their Carrier Qualifications (CQ). In order to graduate, Besal had to safely complete four touch-and-go's and six arrested landings aboard USS *Lexington* in the Gulf of Mexico. On 15 November 1973, Besal was awarded his Wings of Gold.

Following the completion of A-7E Corsair Replacement Pilot Training with Attack Squadron One Seventy Four (VA-174) Hellrazors at Cecil Field in July 1974, Besal reported to Attack Squadron Eighty Two (VA-82) Marauders.

"The Marauders had just returned from a Mediterranean deployment aboard *America*. After a very brief stand down, the squadron prepared to return to *America*. On 27 August 1974, I made my first 'real' *America* arrested landing of 109, trapping aboard in an A-7C."[6]

America departed Pier 12, NOB Norfolk on 6 September with Air Wing Eight (CVW-8) embarked, including VA-82, headed for the North Atlantic to participate in a NATO exercise, Northern Merger.

The exercise, utilizing the air, naval and land forces of eight NATO countries (Belgium, Canada, Denmark, West Germany, the Netherlands, Norway, Great Britain and the United States) was carried out in the North Sea, English Channel and the Norwegian Sea and was meant to simulate operations during times of increasing tensions with the Soviets.[7]

Among the principal objectives of "Northern Merger" were the co-ordination of air operations from aircraft carriers and from land bases, electronic warfare and countermeasures, and mine warfare, in particular, the clearance of mines hampering an amphibious assault.

America joined with HMS *Ark Royal* in providing air support for the NATO task force and the amphibious landing. Throughout the two-week

Lt.(jg) Bob Besal with VA0–82 in 1974 aboard USS *America* (courtesy Robert Besal).

exercise Soviet surface units and aircraft were in the area conducting surveillance missions over and near the NATO forces.

Exercises included anti-submarine attack and submarine warfare, land and carrier-based air operations, mine laying and mine countermeasures, anti-aircraft warfare and control of merchant shipping. The exercise was under the joint control of the three major NATO military commanders; Adm. Sir Terence Lewin, RN, Commander-in-Chief Channel (CINCHAN), Adm. Ralph W. Cousins, U.S. Navy, Supreme Allied Commander Atlantic (SACLANT) and Gen. Andrew J. Goodpaster, U.S. Army, Supreme Allied Commander Europe (SACEUR).[8]

Following a five day visit to Portsmouth, *America* departed in early October and arrived back in Norfolk on 12 October to prepare for a major overhaul, and the Marauders returned to Cecil Field.

Less than a month later, On 2 December, Besal would experience a mid-air collision, an event that would have a profound impact on his leadership style. After the usual post-mishap grind of investigation, analysis, and fitness boards, Besal was returned to flight status, and continued to pilot the A-7. "I became a fervent advocate of 'second chances' as a result of my skipper's personal interest, and, indeed, his understanding. I don't know if that enlightenment was a result of his time as a prisoner-of-war, and his own personal shot at redemption, but I am glad he granted me one. I tried to do the same throughout the remainder of my career, based on his gift to me."

In October 1975, Besal reported to Training Squadron Eighty Six (VT-86) Sabrehawks at NAS Pensacola, for training as bombardier, a tactical jet navigator, and in January 1976, he was granted the designation of a Naval Flight Officer (NFO). He was then assigned as a replacement bombardier-navigator with the Attack Squadron Forty Two (VA-42) Green Pawns, the A-6 Intruder Fleet Replacement Squadron at NAS Oceana, Virginia.

In September 1976, Lt. Besal transferred to Attack Squadron Seventy Five (VA-75) Sunday Punchers upon their return from the Mediterranean. VA-75 was the first, and subsequently last, squadron to fly the Grumman A-6 Intruder.

On 11 July 1977, the squadron deployed to the Mediterranean as part of Air Wing Three (CVW-3) aboard USS *Saratoga* (CV-60), making port calls in Italy and Spain before returning to Virginia just prior to Christmas, on 23 December. A second deployment to the Mediterranean aboard *Saratoga* followed on 3 October 1978, making eleven port calls along the coasts of France, Spain, Italy, and Egypt before returning on 5 April 1979.

That same month, Besal returned to VA-42 as an Instructor Pilot, where he remained until assuming the duties of Asst. Strike Operations Officer aboard USS *Independence* (CV-62) in January 1982. Besal sailed to the Mediterranean aboard the *Independence* on 7 June 1982, with CVW-6 embarked, including two A-6E Intruder squadrons, VA-15 and VA-87.

Besal, now a Lieutenant Commander, was part of Strike Operations, responsible for the planning and daily scheduling of all operations, and served as a link between the ship and the air wing. The cruise included stops in Italy, Spain, and Greece, before returning home on 22 December.[9]

In October 1983, Besal returned to VA-42 for several weeks of refresher training, before rejoining the fleet, and in December 1983, he reported to Attack Squadron Sixty Five (VA-65) the World Famous Fighting Tigers, at NAS Oceana.

During his time with the Tigers, the squadron sailed on three deployments as part of Air Wing Seven (CVW-7) aboard USS *Dwight D. Eisenhower* (CVN-69).

On 8 May 1984, *Eisenhower* sailed to the Caribbean, then the North Atlantic and was present off Omaha Beach on 6 June, as part of an Allied fleet there to commemorate the 40th anniversary of the D–Day landings. The ship had a "visit" from President Ronald Reagan who addressed the crew from a helicopter hovering overhead. After visits to Portugal, France and the U.K., *Eisenhower* returned home on 20 June.

Following a period of carrier qualifications, the ship sailed again on 10 October for the Mediterranean, with scheduled stops in Greece, Italy, Israel, France, and Spain. From 1–20 November, *Eisenhower* took part in Sea Wind, a joint air-defense exercise with Egyptian forces, and in the end of January 1985 she participated in National Week XXXIII, an exercise in the Mediterranean involving NATO ships and aircraft. In February, the squadrons flew exercises with the French Air Force.[10]

On 7 March 1985, while *Eisenhower* was visiting Palma, Spain, she was ordered to make a high-speed transit to the eastern Mediterranean because of increased tensions in the Civil War in Lebanon involving a conflict between Maronite Christians and Druze Muslims that dated back centuries. *Eisenhower* had supported the evacuation of U.S. and foreign civilians from Lebanon in June 1982. A U.S. brokered agreement between Israel and Lebanon on 17 May 1983, had put a temporary end to the civil war, but no peace agreement was reached, and Syria, not a party to the negotiations, refused to cooperate and tensions remained high.

Tensions were reignited when the 17 May Agreement was abrogated by the Lebanese government on 7 March, and the *Eisenhower* remained in the area into April, then sailed for home arriving at Norfolk on 8 May.

Besal went to sea with the squadron for a third time on 8 July when *Eisenhower* departed on 8 July, and following carrier qualifications off Jacksonville, she sailed to the Caribbean, in part due to increased tensions following Marxist rebel attacks in Guatemala and Honduras. By 22 August, she was back at Norfolk.

In May 1986, Besal was appointed to the staff of Commander in Chief—U.S. Atlantic Command (USCINCLANT). "I was the Flag Lieutenant and Aide to the Commander-in-Chief, Adm. Lee Baggett, Jr. Duties were the usual aide stuff: 'care and feeding' of the senior flag officer in the Tidewater area, keeping the admiral's schedule, escort of distinguished U.S. and NATO guests, protocol matters, and the like."

Besal returned to VA-42 in July 1987. "I completed a brief refresher syllabus, and because I had previously been an instructor, I stepped back into that role while serving as the Executive Officer of the squadron. I was 'stashed' there because VA-42 had a vacancy in that XO position. When my ultimate duty station, VA-75, had their change of command, I would then report there as Executive Officer."[11]

In April 1988, Besal rejoined the fleet, reporting to VA-75 as Executive Officer. On 2 August 1988, the squadron set sail for the Mediterranean aboard USS *John F. Kennedy* (CV 67). During the deployment which included flights over seven different countries, twenty-one exercises, and eleven port visits, the Sunday Punchers won the 1988 Norden Pickle Barrel trophy for bombing excellence, and earned the Secretary of the Navy's Meritorious Unit Commendation for superior performance. The squadron returned to NAS Oceana on 1 February 1989.[12]

On 29 September 1989, Besal relieved Cdr. John T. Meister and assumed command of VA-75. During mid-1990, the squadron, embarked on the *Kennedy*, made port visits to New York City in June for Fleet Week and Boston in July for Independence Day.

On 27 July, Besal sat in his office, disappointed at the news that the *America* would not be participating in a North Atlantic NATO exercise due to "budget constraints." "I saw my one chance to deploy in command of the Sunday Punchers evaporating. Later, my two squadron intelligence officers, Ensigns Mark Elliott and Dan Brannick, stopped by to give me an update on the situation in Iraq. There were reports that units of the Iraqi Republican Guard were massing on their border with Kuwait. I was interested, but my involvement seemed unlikely."

Four days later, on 31 July, the Iraqi units pulled back from the border, and senior analysts advised that the threat of invasion was over. Besal's two ensigns disagreed. "They saw things differently, and told me they believed Iraq would invade within forty-eight hours. On 2 August, when Iraq invaded Kuwait, they looked pretty smug."

On August 7, Besal's hopes for deployment were again shot down. "I was directed by COMNAVAIRLANT to transfer four of my SWIP Intruders and five crews to VA-35 ASAP. I was disappointed, to say the least. VA-35 was sailing aboard *Saratoga* on schedule to relieve *Eisenhower*."

On 10 August 1990, *Kennedy*'s skipper, Capt. Herb Browne, made official what most of the crew already suspected. The carrier was to begin making preparations to deploy to the Red Sea in support of Operation Desert Shield, in response to Iraq's invasion of Kuwait. The next few days were spent in air work-ups and general quarters drills, as well as laying in sufficient rations, fuel and munitions to sustain the 5,200 men for an indefinite period. On 15 August 1990, the crew gave their last portside hugs and departed Norfolk for the Red Sea.

On 10 August, while Captain Browne was briefing his crew, Besal was ordered to report to the Medium Attack Wing One commodore, Capt. William J. Fallon. "I was told that the powers that be had decided to deploy *Kennedy* the following Wednesday, 15 August. I would pick up four 'unrestricted' (+6.5 G-limit) jets over the weekend, and transfer all four of my KA-6D tankers, two to VA-42, and two to VA-85. I would also gain an augment of four additional crews from VA-55, which was getting ready to stand down. After we caught up with *Saratoga* on station, we would get our crews and SWIP jets back. I was ecstatic."

On 15 September, the *Kennedy* joined the *Saratoga* on station. Upon arrival in the area, *Kennedy* was made the flagship of the Commander—Red Sea Battle Force, and her Battle Group included three guided missile cruisers; USS *South Carolina* (CGN-37), USS *Mississippi* (CGN-40) and USS *Thomas S. Gates* (CG-51) as well as the Knox-class frigate USS *Thomas C. Hart* (FF-1092).

"We repatriated our four 'lost Puncher crews' and SWIP aircraft, sent the three VA-55 crews home to the States, and transferred four 'straight stick' A-6E's to VA-35. I received Intel reports from our former Deputy CAG, Capt. "Carlos" Johnson, who told us of photographs of 'ten thousand gun barrels' pointed skyward in Baghdad. I was concerned.

"Until the start of Desert Storm, we continued to train to the most challenging mission—low-level night attack. It kept our edge sharp, kept the adrenaline pumping and the crews focused. No one except the XO, Cdr. Kolin Jan had ever seen a missile fired at him. (Kolin had flown during Operation El Dorado Canyon on the Al Azizyah Barracks strike while a department head in VA-34). It's easy to tell someone how to maneuver to defeat a missile but doing it while navigating at low level and then hitting the target, well, that's easier said than done!"[13]

Between port visits to Alexandria, Egypt, Izmir and Antaly, Turkey, and Jeddah, Saudi Arabia, there were daily firefighting drills and weapons training, and daily flight operations.

"At 1:00 p.m. local time on 16 January 1991, CAG Hardin White called a meeting of all squadron CO's in his office. The President's deadline for Iraqi withdrawal from Kuwait had just passed. As we provided updates to CAG on our status of preparations, Rear Admiral Mixson opened the door slightly, stuck his head in and said, 'CAG, we just got an Execute order. We go tonight!' There was a collective swallow by all of us skippers, and then a great feeling of semi-relief. It was almost game time."

On 17 January 1991, Operation Desert Shield transitioned into Operation Desert Storm with the initiation of an air war against Iraqi targets. The Sunday Punchers delivered one of the first naval air wing strikes deep into Iraq. Armed with HARM anti-radar missiles, laser guided bombs and SLAM land-attack missiles, the squadron wreaked havoc on Iraqi targets.

"We briefed at 9:15 p.m. As we suited up in the paraloft, there was a bit of light banter, but mostly quiet as we donned our gear, stowed our sidearms, SERE charts, blood chits, and extra water bottles in our survival vests. We wished each other good luck, and headed to the flight deck to preflight and start engines.

"The launch sequence plan worked flawlessly. First launched were two E-2's, then the A-6E tanker, then six Intruder and eighteen Corsair strikers. Next, four F-14's and three EA-6B's. Thirty-four in all from JFK headed northeast, as a similar number left Saratoga's deck not far away.

"As we pressed into Iraq, I thought about how complicated this whole evolution was. We were part of a seventy plane force hurtling in the dark, each trusting the other to be on track, on altitude, on time. The alternative wasn't a pretty picture. At 3:45 a.m., the ground below us erupted in brilliant flashes as two and three-ship formations of B-52's at low altitude simultaneously struck Iraqi forward airstrips at Mudaysis, Rhadif al Khafi, and Wadi al Khirr.

"The B-52 explosions subsided as we flew overhead. I remember noticing that all the lights in the cities and towns below were still on. In the distance about one hundred miles away, we could see the environs of Baghdad. It was a strange sight, with the lights seeming to pulse. As we neared, we could see that the surreal, occulting lights were really AAA fire; the city seemed like it was alive with tracer rounds streaking everywhere. Reaching our initial point, a distinctive bend in the Euphrates River, we turned right toward the target, twenty-nine miles ahead, and accelerated."

Leading the attack, Besal was dismayed to miss his target, but was satisfied that they "did as I said, not as I did." As he later recalled, "Looking out the left side as we completed our turn off target, I could see the explosions from the rest of my wingmen finding their marks.

"After debriefing with Rear Admiral Mixson in CVIC, we returned to the Ready Room. We were all grins as we entered, and we saw the intense faces of crews preparing to brief for the next wave. We had returned, unscratched, and had delivered some incredibly damaging blows to the enemy. VA-75 maintained that record for the duration of Desert Storm, and I'm convinced that our training and 'intensity' paid off. A little luck didn't hurt, either!"

During their forty-three days of combat, the squadron flew around the clock and delivered over 1.6 million pounds of ordnance, flew 2,150 combat hours in 498 sorties without a loss of life or damage to any aircraft. For their efforts, the Sunday Punchers became the most decorated Navy squadron of Desert Storm.[14]

The ground phase of what came to be known as the Persian Gulf War began on 24 February, and one hundred hours later, on 28 February, the Coalition forces declared a ceasefire. President Bush ordered all U.S. forces to stand-down, and once relieved, *Kennedy*, after a brief visit to Hurgada, Egypt, in early March, returned to Norfolk, arriving on 28 March.

Besal missed what was by all accounts the greatest homecoming celebration and outpouring of public support since World War II. On 15 February, while still deployed on the Red Sea, Besal had turned over command of the squadron to his XO, Cdr. Kolin Jan.

"Kolin and I went back to our first days in the Intruder, and we flew together for carrier qualification aboard the *Forrestal* as new replacements, then we served together as junior officers in VA-75. There was still some Desert Storm to go and it was important to me that Kolin get some combat time as CO of the squadron.

"And my old friend, Capt. Ralph 'Benny' Suggs, who I was scheduled to relieve, kept telling me that Vice Adm. Paul Ilg wanted me in London ASAP to relieve Suggs as Executive Assistant to the Deputy Commander in Chief–U.S. Naval Forces Europe (CINCUSNAVEUR). What he really meant was that HE wanted me in London ASAP because he wanted to proceed to his training for command of USS *San Diego*. I stayed on when Vice Admiral Ilg was relieved by Vice Adm. Ed Clexton. As Executive Assistant, I assisted the DCINC in his duties by ensuring the smooth operation of the 'front office' staff, and I provided an interface with the broader HQ staff."

From November 1992 through March 1993, Besal attended the Surface Warfare Officer Schools Command at Newport, Rhode Island, in preparation for a command at sea.

On 30 April 1993, Captain Besal relieved Capt. Donald Vtipil to assume command of the USS *Savannah* (AOR-4), a *Wichita*-class replenishment oiler. The ship, crewed by twenty-two officers and 398 enlisted carried a wide range of logistic supplies from aviation fuel and missiles to movies and mail. She was known as the "First and Finest Fast Attack Oiler" and carried two CH-46 Sea Knight helicopters, two Phalanx Close In Weapons System (CIWS) and a Mark 29 Sea Sparrow missile launcher.

"Normal command assignments lasted eighteen months back then. My command of *Savannah* lasted for twenty-seven months, because when they made the decision to retire her, the next CO would have had only nine months in command, 'not significant' in their words. It turned out to be my good fortune, because then I got the Haiti operation, a lot more sea time, and the last port visit for the ship to her namesake city, Savannah, Georgia, for St. Patrick's Day. I was the grand marshal of the St. Patrick's Day Parade, and a company-sized contingent of my crew marched in the parade. You couldn't buy a drink for yourself in town, as the locals loved us and we were warmly received!"

The ship made her last deployment to the Mediterranean and Indian Ocean from August 1993 through January 1994, then returned to Norfolk. She was decommissioned at Pier 20 aboard Norfolk Naval Base on 29 July 1995. "My guest speaker was Rear Adm. Jerry Breast, a former *Savannah* CO, my first fleet squadron CO in VA-82, and my captain aboard USS *Independence*."

On 25 September 1995, Besal again relieved Captain Suggs, this time to assume command of USS *America,* on what was to be her twentieth and final deployment. The change of command took place aboard ship during a four-day port visit to Corfu, Greece. It was not to be a routine deployment.

With Captain Suggs in command, *America* had already deployed to the Mediterranean earlier, on 28 August, with CVW-1 embarked and enhanced by two Marine fixed-wing squadrons. She had been ordered to the Adriatic Sea in response to the deteriorating civil war in Bosnia.

On the day that *America* departed Norfolk, a mortar shell had exploded in a Sarajevo marketplace, killing thirty-seven civilians, and the blame had been placed on Bosnian Serbs who were already the subject of international condemnation for attacking into "safe" areas of Bosnia-Herzegovina. The NATO commander, Adm. Leighton Smith, launched a sustained air strike campaign, Operation Deliberate Force, beginning on 30 August 1995, against Bosnian Serb military targets in response to the mortar attack on civilians in Sarajevo.[15]

On 9 September, *America* joined the USS *Theodore Roosevelt* (CVN-71) in the Adriatic, and the two carriers carried out airstrikes against Bosnian Serb positions in support of NATO. The *Roosevelt* was relieved on 12 September, but CVW-1 continued selective strike missions using laser-guided bombs until a NATO declared moratorium on air strikes two days later, on 12 September. In total, *America*'s airwing dropped over thirty tons of ordnance.[16]

Subsequent to taking command, Besal sailed *America* into the Persian Gulf on 25 November in support of Operation Southern Watch, helping to enforce the no-fly zone over Southern Iraq. On 3 December, *America* departed the Gulf to return to Bosnia, operating in support of NATO's Implementation Force (IFOR) as part of Operation Decisive Endeavor and Operation Decisive Edge, with a port visit to Valletta, Malta.

Besal recalls: "Operations in the Adriatic Sea were critical to the success of land forces in Bosnia. The December and January weather over the NATO airfields frequently produced ceilings and visibility below minimums for takeoff. Despite high winds and driving rains, *America* could move to find breaks in the weather to launch close-air support and combat air patrol missions needed for the safety of forces ashore.

"A highlight of the deployment was the visit of Adm. Igor V. Kasatonov, the First Deputy Commander-in-Chief of the Russian Navy. Kasatonov was embarked in the Russian aircraft carrier *Kuznetsov* on her first Mediterranean deployment. During a visit to *Kuznetsov*, the U.S. Sixth Fleet Commander, Vice Adm. Donald Pilling, invited Kasatonov for a reciprocal visit to *America*. Kasatonov and his party arrived in U.S. Navy helicopters, and observed flight operations before returning to *Kuznetsov*."

On 21 February 1996, still three days out from Norfolk, VS-32's Cdr. Robert A. Buehn made *America*'s 319,504th and final arrested landing, and three days later, she docked at Norfolk, completing thirty-one years of service. USS *America* was decommissioned on 9 August 1996, in a ceremony at Norfolk Naval Shipyard. The guest speaker was Adm. Leighton Smith, a former commanding officer.

Following the decommissioning, Besal's next assignment, in August 1996, was to the Naval Military Personnel Command (NAVMILPERSCOM) at the Navy Annex in Washington, D.C., formerly and subsequently known as the Bureau of Naval Personnel (BUPERS). The command, whose mission statement reads "The right person in the right job at the right time," was in the process of transitioning their headquarters to Millington, Tennessee. As Director—Aviation Officer Distribution Division, Besal was responsible for the duty station assignments of more than seven hundred Naval Aviation Captains.

He left BUPERS in December 1997 to take command of the Naval Safety Center (COMNAVSAFECEN) back at Norfolk, Virginia. The center provides training and raises awareness over a variety of safety issues, including risk identification and management.

In August 1998, Besal was detached to Saudi Arabia as Deputy Commander of the Joint Task Force—Southwest Asia (JTF-SWA), a multi-service, multinational coalition comprised of 6,000 troops from the United States, the United Kingdom, Saudi Arabia and, until December 1998, France. He returned to Norfolk in December 1998, but once his assignment at the Safety Center was complete in April 1999, he returned to Saudi Arabia for a second rotation as Deputy Commander JTF-SWA.

The task force was established on 26 August 1992, with the mission of enforcing the United Nations Security Council Resolutions in the Gulf region. The following day, the JTF-SWA initiated Operation Southern Watch, monitoring and controlling airspace south of the 32nd Parallel, later 33rd Parallel, in southern Iraq, by enforcing a "no-fly zone."

The task force, headquartered at Eskhan Village, a compound east of the capital city of Riyadh, was commanded by an Air Force Major General. It planned, coordinated, and executed air operations in support of Operation Southern Watch and reported directly to U.S. Central Command.

Although Operation Southern Watch continued until 19 March 2003, Besal rotated out in August 1999 to take command of the Navy's Operational Test and Evaluation Force (COMOPTEVFOR) back at Norfolk.

Reporting to the Chief of Naval Operations, Besal was the sole authority for U.S. Navy Operational Testing and Evaluation (OT&E). As such, he was responsible for the "independent and objective evaluation for the operational effectiveness and suitability of naval aviation, surface, subsurface,

C⁴I (Command, Control, Communications, Computer and Intelligence), cryptologic and space systems in support of DOD and Navy acquisition and fleet introduction systems."[17]

On 1 August 2002, following 30 years of active duty, Rear Admiral Besal retired from the Navy with more than 4,000 hours in tactical aircraft and over 1,100 arrested carrier landings. His combat awards include two awards of the Distinguished Flying Cross, the Bronze Star Medal, and three Air Medals.

Notes

1. Barnett, Jim. "Naval Aviator returns to underwater site of 1974 Crash." CNN, 1 October 2012 http://www.cnn.com/2012/09/29/us/pilot-wreckage.

2. Interview with Robert Besal, March-April 2013.

3. Ibid.

4. Barnett, Jim. "Pilot Who Survived Midair Collision 37 Years Ago Learns Wreckage Found." CNN, 22 August 2012, http://www.cnn.com/2012/08/22/us/pilot-wreckage.

5. Interview with Robert Besal, March-April 2013.

6. Ibid.

7. Scott, Ian. *Exercise Northern Merger.* http://www.flightglobal.com/FlightPDF Archive/1974/1974 percent20-percent201588.PDF

8. Ibid.

9. USS *Independence* (CV-62) Mediterranean Cruise Book—1982. http://navysite. de/cruisebooks/cv6282/198.htm

10. USS *Dwight D. Eisenhower* (CVN-69). http://www.uscarriers.net/cvn69history. htm

11. Interview with Robert Besal, 1 March 2013.

12. VA-75 Sunday Punchers—Intruder Association. http://www.intruderassociation. org/squadrons/va75.html

13. Interview with Robert Besal, 1 March 2013.

14. VA-75 Sunday Punchers—Intruder Association. http://www.intruderassociation. org/squadrons/va75.html.

15. Operation Deliberate Force. Global Security.Org. http://www.globalsecurity.org/ military/ops/deliberate_force.htm.

16. USS *America* Museum Foundation—http://ussamerica-museumfoundation.org/ history.html.

17. Comoptevfor website http://www.public.navy.mil/cotf/pages/home.aspx.

New USS *America* (LHA-6)

Almost as soon as the news was released about the Navy's plan to decommission the USS *America* (CVA-66) efforts were initiated to ensure that a naval vessel would carry the name *America*. Initially unsuccessful in their effort to have *America* turned into a naval museum, after the decision was made to use her as a weapons testing platform, former crew members, veterans and the public united in an effort to name the Navy's next aircraft carrier, CVN78, the *America*.

Those efforts also proved unsuccessful when on Tuesday, 16 January 2006, at a ceremony held at the Pentagon in Washington, D.C., Navy Secretary Donald Winter officially named CVN78 the USS *Gerald R. Ford*.

Disappointed, they remained committed to the belief that the name *America* belonged on a Navy ship and they continued lobbying to have a future vessel named *America*.

Their efforts finally proved successful when on 27 June 2008, during a reunion banquet hosted by the USS *America* Carrier Veterans Association (CVA) in Jacksonville, Florida, Navy Secretary Winter announced that the first of three in a new class of amphibious assault ships, the *America*-class, would be designated USS *America* LHA-6. To an audience that included former Chairman of the Joint Chiefs Marine Gen. Peter Pace and his wife Lynne, who accepted the invitation to serve as the ship's sponsor, Secretary Winter stated, "I am proud to announce that LHA-6, our newest assault ship, will carry on the proud legacy of her predecessor and be named *America*."[1]

On 1 June 2007, the contract was awarded to Northrop Grumman Shipbuilding, Pascagoula, Mississippi, with an expected delivery to the Navy in 2012. A keel laying ceremony for the *America* (LHA 6) was held at the company's shipyard on 17 July 2009.[2]

Amphibious warships are designed to support the Marine Corps tenets of operational maneuver from the sea. They must be able to provide a rapid buildup of combat power ashore in the face of opposition.

In describing the mission of the new ship, the Navy proclaims, "USS *America* is an amphibious assault ship that will provide forward presence and power projection as an integral part of Joint, Interagency and Multinational Maritime Expeditionary Forces. It will support Marine Aviation requirements, from small-scale contingency operations of an Expeditionary Strike Group, to forcible entry missions in major theater war."[3]

As planned, the new *America* will be 844 feet in length, with a beam of 106 feet and will displace approximately 45,000 tons when fully loaded. Capable of a speed exceeding twenty-two knots and a range of 9,500 miles, *America* will be a gas-turbine powered warship capable of carrying a Marine Expeditionary Brigade with accompanying helicopters and aircraft great distances at high speeds.

Her planned complement of aircraft will include many still in development such as the MV-22B Osprey, a high speed, long range tiltrotor transport capable of both vertical takeoff and landing (VTOL) and short takeoff and landing (STOL) and the F-35B Lightning II fighter, able to carry out ground attack, reconnaissance, and air defense missions. Additionally, she will carry CH-53K "Super Stallion" heavy lift cargo helicopters, AH-1Z Viper attack helicopters, UH-1Y Venom utility helicopters and the MH-60S Seahawk, a multi-mission helicopter capable of anti-submarine warfare (ASW), anti-surface warfare (ASUW), naval special warfare (NSW) insertion, search and rescue (SAR), combat search and rescue (CSAR), vertical replenishment (VERTREP), and medical evacuation (MEDEVAC).[4]

Her planned armament will include two Mk-29 NATO Evolved Sea Sparrow launchers, two MK49 Rolling Airframe Missiles (RAM), three 20 mm Phalanx CIWS mounts, and seven twin .50 cal. machine guns.

The *America*-class LHA(R) will replace the older *Tarawa*-class amphibious assault ship, and will be wider and longer to provide increased vehicle lift, cargo magazine capacity, better survivability, increased habitability standards and greater service life margins.

The ship was launched on 4 June 2012, and christened on 20 October 2012, by Lynne Pace, spouse of retired Marine General and 17th Chairman of the Joint Chiefs of Staff Peter Pace. Delivery is scheduled for February 2013.[5]

Notes

1. "Navy Names New Amphibious Assault Ship (USS *America* LHA-6)." Story #NNS080630-13, Secretary of the Navy Public Affairs—30 June 2008.

2. "U.S. Navy Program Executive Office Ships." Story Number: NNS090718-01, 18 July 2009. http://www.navy.mil/submit/display.asp?story_id=47036

3. U.S. Navy—Commander Naval Surface Force, U.S. Pacific Fleet. http://www.public. navy.mil/surfor/lha6/Pages/ourship.aspx

4. NavSource online: USS *America* (LHA-6). http://www.navsource.org/archives/10/ 07/0706.htm

5. Huntington Ingalls Press Release, 5 June 2012. http://www.globenewswire.com/ newsarchive/hii/pages/news_releases.html?d=258308

Early Ships Named USS *America*

The First USS America—*1782*

The first American ship to bear the name *America* actually predated the republic itself, although in one of history's ironies, it would never serve a day in the American fleet.

On 9 November 1776, less than six months after declaring independence, the Continental Congress voted to authorize the construction of three 74-gun ships-of-the-line for the Continental Navy and the first of these, the *America*, began construction at John Langdon's shipyard on Rising Castle (later Badgers) Island located on the Piscataqua River in New Hampshire.

The ship was to be 2,014 tons with a length of 182 ft 6 in (55.63m) a beam of 50 ft 6 in (15.39m) a depth of hold measuring 23 ft (7m) and a crew of 626. Her armament consisted of 30 eighteen-pounder cannon, 32 twelve-pounders, and 14 nine-pounders, exceeding the planned 74 guns by two.

Under the direction of Master Shipbuilder Col. James Hackett, the keel was laid in May 1777, and although the area was abundant in raw materials, the inability of the Continental legislature to allocate sufficient funds delayed her completion, as did the lack of skilled craftsmen and seasoned lumber.

Impatient with continued delays, the Marine Committee of the Congress voted in November 1779 to replace Hackett with Capt. John Barry with instructions to oversee construction and expedite construction of the *America*.

Barry, a native of Ireland, was one of the nation's earliest naval commanders. He was appointed a captain in the Continental Navy on 7 December 1775, and took command of the 14-gun *Lexington* the same day. His successful command of the *Lexington*, and later the *Raleigh* on 24 June 1778, resulted in the capture of the HMS *Edward* and several privateers.

However successful Barry was as a ship's captain, he was unable to effectively negotiate with the shipwrights, craftsmen and merchants involved in the construction, and frustrated, he applied for leave in March 1780.

Barry was subsequently given command of the 36-gun frigate *Alliance* on 19 September 1780, and he fought the last naval battle of the Revolution from her decks off the coast of Cape Canaveral, Florida, on 10 March 1783, when he inconclusively engaged the British 28-gun frigate HMS *Sybil* under the command of Captain John Vashon, while escorting $72,000 in Spanish silver bullion from Havana to Newport, Rhode Island, for the Continental Congress in Philadelphia.[1]

Granted Navy Commission #1, with the rank of Commodore, by President George Washington, backdated to 4 June 1794, Barry was simultaneously the U.S. Navy's first commissioned officer and first flag rank officer. He commanded the Navy until his death on 13 September 1803 and is considered by many the "Father" of the U.S. Navy.[2]

To encourage rapid completion of the *America*, Congress paid the bill in full, and in late June 1781, appointed Captain John Paul Jones to be her first commanding officer. Jones arrived in August and worked for more than a year to get the work done. He was in the process of placing her cannons when he learned that Congress, in an expression of gratitude to France for her support of America in the war, voted on 3 September 1782 to give the warship to France upon her completion to replace the French Ship-of-the-Line *Magnifique* which had run aground in Boston Harbor on 11 August.

No doubt disappointed, Jones nonetheless continued to supervise the completion of the *America* and although Jones' working relationship with Langdon was little better than Barry's had been, work was finally completed. After an unsuccessful attempt to launch on 23 October 1782, she finally successfully launched on 5 November, the ensigns of France and the United States crossing her stern. Once the *America* was safely moored in the river, Jones, with appropriate ceremony turned command over to Capitaine de Vaisseau de Macarty-Macteigne, the former captain of the Magnifique. Another six months were necessary to add mast, spars and sail before the ship was seaworthy, and she departed Portsmouth for France on 24 June 1783.[3]

America served under the French flag for little more than three years before an inspection found damage from dry rot, likely caused by the use of green, unseasoned timber, that was so extensive as to make repairs impractical, and she was scrapped in 1786; her parts were used on a much larger vessel that was built to replace her, also named *America*.

The Second USS America—*1861*

The second USS *America*, often confused with the USS *American*, was a three-masted, 418-ton former whaling vessel purchased by G.D. Morgan & R.H. Chappell for the Union Navy at a cost of $5,250 on 8 November 1861, at New Bedford, Massachusetts. The intention was to sink a number of vessels in Savannah Harbor, Georgia, to obstruct Confederate shipping; however, Confederate actions to protect Savannah by sinking hulks of ships made Union action unnecessary.

The purchase of aged vessels to be used as sunken barricades of southern ports came to be known as the "Stone Fleet," carried out under the direction of Samuel Francis DuPont, Flag Officer and commander of the South Atlantic Blockading Squadron. The "fleet" then sailed to Charleston, South Carolina, where 24 whaling ships including the USS *America*, under the command of Capt. Charles Henry Davis, were sunk in Charleston Harbor beginning on 19 December 1861.

The USS *America* is sometimes confused with the 329-ton USS *American*, an aging whaler also purchased by Morgan & Chappell at Edgartown, Massachusetts, on 1 November 1861, for $3,370. Loaded with stones, it too was sunk at the mouth of Charleston Harbor on 20 December 1861.[4]

The Third USS America *(ID-3006)—1917*

The third ship to carry the name USS *America* served as a troopship in both World Wars, for both the U.S. Army and U.S. Navy and as a mail steamship and liner between the wars. She began as the *Amerika*, a 22,224 ton steel-hulled twin screw German passenger liner built for the Hamburg American Line by the Harland & Wolff Company of Belfast, Northern Ireland. At 669 feet in length and a beam of 74.3, she was one of the earliest "Grand Luxury" liners, was decorated in the style of Louis XVI , and featured electric elevators, a garden, mineral baths, and her own Ritz Carlton Restaurant. At the time of her launching on 20 April 1905, she was the largest ship in the world.[5]

On 11 October 1905, with a crew of 577, *Amerika* departed Hamburg on her maiden voyage carrying 420 First Class, 254 Second Class, 223 Third Class, and 1,765 steerage passengers, with stops at Dover, England, and Cherbourg, France, before arriving at the Hamburg-America piers at Hoboken, New Jersey, in mid-afternoon of 20 October, to be greeted by a crowd of two thousand.[6]

Amerika spent the next nine years traveling the Hamburg–New York route, later adding Boulogne, France, and Southhampton, England, to her itinerary. On 14 April 1912, at about 11:45 a.m., Captain H. Knuth directed his wireless operator, Otto Reuter, to send the following message to the Hydrographic Office in Washington, D.C.: "*Amerika* passed two large icebergs in 41°27′N, 50°8′W, on the 14th of April." The message was received by the radio operator aboard a nearby liner, the HMS *Titanic*, and passed on to the station at Cape Race, but the message was apparently not passed on to the bridge, and less than three hours later, the *Titanic* sank after hitting one of those icebergs.[7]

Early on the morning of 4 October 1912, *Amerika* struck a British submarine, HMS B2, while steaming through the English Channel four miles off Dover while en route to New York. The ship struck just forward of the conning tower, sinking the submarine, resulting in the loss of fifteen lives and the rescue of one sailor.

In June 1914, the *Amerika* inaugurated a Hamburg to Boston route, but war clouds were gathering over Europe. On 28 July, the Austro-Hungarian invasion of Serbia, followed by the German invasion of Belgium, Luxembourg and France began the First World War, and like countless refugees before her, *Amerika* sought sanctuary in America. Due to depart Boston on 1 August, she remained in the neutral United States rather than hazard a confrontation with the British Royal Navy.

After America's neutrality ended, with a declaration of war on Germany on 2 April 1917, the *Amerika* was seized on 25 July by order of John A. Donald, Commissioner of the United States Shipping Board (USSB) and her crew was detained on Deer Island. Although the ship was filthy, partially sabotaged and in ill repair, she was selected for service as a troop transport and assigned the identification number #3006. On 6 August 1917, *Amerika* was commissioned into the U.S. Navy at the Boston Navy Yard, Lt. Cdr. Frederick L. Oliver in temporary command until Capt. George Calvin Day arrived ten days later to assume command.

Captain Day, an 1892 graduate of the U.S. Naval Academy, had a varied career in the Navy, serving aboard torpedo boats, destroyers and commanding cruisers (USS *Brooklyn* CA-3) and battleships (USS *New York* BB-34) as well as serving as Commander, Submarines, Pacific from 1923–25. He was the navigator for the Great White Fleet and was awarded the Navy Cross for his actions during World War I. He retired in 1935 with the rank of Rear Admiral, and is buried at Arlington National Cemetery.[8]

After several weeks and countless man hours, *Amerika* was transformed from a luxury liner into a more Spartan troopship, and on 1 September 1917, Secretary of the Navy Josephus Daniels issued General Order No. 320 changing the names of several interned German vessels, including the *Amerika* which became the USS *America*.[9]

Repairs completed, the newly christened USS *America* departed the Boston Navy Yard on 18 October 1917, arriving at the port of embarkation at Hoboken, New Jersey, on the 20th to take on supplies and troops for her maiden voyage to France. Besides loading coal, cargo and troops, the ship received a visit from Rear Adm. Albert Gleaves, the commander of the Cruiser-Transport Force.

All troops were aboard by 29 October, and she sailed on the 31st with three other transports (USS *Mount Vernon*, USS *Von Steuben* and USS *Agamemnon*) escorted by the USS *North Carolina* (ACR-12), an armored cruiser, and two destroyers, USS *Terry* (DD-25) and USS *Duncan* (DD-46). It was the first of her nine round-trip voyages to France during the war. An outbreak of influenza on her ninth voyage resulted in the deaths of 53 soldiers and two sailors, and she was in port loaded and prepared for her tenth voyage on 15 October 1918 when without warning she listed to port and sank alongside her pier, killing six.

Raised and refloated on 21 November, ten days after the signing of the armistice, *America* was towed to New York and repaired. She returned to service in February 1919 to complete eight additional round-trip voyages to Europe to transport nearly 47,000 servicemen to America.

Decommissioned on 26 September, she was transferred to the U.S. Army Transportation Service and the USAT *America* completed two more voyages between Hoboken and Brest under the command of Capt. J. Ford, ATS.

Then, on 30 January 1920, *America*, accompanied by the *President Grant* traveled to Russia, then in the midst of a revolution to secretly evacuate members of the Czech Legion from Vladivostok, Russia, to Trieste, Italy , via the Panama Canal, arriving in Trieste on 8 August without incident.[10]

Her military service complete, her guns were removed and her camouflage was painted over and control was transferred to the United States Mail Steamship Company and later the United States Lines which reconditioned her to resume her duties as a transatlantic passenger liner, the SS *America*. On 22 June 1921, she sailed her maiden voyage to Bremen, Germany, with stops at Plymouth, England, and Cherbourg, France, a route she continued for the next eleven years.

Mothballed in 1932 at Point Patience, Maryland, she remained inactive until called back to service in October 1940. With a new war in Europe, the U.S. brokered an agreement with Great Britain, known as Lend-Lease, whereby the United States transferred fifty surplus destroyers to the British Government in exchange for a number of bases. One of these was Pepperell Air Force Base at St. John's, Newfoundland.

Since no barracks existed there, a temporary solution was that the SS *America* was towed to Baltimore and reconfigured by the Bethlehem Steel Company into a floating barracks ship, capable of quartering 1,200 troops, essentially the entire garrison of the new base. To avoid confusion with a new liner, *America*, then under construction by the Newport News Shipbuilding and Dry Dock Company, the ship was renamed USAT *Edmund B. Alexander* in honor of Col. Edmund Alexander, a West Point graduate and veteran of the Mexican and Civil Wars.

As the *Alexander*, she arrived in Newfoundland in January 1941 and remained until barracks were constructed, returning to New York in June.[11]

After briefly operating between New Orleans and the Panama Canal Zone, she was again ordered to Baltimore in May 1942 and spent a year undergoing major renovations, including a conversion from coal to fuel, and was returned to troopship duty. She spent the remainder of World War II transporting troops between the United States, Europe and the Mediterranean. For three years following the end of the war, she transported dependents (primarily war brides and children) until placed in reserve at Hawkins Point, Maryland, on 26 May 1949. Bought by Bethlehem Steel in 1957, she was shortly thereafter broken up as scrap metal.

Notes

1. Brock, Lindsey Cook. "The Last Naval Battle of the American Revolution in American Waters." *SAR (Sons of the American Revolution) Magazine*, Spring, 2008. http://www.revolutionarywararchives.org/lastnavalbattle.html
2. Barry, John. *American National Biography*, Vol.2. New York: Oxford University Press, 1999, 250–252.
3. Morison, Samuel Eliot. *John Paul Jones—A Sailor's Biography*. Annapolis, MD: U.S. Naval Institute, 1989.
4. Official records of the Union and Confederate Navies in the War of Rebellion United States, Naval War Records Office, United States. Office of Naval Records and Library, Government Printing Office, 1921.
5. Famous Liners Online—*Amerika* 1905–1917. http://www.famouslinersonline.com/index.php?page=amerika-1905-1917

6. USS *America*—Navy History http://www.historycentral.com/navy/Transport/America.html;
7. The Titanic Commutator No. 192, The Titanic Historical Society, http://www.titanicl.org/
8. George C. Day—Arlington National Cemetery Website. http://www.arlingtoncemetery.net/gcday.htm
9. Famous Liners Online—*Amerika* 1905–1917.
10. Ibid.
11. *Dictionary of American Naval Fighting Ships*, Naval Historical Center, 1959–91.

Flight Deck Colors

There are numerous functions that need to be performed on an aircraft carrier flight deck in order to safely launch and recover squadron aircraft and all personnel associated with flight deck operations have a specific job, indicated by the color of his/her deck jersey, float coat and helmet. (Officers and Chief Petty Officers are distinguished by khaki, rather than blue, trousers.)

Yellow

Yellowshirts direct the movement of all aircraft, to include: Aircraft handling officers, Catapult and Arresting Gear Officers, Plane directors.

Blue

Plane Handlers—Move, chock and chain aircraft at the direction of Yellowshirts, Aircraft Elevator Operators, Tractor Drivers, Messengers and Phone Talkers

Green

Greenshirts are generally aircraft or equipment maintenance personnel, to include: Catapult and arresting gear crews, Air wing maintenance personnel, Air wing quality control personnel, Cargo-handling personnel, Ground Support Equipment (GSE) troubleshooters, Hook runners, Photographer's Mates, Helicopter Landing Signal Enlisted (LSE) personnel.

Brown

Air wing plane captains and Air wing line leading petty officers—responsible for preparing/inspecting aircraft for flight.

Purple

Aviation Fuels (AKA "Grapes")

Red

Ordnancemen, Crash and Salvage Crews, Explosive Ordnance Disposal (EOD), Firefighter

White

Squadron plane inspectors, Landing Signal Officer (LSO), Air Transfer Officers (ATO), Liquid Oxygen (LOX) crews, Safety Observers, Medical personnel—Senior Medical Officer and Flight Surgeons wear white with Red Cross emblem.

Black and White

Final Checkers wear white with black checks. When a Distinguished Visitor (DV) arrives by air, a call goes out to "Muster the Rainbow Sideboys." Typically two of each colored jersey stand opposite each other in front of the entrance to the ship to render honors to the DV. These sailors in their colored jerseys are referred to as "Rainbow Sideboys."

Career Summary of Medals
Won by the Captions

	Total
Navy Cross	3
Defense Distinguished Service Medal	2
Navy Distinguished Service Medal	1
Defense Superior Service Medal	3
Silver Star	5
Defense Superior Service Medal	1
Legion of Merit	30
Distinguished Flying Cross	20
Bronze Star Medal	10
Purple Heart	2
Defense Meritorious Service Medal	3
Meritorious Service Medal	21
Air Medal	150
Joint Service Commendation Medal	2
Navy Commendation Medal	33
Joint Service Achievement Medal	3
Navy Achievement Medal	1
POW	1
Knight Commander of the Order of the British Empire	1
Ordre National du Mérite (France)	1

Bibliography

Andrew, R.D.M. (Ed.). *1959 USS Lexington CVG-21 Far East Cruise Book.* Tokyo: Daito Art Printing Company, 1959.

Bauer, K. Jack, and Stephen S. Roberts. *Register of Ships of the U.S. Navy, 1775–1990: Major Combatants.* Westport, Connecticut: Greenwood Press, 1991.

Boyne, Walter J. "Breaking the Dragon's Jaw." *Air Force Magazine,* August 2011, Vol. 94, No. 8.

_____. "El Dorado Canyon." *Air Force Magazine,* March 1999, Vol. 82, No. 3.

Brecher, Michael, and Jonathan Wilkenfeld. *A Study in Crisis.* Ann Arbor: University of Michigan Press, 1997.

Burgess, Colin. *Selecting the Mercury Seven: The Search for America's First Astronauts.* New York: Springer-Praxis Books, 2011.

Christmann, Timothy J. "Vice President Bush Recalls World War Two Experience as 'Sobering'." *Naval Aviation News,* March-April, 1985.

Elder, Adam. "Top Gun: 40 Years of Higher Learning." *San Diego Magazine,* October 2009.

Engen, Donald D. *Wings and Warriors.* Washington, DC: Smithsonian, 1997.

Fuller, R. Byron. "Life After the Hanoi Hilton." *National Museum of Aviation Foundation Magazine,* Spring 1996.

Gargus, John. *The Son Tay Raid: American POWs in Vietnam Were Not Forgotten.* College Station: Texas A&M University Press, 2010.

Gray, Stephen R. *Rampant Raider: An A4 Skyhawk pilot in Vietnam.* Annapolis, MD: Naval Institute Press, 2007.

Grossnick, Roy A. *Dictionary of American Naval Aviation Squadrons,* Vol. 1 Washington, D.C.: Naval Historical Center, 1994.

_____. *Dictionary of American Naval Aviation Squadrons: The History of VA, VAH, VAK, VAL, VAP and VFA Squadrons,* Volume 1. Washington, D.C.: Naval Historical Center, Department of the Navy, 1995.

Hattendorf, John B., and Bruce A. Elleman. *Nineteen-Gun Salute: Case Studies of Operational, Strategic, and Diplomatic Naval Leadership During the 20th and Early 21st Centuries.* Washington, D.C.: Government Printing Office, 2010.

Mersky, Peter. *U.S. Navy and Marine Corps A-4 Skyhawk Units of the Vietnam War.* London: Osprey Books, 2007.

_____. *U.S. Navy A-7 Corsair II Units of the Vietnam War.* London: Osprey Publishing, 2004.

Mooney, James L. *Dictionary of American Naval Fighting Ships*, Vol. VI. Washington, D.C.: U.S. Navy History Division, 1976.

_____. *Dictionary of American Naval Fighting Ships,* Vol. VIII. Washington, D.C.: U.S. Navy History Division, 1981.

Nalty, Bernard C. *Air War Over South Vietnam: 1969–1975*. Washington, D.C.: Air Force History and Museums Program, 1995.

Polmar, Norman. *The Naval Institute Guide to the Ships and Aircraft of the U.S. Fleet*, 15th ed. Annapolis, MD: Naval Institute Press, 1993.

Potter, E.B. *Sea Power: A Naval History*. Annapolis, MD: Naval Institute Press, 1981.

Powell, Robert R. "Boom." *RA5-C Vigilante Units in Combat*. Oxford, Great Britain: Osprey, 2004.

Stanik, Joseph T. *El Dorado Canyon: Reagan's Undeclared War with Qaddafi*. Annapolis, MD: Naval Institute Press, 2003.

Sweetman, Jack. *American Naval History: An Illustrated Chronology of the United States Navy and Marine Corps 1775–Present*. Annapolis, MD. Naval Institute Press, 2002.

Symonds, Craig, and William J. Clipson. *Naval Institute Historical Atlas of the U.S. Navy*. Annapolis, MD: Naval Institute Press, 2001.

Wilcox, Robert K. *Scream of Eagles: The Dramatic Account of the U.S. Navy's Top Gun Fighter and How They Took Back the Skies Over Vietnam*. London: Simon & Schuster, 2005.

Wingo, Hal. "Rescue by Copter and Bo'sun's Chair." *Life Magazine*, 8 January 1965.

Index